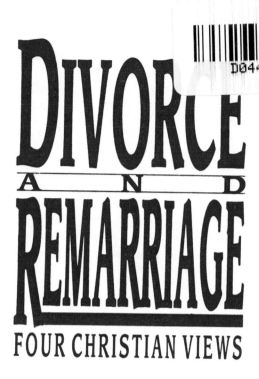

DIVORCE AND REMARRIAGE

FOUR CHRISTIAN VIEWS

H. WAYNE HOUSE, *EDITOR*

with contributions from

J. Carl Laney

William Heth

Thomas Edgar &

Larry Richards

INTERVARSITY PRESS
DOWNERS GROVE, ILLINOIS 60515

InterVarsity Press is the book-publishing division of InterVarsity Christian Fellowship, a student movement active on campus at hundreds of universities, colleges and schools of nursing. For information about local and regional activities, write Public Relations Dept., InterVarsity Christian Fellowship, 6400 Schroeder Rd., P.O. Box 7895, Madison, WI 53707-7895.

All Scripture quotations, unless otherwise indicated, are from the Holy Bible, New International Version. Copyright © 1973, 1978, International Bible Society. Used by permission of Zondervan Bible Publishers.

Chart on p. 230 is used by permission of Zondervan.

The material from chapter one is used by permission of Bethany House.

Cover photograph: Carlos Vergara

ISBN 0-8308-1283-0

Printed in the United States of America

Library of Congress Cataloging-in-Publication Data

Divorce and remarriage: four Christian views/H. Wayne House,
 general editor.
  p. cm.
  Contents: No divorce & no remarriage/J. Carl Laney—Divorce,
 but no remarriage/ William A. Heth—Divorce & remarriage for
 adultery or desertion/Thomas Edgar—Divorce & remarriage under a
 variety of circumstances/Larry Richards.
  ISBN 0-8308-1283-0
  1. Divorce—Religious aspects—Christianity.   2. Remarriage-
 -Religious aspects—Christianity.   I. House, H. Wayne.
  BT707.D58   1990   90-30839
  241'.63—dc20   CIP

21 20 19 18 17 16 15 14 13 12 11 10

10 09 08 07 06 05 04 03 02 01 00

other books by H. Wayne House

Chronological and Background Charts of the New Testament
Civilization in Crisis
Dominion Theology: Blessing or Curse?
Restoring the Constitution
Schooling Choices
The Place of Women in Ministry Today

To Dr. Stanley Ellisen, professor of biblical literature
at Western Conservative Baptist Seminary,
who led me through the issues in this book
as my thesis advisor for my master of theology.
Thank you, Dr. Ellisen, and may you have
many more wonderful years of study in the Word of God,
helping students as you did me.

Introduction

H. Wayne House

*D*ivorce has permeated our society so that the marriage rate and divorce rate are almost equal. This is not restricted merely to the non-Christian community. Christians are also flooding psychologists and marriage counselors, seeking to resolve seemingly irreconcilable conflicts.

Not only are personal lives in a quandary, but the way pastors and biblical scholars have varied on the issue of divorce and remarriage must leave the layperson with much confusion: if the experts can't agree, what is the laity to do or think? Therefore four standard arguments are presented here from various positions, as well as refutations from each of the other three. With this kind of framework the average reader can evaluate the validity of divorce and remarriage.

Each of the persons contributing to this volume has spent an unusual amount of time studying the question of divorce and remarriage. Each has written either books or manuscripts on the matter, having looked in detail at each of the views presented in this volume. Yet, they have come to different conclusions on many points. Part of the reason for this is that they differ initially on such questions as what marriage is, the meaning of "one flesh," and the importance or understanding of the grammar of pertinent biblical passages. Readers will see some of these and other influences as they read the chapters.

Another feature of the book is the case study that each author includes at the end of his section. This allows readers to move beyond technical argument to see how such a view would work out in real life.

The responses provide important insights into each author's position. Here the other authors have the opportunity to note points of agreement as well as to further explain points of difference. Often the responses are the most helpful in that the major points of disagreement are highlighted and more succinctly argued.

You will soon discover that the writers of this book refer to a plethora of biblical verses. You will do well to read these verses along with the arguments that each author makes, often in different versions or translations, so that you can fully benefit from the biblical presentation the various authors make. Some of the major passages are Genesis 2:24, Leviticus 18:6-18, Deuteronomy 24:1-3, Matthew 5:32, Matthew 19:3-12—especially verse 9—Mark 10:2-12 and 1 Corinthians 7:12-16.

You will also observe that there is considerable controversy over the meaning of certain Hebrew or Greek words. If you are untrained in Greek or Hebrew, you may find this difficult to follow, but the need for such discussion becomes obvious. Since the Scriptures were written in these languages, often the meaning of a passage will turn on the correct understanding of the words used by the biblical author. Paying special attention to the other writers in the book will help you in this area. Also, you may want to look up the appropriate words—

the original, as well as the translation—in a Bible dictionary or the Greek or Hebrew dictionary in a large concordance. Good common sense will help, as well as comparing passages of Scripture with other passages.

The contributors come to different conclusions because of the differing weight they give to the various passages. What is the meaning of "one flesh"? Does it refer to blood relation? What is the nature of marriage? Is it inherently indissoluble? How does one explain the divorcing of foreign wives in Ezra and Malachi?

Is Jesus speaking of the betrothal period by the word *fornication* in Matthew 19:9? Or is this a reference to an "incestuous" act? Does Jesus offer new teaching that sets aside the teaching of Moses in Deuteronomy? Is only divorce in view in Matthew 19:9 and not remarriage, or is remarriage inherent in the understanding of divorce? If "fornication" includes adultery, as well as other sexual sins, does it refer to a single act or does it refer to a continual state?

Does Paul introduce another exception besides "fornication" or "sexual immorality" in 1 Corinthians 7, namely, desertion by an unbelieving spouse? Does this require the believing spouse to remain unmarried or does it allow a new marriage to be contracted?

A broader question to be asked concerning divorce and remarriage for the Christian is how does God's grace affect this issue. Where and how does God's forgiveness come into play? These and many more questions await you in your reading of this book. I pray that God will use this book to help you find his answer.

1
NO DIVORCE &
NO REMARRIAGE

No Divorce
& No Remarriage

J. Carl Laney*

*S*peaking at the 1982 International Council on Biblical Inerrancy, the late Francis Schaeffer stated, "If we believe the Bible is totally true, we cannot dodge its claims on our lives in sensitive areas such as divorce."

Divorce and remarriage—the mere mention of this topic at a pastors' workshop, deacons' meeting or ordination council is guaranteed to generate heated discussion. But often the issues are confused by personal feelings, experiences and emotions.

In a discussion with a seminary colleague on this subject, I was asked the question, "How would your views change if your son or daughter were divorced?" The question implies that personal expe-

*The material in J. Carl Laney's section is based on his book *The Divorce Myth* (Bethany House Publisher, 1981) and is used by permission.

rience is the ultimate criterion in determining a position on this controversial subject. In such a perspective, the scriptural data either serves as a secondary consideration or is pressed to conform to the inclinations of personal experience.

Recently, I was asked not to speak on the subject of divorce and remarriage when invited to speak at a church Bible conference. The pastor explained, "We who are in the pastoral ministry have a different perspective on this subject than those who teach in a seminary." The implication: no one can determine God's truth on this matter by a study of Scripture alone. Interpretations must be tempered or modified by personal experience with those who are divorced or remarried.

While personal experience and feelings have a significant role in determining who we are and what we think, these factors cannot be the ultimate basis for providing pastoral counsel to those facing divorce or considering remarriage. God's Word must be the foundation of all practical theology. It is on Scripture, not experience, that a biblical theology of divorce and remarriage must be grounded.

But what does the Bible say? As presented in my book *The Divorce Myth,*[1] I believe Scripture teaches that marriage was designed by God to be permanent unto death, and that divorce and remarriage constitute the sin of adultery. In the following argument we will examine the major texts dealing with marriage, divorce and remarriage. It is not my ultimate objective to convince you of my own position; rather I want to help you explore what Scripture teaches on this contemporary moral issue.

On the subject of the pursuit of truth, William Sanford LaSor, professor of Old Testament at Fuller Theological Seminary, has remarked, "We have nothing to fear from truth; only ignorance can hurt us. ... New truths always challenge old opinions. But new truths never destroy old truths; they merely separate truth from falsehood."[2] In this spirit, I trust that you will weigh carefully my arguments and exegesis as you determine your own viewpoint on divorce and remarriage.

God's Plan for Marriage
Any biblical study of divorce must begin with a consideration of God's

original plan for marriage. That plan is revealed in Genesis 2:24, a text which is quoted twice in the Gospels (Mt 19:5; Mk 10:7-8) and once in the Epistles (Eph 5:31). This foundational passage reveals that marriage was divinely designed and instituted as a lifelong relationship.

The words of Genesis 2:24 are frequently interpreted as being those of Adam. However, it is unlikely that Adam, even in his pre-Fall state, would have had such insight into marriage and family life. The New Testament comes to our aid at this point. In Matthew 19:4-5 Jesus answered the Pharisees: "He who created them from the beginning made them male and female, and said, 'For this cause a man shall leave his father and mother, and shall cleave to his wife, and the two shall become one flesh' "(NASB). According to Jesus, the words of Genesis 2:24 are not those of Adam, but of the Creator himself.

This verse has three parts and mentions three things which are essential to marriage: (1) a public act, "leaving" one's family with a view to establishing a new home; (2) a permanent bond, "cleaving" or being permanently bound in a partnership as husband and wife; (3) a physical embrace, becoming "one flesh" physically through sexual union.

Leaving. God's plan for marriage first involves "leaving." The Hebrew word for "leave" *('āzab)* means to "leave behind" or "depart from." In Exodus 23:5 it has the sense of "set loose" or "let go." The phrase "for this cause" refers back to verse 22, "And the LORD God fashioned into a woman the rib which He had taken from the man, and brought her to the man" (Gen 2:22 NASB). Because God made woman, man must let go of his parents, with a view to establishing his own home and family. There can be no firmly established and lasting marriage without this first essential step.

While some young people can hardly wait to cut loose from their parents, for others this is not an easy step. Frequently, it is even harder for parents to let their children go. There are many marriages where the husband or wife is still emotionally bound to parents, answering to their demands, living under the authority of Mom and Dad. This kind of a situation creates unnecessary tensions for the newly married couple. Someone has said that the two best legacies parents can give their children are roots and wings—the security of knowing that Mom and Dad are always there to help and encourage in time of special need, but also the freedom to live one's own life and develop one's own family.

Leaving does not, of course, imply abandoning parents. The responsibility to "honor your father and mother" (Ex 20:12) is applied by Jesus to adult Pharisees (Mk 7:6-13). In his instructions on caring for widows, Paul asks that believers make some recompense or return to their aged parents—that is, to provide for their needs (1 Tim 5:3-4). The "leaving" of Genesis 2:24 does not mean the young couple should avoid contact with their parents. Rather, they must "let go" of their former lives as son or daughter in order to cement their partnership as husband and wife.

Cleaving. The second essential ingredient for a marriage is cleaving. "A man shall leave his father and mother and cleave to his wife." There is a divine order and purpose in this process. It is impossible to "cleave" until you "leave." And the purpose of this leaving is to establish a new marriage relationship and home.

The word *cleave (dābaq)* means to "cling" or "keep close." While retaining the idea of physical proximity, it is used in the Old Testament as a figure of loyalty and affection. The word is used by Joshua of a military alliance (Josh 23:12), by Ruth of her commitment to Naomi (Ruth 1:14), and of the men of Judah who remained faithful to David during Sheba's rebellion (2 Sam 20:2). The noun form of the word is used of joining metal by soldering (Is 41:7).

A study of the word *cleave* suggests that marriage involves a partnership commitment to which the husband and wife must be loyal. It is significant that the term *covenant (bƙrît)* is used of marriage in Malachi 2:14 and Proverbs 2:17. The word is used of a pact made between two persons and of the constitutional agreement made by God with Israel at Sinai. It is also used of the alliance of friendship between David and Jonathan (1 Sam 18:3). Implicit in the idea of a *covenant* is that of a binding relationship which shall not be broken (Ps 89:34; Dan 9:4).

The biblical concept of "cleaving" suggests the idea of being "superglued" together—bound inseparably by a commitment to a lifelong relationship.

While tape is used to bind things temporarily, glue is normally used to bind things together permanently. Only with great difficulty can two articles which are glued together be separated. If you try to separate two pieces of wood which have been glued together, you will discover that they usually don't separate at the joint. While the glue holds the joint firm, the wood pulls away from its own grain and breaks! Items which are glued together often cannot be separated without great damage. The same is true of persons bound together in a marriage covenant.

You or I might have used the word *love* in place of *cleave.* God used a word which would be less affected by changes in feelings and emotions. Cleaving includes love—*agapē*—a sacrificial commitment patterned after Christ's own example of personal sacrifice (Eph 5:2, 25).

It may be well to point out in this day of moral looseness that cleaving to one's spouse would obviously exclude marital unfaithfulness. Being "glued" to one's wife and at the same time engaging in sexual intercourse with another woman are mutually exclusive concepts. Marital faithfulness is essential to the biblical cleaving relationship.

Becoming One Flesh. The third essential ingredient to marriage is the physical union, "they shall become one flesh." This phrase refers to the physical or sexual aspect of marriage. Becoming one flesh symbolizes the identification of two people with one community of interests and pursuits, a union consummated by the physical act of sexual intercourse. Although they remain two persons, the married couple becomes one in a mystical, spiritual unity. Through acts of physical union, married couples celebrate and renew their oneness in the most intimate and personal way.

Becoming "one flesh" does not in and of itself make a marriage. The "leaving" and "cleaving" must also be included. And the leaving must be recognized by society and regulated by the laws of the government.

On the other hand, there is no sexual intercourse which does not result in two people becoming one flesh (1 Cor 6:16)! A married man who has intercourse with a prostitute becomes one flesh with her, thus destroying the uniqueness of the one-flesh relationship with his wife. By God's grace, forgiveness and healing are always available to the repentant. Yet unfaithfulness to that most unique and intimate of relationships will always leave hurt, sorrow and scars.

Notice that Genesis 2:24 says nothing about children. A childless marriage is a marriage in every sense of the word. God may in his wisdom withhold children to enable a couple to have a ministry which would be impossible with the responsibilities of childrearing. Yet, while the couple may be one flesh without children, procreation and the raising of children is a significant aspect of marriage (Gen 1:28). This means that while sexual union in marriage is beautiful and honorable (Heb 13:4), "sexual gratification was not designed as an end in itself."[3]

The concept of "one flesh" is beautifully illustrated in the children God may be pleased to give a married couple. In their offspring, husband and wife are indissolubly united into one person. My children—John, Elisabeth and Laura—possess my features and Nancy's. They are my flesh and my wife's. There is no way that I can retrieve my features from my child, nor could my wife retrieve hers. Something unique and permanent is formed when a child is born, and similarly when the one-flesh relationship is established in marriage.

The concept of one flesh seems to imply that the marriage bond is indissoluble. Certainly, Genesis 2:24 makes no provision for divorce. Jesus himself acknowledges that "from the beginning" marriage was designed to be lifelong and permanent (Mt 19:8).

It is important to note that a divine order is involved in establishing the one-flesh union. Becoming one flesh—the physical union—follows the leaving and cleaving. In our modern, promiscuous society the steps are often reversed. Yet the Bible knows nothing of "trial marriages" where couples live together apart from wedlock. Premarital sexual intercourse is not only immoral, it defrauds one's future spouse of the right to take a virgin in marriage (see 1 Thess 4:3-5).

A Biblical Definition. What is marriage anyway? While many have thought of it merely as a legal agreement, the Bible reveals that the marriage union involves much more. Based on our study, marriage could be defined as God's act of joining a man and a woman in a permanent, covenanted, one-flesh relationship.[4]

The Bible calls marriage a "covenant" (Mal 2:14; Prov 2:17), and God is not in the business of breaking covenant relationships. Marriage involves a vow or promise which makes the obligation binding. God's Word instructs that "a man shall not violate his word; he shall do according to all that proceeds out of his mouth" (Num 30:2 NASB). Ecclesiastes 5:4-6 warns of God's displeasure toward those who make a vow they refuse to keep. Psalm 15:4 highlights the priority of faithfulness to one's word in spite of the personal cost.

Marriage is built on a promise made before God, friends and family members. Perhaps promise-keeping is the key issue for the doctrine of the permanence of marriage. Lewis B. Smedes, professor of theology and ethics at Fuller Seminary, has written, "When you make a promise you have created a small sanctuary of trust within the jungle of unpredictability. Human destiny rests on a promise freely given and reliably remembered."[5] What a different place this world would be if we would keep our promises!

Divorce in Deuteronomy

Not long after the Fall, God's standard of one man, one woman was violated (Gen 4:19). By the time of Moses, Israelite men were orally divorcing their wives as was the custom among heathen nations. Observing something that displeased him, a husband could simply declare before witnesses, "I divorce my wife," or declare, "You are no longer my wife."[6] The rejected wife would have no recourse but to leave home. She was entitled to none of her husband's property. For this reason, the wedding present or dowry (1 Kings 9:16) provided an important resource should a woman be divorced by her husband.

Increased laxity regarding divorce and remarriage among the Hebrews necessitated legislation to deal with this matter. Deuteronomy 24:1-4 is a key Old Testament text dealing with this issue. It is crucial to understand that this passage does not institute or approve divorce, but merely treats it as a practice already known and existing.[7]

Stylistically, Deuteronomy 24:1-4 is an example of biblical case law where certain conditions ("if") are stated which become the basis for a command ("then"). In this text, verses 1-3 specify the conditions that must apply for the execution of the command in verse 4. The legislation actually applies to a particular case of remarriage. Its grammatical intent is not to give legal sanction to divorce or regulate the divorce procedure, but to prohibit the remarriage of a man to his divorced wife in cases where the wife has had an intervening marriage.

The Circumstances of Divorce (Deut 24:1-3). The first three verses describe the situation of a woman who is twice divorced by different men or once divorced and then widowed. It should be noted that divorce is neither encouraged nor commanded in this text. The circumstance leading to the divorce is described. But the text does not suggest that divorce is necessarily sanctioned under such circumstances.

In this case, the married woman lost favor with her husband because of "some indecency in her" (literally, "nakedness of a thing" or "a naked matter"). The precise meaning of the phrase *('erwat dābār)* is uncertain and consequently was the subject of heated rabbinic debates on divorce. This may refer to some physical deficiency—such as the inability to bear children. This is suggested by a possible parallel between our text and an old Assyrian marriage contract.[8] Or perhaps it refers to some shameful or repulsive act such as the indecency referred to in Deuteronomy 23:13 where the same expression is used as a euphemism for excrement. At any rate, it is very unlikely that the phrase *('erwat dābār)* refers to adultery since adultery was punished by death (Lev 20:10, Deut 22:22-24), not divorce.

There are several circumstances mentioned in the Old Testament for which divorce is specifically prohibited. A man who morally defiled his wife before marriage was not permitted to divorce her (Deut 22:28-29). Nor could a man divorce his new wife, having falsely accused her of not being a virgin (Deut 22:13-19). Apparently, however, in the case of the "naked matter" of Deuteronomy 24:1, divorce was *not* prohibited.

Many have concluded that since, in this case, divorce was not prohibited, both divorce and remarriage are permitted with divine sanction. However, the text is far from approving the second marriage. In verse 4, the second marriage is viewed as bringing defilement ("after she has been defiled"). The word *defiled (ṭāmē')* means "to become unclean" and is used in Leviticus 18:20 and Numbers 5:13-14 of the defilement of adultery. The implication is that a woman's remarriage after divorce is similar to adultery in that she cohabits with another man.[9] This Mosaic perspective is certainly consistent with Jesus' teaching that divorce and remarriage by either the husband or wife constitutes adultery (Mk 10:11-12).

The rejected wife was sent out with a "certificate of divorce." According to the Mishnah, the essential words of such a document are "Behold, you are free to marry any man."[10] It is important to note that the bill of divorcement is not required by this text. The case being described includes the giving of a divorce document, which implies only that it was a matter of custom. Such a document would protect the rejected wife from any further responsibility to her husband. It would also protect any subsequent marriage from interference by the former husband.

The Prohibition against Remarriage (Deut 24:4). The main point of this legislation, stated in the "then" clause of verse 4, relates to a particular case of remarriage. Moses declares that a man may not remarry his former wife if she has in the meantime been married to another man. Even though her second husband should divorce her or die, she must not return to her first husband. The prohibition is backed up with a reason and a command.

The reason: to commit this sin (that is, to remarry one's original husband after an intervening marriage) is "an abomination before Yahweh."[11] The reason is followed by the command, "You shall not bring sin on the land which Yahweh your God gives you as an inheritance." To commit the act prohibited in this case law amounts to bringing the guilt of sin on the land of Israel. These words bring to mind the warning God gave the Israelites in Leviticus 18:24-25 regarding the wicked ways of Canaan,

> Do not defile yourselves by any of these things; for by all these the nations which I am casting out before you have become defiled. For the land has become defiled, therefore I have visited its punishment upon it, so that land has spewed out its inhabitants. (NASB)

This legislation was designed to prevent the defilement of the land which God would soon be giving His people as an inheritance. Does Deuteronomy 24:1-4 have a similar purpose?

The Purpose of the Legislation. I have argued that this legislation was intended to discourage divorce among the Israelite people. Since there was a good possibility of not being able to remarry one's former wife, the husband would not be so likely to put his wife away hastily.[12] Yet, would this really deter an angry husband? In biblical times the chief deterrent to divorce was financial. Usually the husband forfeited the dowry and sometimes had to make a divorce payment as well.[13]

In a lectureship delivered at the University of Oxford on Polygamy in Jewish Law, R. Yaron suggested that legislation was designed to protect the second marriage.[14] Remarriage of a divorced wife creates the possibility of tension within a "lovers' triangle." Having repented of dismissing her, the first husband may want to get his wife back. The wife may draw comparisons and find her second husband less desirable than her first. By outlawing the remarriage, the stability and continuation of the second marriage is assured. Yaron's view, however, fails to explain why the rule would apply after the death of the second husband.

More recently Gordon Wenham, lecturer in Semitic studies at The Queen's University of Belfast, pointed out that the reasons the husband should not take back his former wife—defilement, abomination and pollution of the land—occur repeatedly in connection with the sexual offenses listed in Leviticus 18 and 20.[15]

Wenham points out that marriage establishes a close and lasting one-flesh relationship which does not terminate with divorce. From a biblical perspective, marital intercourse makes a husband and wife as closely related as parents and children. If a man may not marry his sister-in-law because she has in effect become his sister (see Lev 18:16; 20:21), may he remarry his former wife? Wenham suggests that Deuteronomy 24:1-4 uses the logic of incest laws to deny it. If a divorced couple should come together again after an intervening marriage, it would be as bad as a man marrying his sister. To reconstitute the first marriage would be a "type of incest" which is explicitly prohibited in Leviticus 18:6-18.[16]

Concluding Observations. Moses did not institute divorce; he acknowledged it as taking place and sought to curb that which clearly contradicted God's original design for marriage. Although divorce was "permitted" in the sense that it was not specifically prohibited by law, it was not looked on with favor. The lot of a divorcée was not pleasant (see Is 54:6). Although she was free to remarry, she could not marry a priest (Lev 21:7). This suggests that there was something of a stigma (social or moral) attached to her as a divorced woman. And there would be some measure of moral or ceremonial defilement associated with her should she remarry (Deut 24:4).

Many have wondered why God did not outlaw divorce and remarriage in the Mosaic Law and terminate all the future haggling over this issue. The answer is found in the words of Jesus, "Because of your hardness of heart, Moses permitted you to divorce your wives; but from the beginning it has not been this way" (Mt 19:8). Because of Israel's hard-hearted rejection of God's design for marriage (Mt 19:8), it is not likely that a general prohibition against divorce would have been obeyed. Instead, God chose to progressively reveal his displeasure with divorce and direct his people back to his standard.

In a study of the Old Testament's teaching on divorce and remarriage Wenham concludes, "Thus the laws in the OT not only promote the ideal of a lifelong partnership, they are based on the idea that a permanent relationship is established between the parties."[17] Deuteronomy 24:1-4 does not alter God's original plan for marriage. It simply provides recourse and direction where God's original plan for the permanence of marriage has not been followed.

Divorce in Ezra

In 458 B.C. Ezra the scribe led a small group of Jewish exiles back to Jerusalem from captivity in Babylon.[18] Ezra had been in Jerusalem about four and one-half months when the officials of the city brought to his attention a serious problem. Many of the Jews who had recently returned from Babylon had married the unbelieving Gentiles living in the land of Judah (Ezra 9:1-2).

Ezra's Response. Ezra knew that the intermarriage of Jews with foreigners was strictly forbidden by the Mosaic Law. Marriage with unbelieving heathen would almost inevitably result in worshiping heathen gods (Deut 7:1-4; Mal 2:11). This sin had plagued Israel in the past (Judg 3:5-6). Even Solomon had succumbed to the temptation to marry foreign women, and as a result his heart was turned away to other gods (1 Kings 11:1-8).

Ezra was facing the first major crisis of his ministry. He fully understood that if this practice continued, the Jews of the restoration community would soon lose their national identity and fall into idolatry. The people of Judah were on the verge of duplicating the very circumstances that led to the Babylonian Exile. Responding quickly to this critical situation, Ezra took the matter to God in prayer (Ezra 9:5-15).

As a result of Ezra's prayer, the hearts of the people were changed. While Ezra was still praying in the Court of the Temple, a multitude of repentant people gathered to him (Ezra 10:1). Although not among the offenders who had married foreign wives (see Ezra 10:18-44), Shecaniah represented the group. On behalf of the people, Shecaniah confessed the nation's sin and proposed a solution to the problem (Ezra 10:2-3). He recommended that the people covenant with God to "put away" their foreign wives.

The word *put away* (Hiphil of *yāṣā'*, lit. "cause to go out") is not the customary word for divorcement.[19] The normal verb for "divorce" in the Old Testament is the Piel form of *šālaḥ*, "to send away" or "dismiss." It is possible that Shecaniah intended merely a legal separation rather than a traditional divorce with implied rights of remarriage.

The words "let it be done according to the law" (Ezra 10:3) have been taken as a reference to Deuteronomy 24:1-4. However, it is clear from our previous study that Deuteronomy 24:1-4 provides no direct instruction on the circumstances or conditions of divorce. More likely, Shecaniah is referring to the law of Deuteronomy 7:1-3 which prohibits mixed marriage with unbelieving Gentiles.

Acting on the suggestion of Shecaniah, Ezra issued a proclamation for the returned exiles to gather in Jerusalem. The offenders were then ordered to separate themselves from their foreign wives (Ezra 10:10-11). Again, the customary word for divorce *(šālaḥ)* is not used. The word which appears in Ezra 10:11 is the Niphal (reflexive) form of *bādal*, "to separate oneself from." In Ezra 9:1 the word clearly means separation, not divorce. Instead of separating themselves from the foreign people of the land, the returned exiles took the daughters of these idolaters in marriage.

The people affirmed their agreement with Ezra's proposal (Ezra 10:12). To facilitate the plan, judges were appointed to circulate through the land and deal with the separation proceedings individually (Ezra 10:13-15). A total of 113 Jews were involved, almost one-quarter of whom were religious leaders. Each offender separated from his foreign wife and offered a ram as a guilt offering according to the provision of Leviticus 6:4, 6 (Ezra 10:19). The crisis had been resolved and Israel's identity and religious purity had been preserved.

The Application for Today. How does this incident relate to the biblical teaching on divorce and remarriage? One must be very cautious in drawing conclusions from this account in light of the uncertainty of whether legal divorce with rights of remarriage is actually in view. Not only is the customary word for divorce absent from the narrative, there is nothing mentioned in the account which suggests that remarriages took place. One could assume that the gentile wives remarried. It is possible that the Jewish men did as well. However, it would be unwise to be dogmatic either way in light of the Scripture's silence on the subject.

It must be acknowledged that there was at least one alternative to the actions taken by Ezra and the restoration community. This can be illustrated by Israel's establishing a covenant with the Gibeonites under the leadership of Joshua (Josh 9:11, 14-15). Wrongful as it was (Deut 7:2), the covenant was honored by Israel (Josh 9:18, 20; see also Ps 15:4). Later in Israel's history when the covenant was broken, God brought judgment on the land (2 Sam 21:1-6).

It should not be overlooked in Deuteronomy 7:2-3 that the prohibition against making covenants with Canaanite nations immediately precedes the prohibition against marrying foreign wives. The prohibitions are linked together because violations of both tend to lead people toward idolatry. Thus, the parallel between Joshua 9 and Ezra 10 is significant.[20] Perhaps instead of separating from these foreign wives, the Judeans could have treated them as captive women applying the instructions of Deuteronomy 21:10-14. Following this pattern, the Israelites could have separated from their wives, allowing for a period of consecration from foreign ways, and then been reunited in marriage.

While this was a possible alternative to Ezra's actions, our purpose is not to speculate on what might have been, but rather to understand what history records. The key is to understand this incident in light of the covenant prohibition against marriage to unbelieving Gentiles (Deut 7:3-4). The prohibition was based on the premise that intermarriage would lead to idolatry, and idolatry to divine judgment—possibly even exile from the land (Deut 28:41, 63, 64). Ezra was facing the possible destruction of the recently restored Jewish state (see Ezra 9:14)! Although his actions were severe and drastic, he apparently regarded them as the best means of offsetting the dangerous predicament. A. E. Cundall, lecturer in Old Testament studies at London Bible College, comments:

> The unhappiness caused by these broken homes must be set not only against the initial transgression involved in the contracting of the marriages, but also against the ultimate blessing to the whole world that could only come through a purified community.[21]

Another important factor in biblical interpretation is determining the author's purpose for including a particular incident or account. Ezra 9—10 certainly does not record the high point of Ezra's ministry! Yet he deemed it necessary to include this tragedy in his account of the restoration history. What was he seeking to accomplish?

The account is certainly not designed to provide us a biblical pattern for divorce and remarriage. Ezra's goal as a leader, priest and scribe in the restoration community was to teach the people the laws of God (Ezra 7:10, 25). By recording this near disaster as part of Israel's sacred history, Ezra intended to teach the returned exiles the dangers of apostasy (9:10-14), the drastic measures necessary to maintain religious purity (Ezra 10:2-3) and the tragic consequences of violating God's laws (Ezra 10:1, 14, 44). These are the lessons to be learned from Ezra 9—10, not a theology of divorce and remarriage.

Any tendency to make application of this unique incident to modern marriages, suggesting that a Christian should divorce an unbelieving spouse, would contradict the clear teaching of Paul in 1 Corinthians 7:12-13, "If any brother has a wife who is an unbeliever, and she consents to live with him, let him not send her away. And a woman who has an unbelieving husband, and he consents to live with her, let her not send her husband away" (NASB). Paul plainly does not want believers to dissolve their marriages with unbelieving spouses.

Divorce in Malachi
Between the first and second governorships of Nehemiah in Jerusalem, around 432-431 B.C., God raised up the prophet Malachi to

protest the spiritual corruption of the people of Judah. In addition to the problem of hypocrisy (Mal 2:17) and the neglect of giving (Mal 3:7-9), the people of Jerusalem had become involved in the scandal of mixed marriages. Ezra had already dealt with this matter (Ezra 10), but the problem reoccurred. This time it was even worse. The offenders were divorcing their Jewish wives to marry unbelieving Gentiles.

The Sin of Mixed Marriage (Mal 2:10-12). Malachi protests the violation of the Mosaic Law which prohibited marriages with unbelieving Gentiles as a safeguard against idolatry (Ex 34:14-16; Deut 7:1-4). He argues in verse 10 that since God is Israel's Father and Jews are his children (Ex 4:22), brotherly love and family loyalty should be upheld. Instead, the Jews were dealing treacherously with one another by marrying idolatrous heathen women.

The phrase "daughter of a foreign god" refers to a woman of a foreign people who is dedicated to worshiping a heathen god. Such mixed marriages, declares Malachi, profane God's covenant with the patriarchs, for they threaten Israel's distinctive faith and national existence. The sin also profaned the sanctuary (literally "the holiness") of Yahweh. What was profaned or made common was not the Lord himself, but those who were "holy" by virtue of their relationship with a holy God. The designation "holiness of Yahweh" is a reference to God's chosen people (see Jer 2:3, Ezra 9:2), not the Temple, as the NASB translation suggests.[22]

In verse 12 Malachi calls for divine judgment on all who would profane the marriage relationship in this way. The phrase "cut off" means to put one to death (see Ex 31:14). The universality of this divine retribution is suggested by the fact that not even the priests and Levites who officiate at the Temple will be spared.

The Sin of Divorce (Mal 2:13-16). Malachi declares that their excessive displays of emotion, intended to procure answers to prayer (v. 13), would have no effect because of their broken marriage vows (v. 14, see also 1 Pet 3:7). Malachi condemns those who have violated their marriage commitments as dealing treacherously with their wives. The Hebrew verb *(bāḡaḏ)* means "to act or deal treacherously, faithlessly or deceitfully."

The offense of divorce is graphically illustrated by Malachi's use of three phrases: "wife of your youth," "your companion" and "wife of your covenant." The woman was taken as a wife in the bloom of her young beauty and cruelly cast off after years of faithful service to her husband and family. She was a "companion" or "partner," a term derived from the Hebrew verb meaning "to unite or be joined together." David Garland points out that this term is normally used of men to designate their equality with one another. To use this term for a wife suggests that she is not a piece of property, but one to be regarded as a "covenant partner."[23] Walter Kaiser suggests that there may be "an echo" of the "one flesh" of Genesis 2:24 in this term for the spouse.[24] Finally, she was united "by covenant," an allusion to the marriage contract made before God and witnesses (see Prov 2:17, Ezek 16:8). God does not break covenants (see Lev 26:40-45), and since divorce violates a marriage covenant made before God, it cannot meet with his approval.

While verse 15 is a difficult verse to translate and interpret, it is clearly Malachi's intention to encourage husbands to remain true to their first wife.[25] Following the marginal reading of the NASB, the verse appears to refer to the original institution of marriage when God made one partner for Adam (Gen 2:24). And why only one? God's design was to produce a godly offspring. In other words, while God had the creative power to make Adam any number of wives, he designed that marriage involve one man united to one woman. God knew that a plurality of relationships would not be conducive to raising a godly family. On the other hand, when parents remain faithful to their marriage vows, their children will enjoy the security and nurture which encourages godly living.

Two reasons are provided in verse 16 in support of the warning in verse 15 regarding treacherous dealings against one's wife.[26] First, God hates "putting away" (šālaḥ), a commonly used term for divorce. As God hates (sānē') hypocrisy in worship, idolatry and evil (see Amos 5:21, Is 1:14, Jer 44:4, Prov 6:16-19), so he has a strong and active aversion to divorce.

The second and coordinate reason given for the warning in verse 15 is that God hates "him who covers his garment with wrong." This expression has been understood as being derived from the custom of spreading a garment over a woman to claim her as a wife (see Ruth 3:9, Ezek 16:8).[27] In this case, a symbol for "wedded trust" has been employed as a metaphor for marital treachery. The expression may also be understood to refer to the stain which the sin of divorce leaves, like the blood of a victim on the garment of the murderer.[28] This is seen in Zechariah 3:4 where a soiled garment is indicative of an unclean heart. To corroborate this, the word translated "wrong" is used elsewhere of physical violence and harsh treatment (see Judg 9:24; Gen 16:5).

As God hates the wicked (Ps 5:6; 11:5), so Malachi declares that he hates those who deal treacherously by the act of divorce. Yet it is important to note that God does not say, "I hate divorced people." In view of Christ's gracious dealing with the woman at the well, who had been married five times, believers should be extremely careful to avoid giving a divorced person a feeling of rejection. Rather, they should reflect Christ's attitude of forgiveness and loving concern.

Verse 16 concludes by repeating, for emphasis, the warning given in verse 15. According to the prophet Malachi, divorce is not only a violation of God's original plan for marriage, it violates the marriage covenant to which the Lord is a witness. Divorce is treachery against life's most intimate companion and is a grievous sin which God hates.

The Teaching of Jesus

Two major passages record Jesus' teaching on divorce and remarriage—Matthew 19:1-12 and Mark 10:1-12 (see also Mt 5:31-32; Lk 16:18). While both record the same incident, each Gospel has unique contributions which must be considered in determining what Jesus taught regarding divorce and remarriage.

The Original Permanence of Marriage. Jesus' teaching on divorce, recorded in Matthew 19 and Mark 10, was given while he was traveling through Transjordan on his way to Jerusalem for his last Passover (Mt 19:1; Mk 10:1). In Perea, the territory ruled by Herod Antipas, the Pharisees confronted Jesus with the question, "Is is lawful for a man to divorce his wife for any cause at all?" (Mt 19:3 NASB).

Both Matthew and Mark inform the reader that the Pharisees were "testing" Jesus with their question. Perhaps they wanted to confront Jesus with the fact that his teaching conflicted with their understanding of the Mosaic Law. Or they may have wanted to lure Jesus into making a politically dangerous remark about the marriage of Herod

Antipas to his brother's wife (also Antipas's niece).[29] Such a statement against Herod Antipas's incestuous marriage (see Lev 18:16; 20:12) had resulted in the arrest, imprisonment and execution of John the Baptist just a year or two earlier (Mt 14:4-12). The Pharisees had already determined to destroy Jesus (Mt 12:14; Mk 3:6). Now they were scheming to give Herod Antipas cause to carry out their desire.

The question raised by the Pharisees was asked in the context of the rabbinic debates concerning the meaning of the phrase 'erwat dāḇār ("the nakedness of a thing" or "a naked matter") in Deuteronomy 24:1. While virtually all Jews in Palestine accepted the principle of divorce, there was a major debate among the rabbis over the legitimate cause for which one might divorce his wife. According to the Mishnah, the liberal school of Hillel said that divorce for any reason was legitimate, while the conservative school of Shammai allowed divorce only on the grounds of adultery.[30] The question put to Jesus was "What side of the controversy are you on?" The Pharisees could expect Jesus to reject a lenient view (see Mt 5:21-48). But to side with the conservative school of Shammai would be to condemn the marriage of Herod Antipas, endangering Jesus' own life—precisely what the Pharisees wanted.

In responding to the Pharisees, Jesus rejects both the liberal and conservative views on divorce held by the leading rabbis of his day. Matthew records Jesus' explanation that divorce has no part in God's original design; marriage is permanent (Mt 19:4-6). First, Jesus appeals to Genesis 1:27 and 2:24 to point out that in the beginning God made one male for one female. Second, he appeals to Genesis 2:24 to show that in marriage two people actually become united together in a family (one-flesh) relationship. Third, Jesus affirms that God is the One who actually joins a couple in marriage, and that which God has joined, no man should separate. The phrase "let no man separate" is a present imperative of prohibition and demands the cessation of something in process (that is, divorce). The last part of verse 6 could be paraphrased, "Stop severing marriage unions which God has permanently bound together."

Jesus' answer to the Pharisees' question "Is it lawful for a man to divorce his wife for any cause at all?" (Mt 19:3) is clearly "No!" In contrast to the religious leaders of his day, Jesus affirmed the permanence and inviolability of the God-ordained marriage union. His answer indicates, "There is no valid reason at all" for divorce.[31] Yet, by making no mention of Herod Antipas, he avoided a confrontation with the ruler through whose district he was traveling. By so doing, he successfully skirted the trap of the Pharisees.

The Pharisees clearly understood Jesus to be teaching a "no divorce" viewpoint and sought to challenge him on the basis of Deuteronomy 24:1-4. They questioned, "Why then did Moses command to give her a certificate and divorce her?" (Mt 19:7). Like many evangelicals today, the Pharisees had missed the point of the Mosaic legislation. Moses did not institute divorce or even command the issuance of a divorce document. The only command in Deuteronomy 24:1-4 is that a husband not remarry his divorced wife if she has had an intervening marriage.[32] This passage provides direction for cases in which divorce and remarriage has already occurred.

While the Pharisees thought that Moses commanded divorce, Jesus explains that he only "permitted" it. The words "Moses permitted you to divorce your wives" simply mean that God did not give Moses a specific commandment prohibiting divorce. Jesus then points out that the Mosaic legislation was necessitated by Israel's hard-hearted rejection of God's original design for marriage (Mt 19:8). Jesus then explains, "But from the beginning it has not been this way." Thus he sets the Mosaic concession in stark contrast with God's original plan for marriage as set forth in Genesis 2:24.

Where should the focus of evangelical Christians be in relationship to the issue of divorce and remarriage—on God's original plan or on a concession made because of hard hearts?

The Meaning of Porneia. Continuing his instruction on this controversial issue, Jesus puts himself in contrast to the other rabbis of his day by declaring that divorce and remarriage constitute adultery: "And I say to you, whoever divorces his wife, except for *porneia,* and marries another commits adultery" (Mt 19:9). According to Jesus, mere formal or legal divorce does not dissolve the actual marriage that was made permanent by God. Except in the case of *porneia* (translated "immorality" in the NASB), God does not recognize divorce. Therefore, the subsequent marriage of a divorced person would involve the sin of adultery. Both in Mark 10:1-12 and Luke

16:18 Jesus clearly teaches that divorce and remarriage constitute adultery—without exception. This also appears to be his teaching in Matthew 5:32, "whoever marries a divorced woman commits adultery" (no exception).

But what is the meaning of the phrase "except for porneia"? A proper understanding of this word is crucial to determining the teaching of Jesus on divorce and remarriage.

Porneia is related to the noun *pornē* which is derived from the root "to sell." The original concept behind the word was the offering of one's body for a price. The word *pornē* was especially used of slaves and meant "a harlot for hire." From *pornē* comes the word *porneia*, found in Matthew 5:32 and 19:9. It basically refers to unlawful sexual activity, including prostitution, unchastity and fornication. *Porneia* is a general term which can be interpreted in various ways. The context is the key to determining the meaning in any specific passage.

Many evangelicals have equated *porneia* with adultery. By this interpretation, Jesus' teaching did not rise above that of Shammai and the Pharisees, contrary to his usual pattern (see Mt 5:21–48). The majority of the Patristic writers took this view, although they did not permit remarriage after divorce for "adultery."[33] The word *porneia*, however, does not normally mean adultery. The usual word for adultery is *moicheia,* and Matthew recognizes a distinction between the two terms (Mt 15:19).[34] Had Jesus intended to side with Shammai and permit divorce in the case of adultery, he would have used the more proper and explicit term.

Others have suggested that Jesus chose the broader term *porneia* in order to allow for divorce on the basis of any general sexual irregularity, including adultery. According to this view, Jesus would be taking a more lenient position than Shammai who allowed divorce only in the case of adultery. Yet giving *porneia* the wider meaning introduces internal contradictions in Matthew's text.[35]

Jesus has argued that the permanence of marriage is the will of God according to his created order (Mt 19:4–5; see also Gen 2:24). In the face of the Pharisaic challenge, Jesus made a strong statement against divorce (Mt 19:6). It would be inconsistent for him to suddenly broaden his position taking a more lenient view than the rabbis. Such a lenient view would be inconsistent with the response of Jesus' disciples, "If the relationship of a man with his wife is like this, it is better not to marry" (Mt 19:10 NASB). This comment reflects the fact that Jesus took a more narrow viewpoint than his disciples had expected. The comment is inexplicable if a wider meaning is ascribed to *porneia* in Matthew 19:9.

Another popular interpretation of *porneia* is that it refers to unfaithfulness during the betrothal or engagement period. According to Jewish custom, betrothal was as binding as marriage involving a legal contract which could be broken only by formal divorce or death (see Deut 20:7; 24:5). According to this view, Jesus was teaching that if the betrothed proved unfaithful during the waiting period, then the partner divorced her (see Mt 1:19). The exception clause would have application only to betrothal and not the actual marriage.

The most obvious objection to this view is that Jesus and the Pharisees were not discussing betrothal, but marriage (see Gen 2:24; Deut 24:1-4). In addition, this view would not account for the absence of the exception in Mark and Luke, for both the Greeks and Romans, as well as the Jews, had such a betrothal period to which the exception might apply.

An increasing number of scholars are interpreting Matthew's "except for *porneia*" to refer to marriage within the prohibited relationships of Leviticus 18:6-18.[36] This view fits well with the historical, geographical and cultural context of Matthew's Gospel—a book clearly designed to benefit Jewish readers, showing them that Jesus fulfilled the Messianic prophecies (see Mt 1:23; 2:5-6, 15, 18, 23).

Leviticus 18:6-18 forbids marriages between near relatives. Wenham summarizes the basic prohibition:

A man may not marry any woman who is a close blood relation, or any woman who has become a close relation through a previous marriage to one of the man's close blood relations.[37]

The phrase used repeatedly, "to uncover the nakedness of," is a Hebrew euphemism for sexual intercourse (see Deut 22:30) and refers here to marriage (18:18). Yet because of their illicit nature, they "cannot be regarded as genuine marriages."[38] According to this view, the exception clause in Matthew 19:9 simply states that Christ's prohibition against divorce (Mt 19:6) does not apply in the case of an illegal, incestuous marriage—one that should not have been consummated in the first place. Jesus, then, is teaching "no divorce," save the exceptional situation where marriage has taken place within the prohibited relationships of Leviticus 18:6-18. This view of "except for *porneia*" is supported by the following considerations.

New Testament Usage. Since one lexical meaning of *porneia* is "incest" or "incestuous marriage"[39] this must be considered as a possible interpretation of the exception. In 1 Corinthians 5:1 Paul uses *porneia* to refer to the incestuous marriage of a man to his father's widow—a flagrant violation of Leviticus 18:18. A careful comparison of Acts 15:20, 29 with Leviticus 17:8-18:18 indicates James had incestuous marriage in mind when he used the term *porneia* in the Jerusalem Council discussion.[40] All this implies is that "incestuous marriage" must be considered as a *possible* interpretation of *porneia* in Matthew 5:32 and 19:9. The context will ultimately determine how the word is actually being used.

Jewish Literature. In support of the incestuous marriage view, Joseph Fitzmeyer appeals to the Qumran scrolls to present evidence that there is first-century Palestinian support for this interpretation of *porneia* in Matthew 5:32 and 19:9.[41] He demonstrates that *porneia's* Hebrew counterpart, $z^e n \hat{u} \underline{t}$ (see LXX Jer 3:2, 9), is used of marriage with the forbidden degrees of kinship. This interpretation of *porneia* has had literary support in writings of later Judaism,[42] but now there is evidence from the literature of first-century Judaism.

Jewish Context. There is no question that Matthew addressed his Gospel to a Jewish audience who would understand and appreciate his many references to Old Testament prophecy and fulfillment. Accordingly, the matter of *porneia* would be a problem of primary concern for Jewish readers acquainted with the Old Testament law. This would account for the inclusion of the exception clause in Matthew, and its absence in Mark and Luke, which are addressed to Roman and Greek readers respectively. If *porneia* were to be interpreted broadly, there is no reason for Mark to have omitted the exception from Jesus' teaching on divorce.

Historical Background. The "incestuous marriage" interpretation of *porneia* fits well with the historical background of Jesus' confrontation with the Pharisees. The Jewish readers of Matthew's Gospel were well aware of the incestuous marriage of the Herods—Archelaus,

Antipas and Agrippa II—as reported by the historian Josephus.[43] Since Jesus was in the jurisdiction of Herod Antipas when confronted by the Pharisees, it is reasonable to assume that he might refer to Herod's marital situation. In fact, it appears that the Pharisees attempted to lure Jesus into making a statement against this marriage as had John the Baptist (Mt 14:4). In his response, Jesus declared that divorce was wrong. But he avoided a confrontation with Herod Antipas and a possible premature culmination to his ministry by simply stating that in the unique case of incestuous marriage the prohibition against divorce did not apply.

Immediate Context. One final argument for this specialized use of *porneia* in Matthew 19:9 is the immediate context in which the exception is found. If *porneia* refers to the prohibited relationships of Leviticus 18:16-18, then Jesus' teaching is consistent with God's ideal for marriage as set forth in Matthew 19:4-6 and Mark 10:6-8. God's plan for marriage does not include divorce except in the case of what would constitute an illegal, incestuous marriage. This narrow view of *porneia* would also explain the reaction of the disciples: "If the relationship of a man and his wife is like this, it is better not to marry" (Mt 19:10). Had Jesus permitted divorce for adultery or other illicit sexual behavior, his teaching would not have risen above that of Shammai and would not have provoked such a response.

While *porneia* can be used in a broad sense in the New Testament, the Jewish setting, historical background, and immediate context of Matthew 19:1-12 would indicate that Jesus was using the term in a specialized sense to refer to incestuous marriage.

The Question of Remarriage

Most of those who hold that the exception clause applies to adultery, or some sexual sin, believe that the exception allows for both divorce *and* remarriage.[44] It is not conclusive, however, that the exception applies *both* to divorce and remarriage. In fact, the evidence is to the contrary.

The Placement of the Exception. There are three possible places in Matthew 19:9 where the exception could be placed—at the beginning, in the middle or at the end of the sentence. The careful analysis of Wenham and Heth demonstrates that the precise placement of "except for *porneia*" in the Greek text indicates that the exception applies to divorce, but not to remarriage.[45]

The History of Interpretation. While the church fathers held that divorce was permitted for adultery, with the exception of Ambrosiaster (A.D. 375), they did not interpret the exception clause to allow for remarriage. This interpretation of the divorce texts remained the standard view of the church in the West until the sixteenth century when Erasmus suggested that the "innocent" spouse had the right not only to divorce, but also to contract a new marriage.[46] It is significant that those who had the closest contact with the language and culture of the New Testament did not regard the exception to apply to remarriage.

The Eunuch Passage. Many have interpreted Matthew 19:10-12 as Jesus' teaching on celibacy. Yet Paul, who otherwise appeals to the teaching of Jesus (1 Cor 7:10), writes, "Now concerning virgins I have no command of the Lord" (1 Cor 7:25). It appears that neither Paul nor the church fathers interpreted Matthew 19:10-12 as Jesus' teaching on celibacy. A careful study of the context and the history of interpretation indicates that "the eunuch passage" addresses the issue of remarriage for the one who has divorced for *porneia.*[47] The one who "makes himself a eunuch for the sake of the kingdom" is a divorced person who chooses the single life, not remarriage, for the sake of Christ's kingdom.

The Contribution of Matthew 5:32. In the other divorce text in Matthew (5:31-32), Jesus refutes the Pharisaic interpretation of Deuteronomy 24:1-4 by pointing out that any man who divorces his wife exposes her to the temptation to commit adultery by marrying again. According to 5:32, divorce by itself is adultery, unless it be for *porneia.* But Jesus' words "whoever marries a divorced woman commits adultery" indicate that remarriage after divorce is not permitted.

The Contribution of Mark and Luke. Both Mark and Luke contribute to our understanding of what Jesus taught concerning divorce and remarriage. First, Mark alone mentions the possibility of a woman divorcing her husband (Mk 10:12). While Jesus clearly mentioned this, Matthew did not record it in his Gospel to the Jews since Jewish law did not permit a woman to divorce her husband.[48]

Second, Mark and Luke omit any mention of the exception to the

permanence of marriage in the case of *porneia.* They clearly understood that the exception would relate only to the Jews living under
the Mosaic regulations of Leviticus 18:6-18.

Third, Mark records that Jesus' conversation with the Pharisees
ended with his affirmation of the inviolability and permanence of
marriage (Mk 10:6). Further teaching concerning the consequences
of divorce and remarriage was given to the disciples "in the house"
(Mk 10:10), probably after Jesus found lodging for the evening.

Fourth, Luke records Jesus' teaching that to marry a divorced person—no exception given—would be to enter into an existing marriage and hence to commit adultery (Lk 16:18). This is consistent with
Jesus' instruction in Matthew 5:32.

Is Adultery Once or Continual? It has been argued that the present
tense of the verb *moichaō,* "commits adultery," indicates that divorce
and remarriage involves acts of repeated adultery and that the only
way to cease sinning and demonstrate genuine repentance is to end
the "adulterous marriage." While the present tense of *moichaō can*
be interpreted in this way, it is also possible that the present tense,
"commits adultery," may be used in an aoristic sense expressing the
idea of a present fact without reference to progress. The aoristic
present sets forth an event as now occurring.[49] So interpreted, the
adultery would involve one punctiliar action at the time of the remarriage.

The context of the passage, which contains a succession of aorists,
and the prohibition against returning to one's former spouse after a
second marriage (Deut 24:1-4) would point in the direction of the
second view. It has been objected that this viewpoint may encourage
a couple to remarry, commit adultery, confess it and go on their
blissful way. But it should be noted that even one act of adultery is
a serious sin in God's sight (Heb 13:4; Prov 6:33). To presume on God's
grace by sinning willfully against the light of knowledge would be to
provoke his wrath. True believers could not sin in such a manner
without incurring God's discipline (see Heb 12:6-11).

Since the present tense, "commits adultery," can be used to argue
in favor of either view, it seems that the matter must be decided on
the basis of other clear statements of Scripture. Should sexual intercourse between married partners cease? Not according to Paul (1 Cor

7:5). Should marriage end in divorce? Not according to Jesus (Mk 10:9; Mt 19:6). It may be that confessing the sin, but continuing the marriage is the *least* culpable course of action for the divorced and remarried Christian.

Many people argue that God's grace means that a divorced Christian gets a second chance at marriage. This smacks of license, not grace. It implies that God has a standard, but it really doesn't matter if it is violated. What grace means is that a divorced and remarried couple need not break up. Although entering their marriage wrongfully, they should remain in that marital state in which they find themselves (see 1 Cor 7:17-24).

There is no place for absolute dogmatism on this issue. Ultimately the couple involved must determine their responsibilities from a study of Scripture. Those who choose to end their marriage because it was consummated wrongfully must be respected. Those who recognize their wrong (see 1 Jn 1:9), appropriate God's forgiveness and choose to continue their marriages in good conscience must not be condemned (see Rom 14:3-12).

The Teaching of Paul

Christians struggling with the issue of divorce and remarriage are faced with confusing and often contradictory arguments. It would be most helpful to know how a first-century Greek scholar and theologian understood Jesus' teaching on this topic. Fortunately, we have such a first-century interpreter of the words of Jesus in the apostle Paul. His analysis and understanding of the teachings of Jesus in 1 Corinthians sheds much needed light on the present divorce and remarriage controversy.[50]

First Corinthians contains Paul's replies to a number of inquiries made by the Corinthian believers. This is evidenced by his words "Now concerning the things about which you wrote" (7:1) and the repeated use of the introductory phrase *peri de* ("now concerning"— 7:25; 8:1; 12:1; 16:1). In chapter 7 Paul responds to several questions which the Corinthian believers were asking concerning marriage.

Is Divorce Permitted? (1 Cor 7:10-11). In verses 10-11 Paul addresses married believers about maintaining their marriage relationship. Appealing to the authoritative command *(parangellō)*[51] of Jesus (see Mt 19:6; Mk 10:9-12; Lk 16:18), Paul declares in no uncertain terms that married persons should not seek divorce. Twice he affirms the principle of no divorce: "the wife should not leave her husband" (7:10), and "the husband should not send his wife away" (7:11). The word translated "leave" *(chōrizō)* means "to divide" or "separate" and was something of a "technical term in connexion with divorce" in the first century.[52] The word "send away" *(aphiēmi)* means to "send away," "dismiss" or "let go." It is used in the papyri of a girl to her lover asking that she not be "forsaken."[53] Here the term is used as a virtual equivalent of *chōrizō* and means "send away by divorce."

Paul interpreted Christ's "command" as prohibiting divorce among married believers. Hans Conzelmann observes that "the regulation is absolute; for it comes from the Lord himself."[54] F. F. Bruce adds this comment:

> For a Christian husband or wife divorce is excluded by the law of Christ: here Paul has no need to express a judgment of his own, for the Lord's ruling on the matter was explicit.[55]

It has been noted that in Paul's quotation of Christ's command, no "exceptive clause" is present. It appears that in the teaching of Jesus known to the apostle Paul, the word of Jesus concerning divorce had no "exception clause."[56] Another possible explanation for its absence is that Paul may not have viewed the "exception clause" as applicable to believing Gentiles.

Yet Paul concedes that in a fallen world, divorce does occur. What, then, should be the course of action followed by believers who disobey Christ's command and become divorced or separated? Paul addresses this question in the parenthesis found in verse 11. He leaves the divorced believer with only two options. The first option is to remain permanently unmarried—the present tense of *menō* ("remain") emphasizing the permanent situation. The active voice of the verb suggests that the believer must actively pursue this single state. This would prevent any third-party involvement and encourage the possibility of reconciliation. As Gordon Fee comments, "The wife who may happen to divorce her husband may not use her present unmarried condition as an excuse for remarriage to someone else."[57]

The second option mentioned by Paul is that of reconciliation to one's partner—the aorist tense of *katallassō* ("reconciled") emphasizing attaining the end of the reconciliation process. Harold Mare comments, "The stress of the passage on maintaining the marriage bond unbroken definitely strengthens the injunction for separated marriage partners to become reconciled."[58]

The priorities of responsibility are clear. A married person should not divorce a spouse. But if this command is disobeyed, then there are but two options for the divorced or separated believer—to remain single or be reconciled. Paul gives no other options, for according to his understanding, neither did Jesus.

Is a Mixed Marriage Binding? (1 Cor 7:12-16). Paul goes on in verses 12-16 to deal with the responsibility of a believer in a mixed marriage. Is a marriage between a Christian and a pagan binding? Does the marriage relationship change when one of the partners becomes converted? In view of the pagan practices in Corinth, would it be advisable for a believer to terminate a marriage with an unbeliever?

In terms of structure, the text prohibits divorce (vv. 12-13) and then presents a reason *(gar)* for preserving the union (v. 14). This is followed by a declaration of freedom from slavery (v. 15) and a reason *(gar)* for allowing release (v. 16).

While Christ did not give any command regarding mixed marriages ("I say, not the Lord," v. 12), Paul does, and his teaching is divinely inspired and authoritative. As in the case of two married believers, Paul's instruction is "no divorce" *(mē aphietō).* If the unbelieving partner is willing to remain with the Christian, then the Christian partner must not seek a divorce. The believing husband is not to divorce his unbelieving wife (7:12). Nor is the believing wife to divorce her unbelieving husband (7:13). The prohibition against divorce is given four times in verses 10-13! According to Paul, a marriage is binding even if one of the partners is an unbeliever. The marriage covenant which binds a couple together is in no way changed when one of the partners is converted.

Paul points out in verse 14 one reason *(gar)* for preserving the marriage. Paul asserts that by continuing the marriage the unbelieving partner "is sanctified" *(hagiazō),* literally "set apart," through the believing spouse. What is the unbelieving partner "set apart" to? The pagan partner is set apart to receive a Christian witness and influence which would not be the case otherwise. In addition, the children of the couple are "holy." This does not mean they are "saved," but rather that they too are "set apart" to receive a testimony and may well avoid the entanglements of pagan worship and its evil practices.

While marriage was not designed by God as a program for personal evangelism (see 2 Cor 6:14-18; Eph 5:31-33), in the case of a spiritually mixed marriage, the Christian partner is not to seek divorce. By maintaining the union, the home will be provided with a Christian witness and influence it might otherwise not receive.

In verse 15 Paul acknowledges that the unbelieving partner may insist on ending the marriage when his or her spouse converts to Christianity. If the unbelieving partner insists on ending the marriage, is the believing brother or sister required by the command of Jesus and teaching of Paul to preserve the union at all cost? Verse 15 is interpreted by some as allowing for divorce and remarriage in the case of abandonment in the interests of preserving peace. Paul is understood to be exercising his "pastoral privilege" in modifying the teaching of Jesus by adding another exception—desertion. Jay Adams is representative of those who take this view:

> All the bonds of marriage have been removed. He is released entirely from every marriage obligation, and is a totally free person.
> Nor is there any obligation to be reconciled in marriage.[59]

While Adams's interpretation is popular among evangelicals, it lacks strong support from the biblical text. First, it is very unlikely that Paul would permit in verse 15 something forbidden in verses 10-13.[60] Second, while Paul recognized the possibility of unapproved divorce among Christians, under the command of Jesus remarriage to another partner was not allowed (vv. 10-11). It is difficult to see why remarriage should be allowed in this case (v. 15) and not in the preceding one (vv. 10-11), since Paul taught that marriage with a believer is no different from marriage with an unbeliever. Third, the winning of the unbelieving partner to Christ (v. 14) would take place only through a continued or reconciled marriage, not through divorce and remarriage to a new partner.

In verse 15 Paul is simply saying that if the unbelieving partner demands separation, then the believer is not "under bondage" *(dedoulōtai,* literally "enslaved") to preserve the union through legal maneuvers or by pursuing the unwilling partner all over the Roman Empire. The word *enslaved* has to do with how the partners relate. Is the believer to function like a slave in relationship to the partner who is unwilling to maintain the marriage? Paul answers, "No!" The word *enslaved* is set in contrast with the words *at peace.* The rejected Christian partner is either "enslaved" or "at peace." Peace in the midst of a difficult situation is God's portion for a rejected Christian partner, not a new marriage. Paul is simply saying in verse 15 that Christ's prohibition against divorce does not enslave the believer to maintain the union against the wishes of an unbelieving partner who insists on ending the marriage.

Some have mistakenly concluded that the words "under bondage" in verse 15 are identical or related to the word *bound* in verse 39, and that verse 15 contains an exception to the permanence of marriage expressed in verse 39. One popular expositor has stated that Paul uses the same root word *doulos* in verse 39 as he does in verse 15.[61] But this is simply not the case. The words are quite different. The Greek word *douloō* used by Paul in verse 15 means "to enslave" or "bring into bondage."[62] The believing partner does not have to make him or herself a slave to the unbelieving spouse. The Greek word *deō* used by Paul in verse 39 means "to tie, bind, or fasten."[63] The words used by Paul in verses 15 and 39 are obviously not the same word, and they are not even related to the same root. *Douloō* is derived from *doulos* and is used in the Septuagint to translate *'ābaḏ* ("to serve"), while *deō* is its own root and is used in the Septuagint to translate *asar* ("to tie up").

The word *deō* is used by Paul in Acts 20:22 to describe his sense of constraint or obligation to go to Jerusalem. "And now, behold, *bound* in spirit, I am on my way to Jerusalem, not knowing what will happen to me there" (NASB). Paul uses *deō* in Romans 7:2 and 1 Corinthians 7:26, 39 to describe the marriage commitment which is "binding" until death. Paul is saying in 1 Corinthians 7 that the marriage relationship is binding until death (v. 39), but a rejected spouse is not "enslaved" to the extent of having to maintain the marriage against the wishes of the unbelieving and unwilling partner.

Many of those who take verse 15 as allowing for divorce in the case of desertion also argue that a second marriage is permitted. David

Atkinson comments, "This ['not enslaved'] must presumably mean 'not bound to the marriage bond.' "[64] A pastor asserts:

> Being free of that "bondage" obviously means being free of the responsibility of that marriage. The desertion of the unsaved partner breaks the bond thus freeing the believer to divorce and remarry.[65]

But note carefully that Paul says nothing in the verse about a second marriage for the deserted spouse. Allowance for the deserted spouse to remarry is simply not stated here and cannot be substantiated by an exegesis of this verse. Robertson and Plummer conclude:

> All that "he is not bound" clearly means is that he or she need not feel so bound by Christ's prohibition of divorce as to be afraid to depart when the heathen partner insists on separation.[66]

Dungan agrees that "nothing more is permitted the Christian than accepting the unbelieving partner's wish for divorce."[67] To conclude that remarriage is allowable is to go beyond the clearly stated words of the text.[68]

Paul makes no reference to remarriage except in the case of the death of the spouse (Rom 7:2-3; 1 Cor 7:39; 1 Tim 5:14). For a marriage that ends short of death, reconciliation or a single life are the only two alternatives Paul acknowledges (7:11).

As verse 14 provides the reason *(gar)* for maintaining the marriage, so verse 16 provides reasons *(gar)* for allowing separation. If the unbeliever demands divorce, it should be granted for the sake of peace. While the continuation of the marriage may provide the unbelieving partner with a gospel witness, the conversion of the unbeliever is not guaranteed by the continuation of the marriage.

Is a Virgin Permitted to Marry? (1 Cor 7:25-38). Having stated and illustrated the principle that Christians should not try to change their marital status, but should be content with their present calling, Paul responds to the question of whether unmarried women should marry. The fact that they are called *parthenon* ("virgins") is quite significant and is the key to understanding the verses that follow. That these "virgins" are women is evident from the context (see vv. 28, 34, 36, 37, 38). While Jesus gave no command on this matter, Paul addresses the issue providing the Corinthians with his divinely inspired and authoritative instruction. Paul's conviction is that in view of the "present distress" it is best for believers to remain in their present state (v. 26). The "present distress" is not identified specifically and probably refers to the general difficulty of supporting and caring for a family in a world that is rapidly changing (v. 31). It can be assumed from the general nature of Paul's statements that the "present distress" was not unique to Corinth or to the first-century setting.

According to Paul, the single life is the best course to follow in light of (1) the burdens of family life in an unfriendly world (7:26-28), (2) the transitory nature of things in view of the Lord's imminent return (7:29-31) and (3) the greater freedom and opportunity afforded a single person in serving Christ (7:32-53). Paul views the single life not as morally better, but as providing greater opportunity to be useful for Christ.

However, Paul assures his readers that for a "virgin" to marry is not sinful, but marriage will incur greater responsibility and potential trouble in life (7:28). Therefore, he says, it is best to remain in the marital state you find yourself in. He warns that those who are married ("bound") should not seek the unmarried state. The present imperative, *mē zētei lusin* (v. 27), may be translated, "never at any time seek freedom." Married persons should always strive to maintain their marital status quo.

Paul adds in verse 27 that those who are "released" *(lelusai)* from a wife should not seek a wife. Some would argue that Paul is referring to those who have been divorced, and that they may remarry without sin (v. 28).[69] But does "released from a wife" mean divorced? A reading of the English text might lead one to conclude that Paul is referring to those who have been divorced ("released"). But a careful study of the Greek text indicates that this is not the case.

The words "bound" *(dedesai)* and "released" *(lelusai)* are in the perfect tense, expressing a state or condition. These words contrast two opposite states, not actions. Paul is not saying "Did you get married?" looking back to the event but merely "Are you married?"—describing the present state. So the contrasting question is not "Did you get divorced?" but rather "Are you single?"—also describing the present state. The words of Paul in verse 27 portray a state of singleness with no suggestion of a previous marriage.

There is no question of divorce in Paul's instruction of verse 27. He is simply acknowledging the existence of two general groups: those who are bound by matrimonial ties and those who are in a state of freedom from matrimonial ties. Paul's thought is expressed well by the NIV translation: "Are you married? Do not seek a divorce. Are you unmarried? Do not look for a wife." The English translation "loosed" or "released" in verse 27 demands a situation not called for by the Greek word *lelusai.*

But if Paul is thinking only of "virgins," as verse 25 suggests, why must he repeat his words in verse 28, "But if you should marry, you have not sinned; and if a virgin should marry, she has not sinned" (NASB)? Is Paul suggesting that a divorced person as well as a virgin may marry without sin? The context is the key to understanding the meaning of this verse.

In verse 26 Paul states his general guideline that it is best for believers to maintain their marital status quo. In verses 27–28 he addresses the issue from a man's perspective. Paul essentially says, "Remain in the marital state you find yourself in whether attached or unattached to a wife. But don't consider it to be a sin if you decide to marry." Then he goes on to make specific application of his teaching to the situation of the young unmarried women ("virgins," see v. 25), "and if a virgin should marry, she has not sinned." Phillips captures the flow of Paul's thought in his translation of verse 28: "But if you, a man, should marry, don't think that you have done anything sinful. And the same applies to a young woman."[70]

Is a Widow Permitted to Remarry? (1 Cor 7:39-40). Paul concludes his discussion concerning marriage with a brief word concerning the remarriage of widows. He states quite clearly that marriage is a lifelong relationship. "A wife is bound as long as her husband lives" (7:39). The word dedetai (perfect tense of *deō)* is "a strong expression for the unbroken ties of marriage."[71]

Paul's view expressed here is in harmony with his words in Romans 7:1-3. There he uses the binding and lifelong nature of marriage to illustrate the theological point that death dissolves the dominion of the law (Rom 6:14; 7:1). Paul states that a woman is bound to her husband as long as he lives, but that when he dies she is released from the marital relationship (Rom 7:2). If while her husband yet lives she is "joined" (that is, "married") to another man, she shall be called an adulteress. Only on the death of the husband is the woman free to remarry without sin (Rom 7:3).

The teaching of Paul serves as the culmination of God's revelation on the issue of divorce and remarriage. The illustration in Romans 7:2-3 reflects Paul's view, expounded in 1 Corinthians 7, on the indissolubility of marriage. This perspective on marriage as permanent until death is consistently reflected throughout the Hebrew and New Testament Scriptures.

Conclusion

Is an unhappily married person allowed to divorce? Is a divorced person allowed to remarry? For those who are willing to hear and heed, the Bible gives clear answers to these questions.

On the basis of our survey of the major scriptural passages on marriage, divorce and remarriage, we can conclude the following: (1) the original creative intention and desired will of God is that marriage be permanent until death; (2) neither God himself nor God through Moses commanded divorce; (3) the explanation the New Testament gives for allowing divorce in the Old Testament is the hardness of the people's hearts—hearts unsubmitted to the restraints of a high and holy God; (4) Paul asserts that the fundamental teachings of Jesus must be followed precisely, that the wife should not leave her husband and that the husband should not divorce his wife; (5) remarriage is permissible without sin for a widow or widower, if the marriage is to another believer; (6) remarriage following divorce, by either the husband or wife, constitutes an act of adultery; (7) marriage to a divorced person constitutes an act of adultery; (8) when a divorce does occur, the only two scriptural options for the divorced person are reconciliation or the single life.[72]

If a biblical view on divorce and remarriage were taught in today's churches, marriage would be entered into with greater caution and partners would commit themselves to making their marriage work. Marriages would be stronger and longer lasting were divorce not viewed as a way out of a difficult relationship.

Case Study

John has been on the elder board for twelve years. He is growing in the Lord and from every indication he appears to have a hunger to know the Word and apply it. Early in his fifteen-year marriage, John's wife discovered that John had relations with another woman before they were ever married. John had never told his wife about it because his relationship was a one-night collegiate stand and it happened while he was a non-believer. He didn't try to hide the past from his wife, he just didn't feel that it was a necessary thing that needed to be known by his wife. For ten of those fifteen years of marriage, John's wife, Sue, has nursed a resentment for being deceived. Her anger has been carefully hidden. Most people in the church see Sue as a godly woman. Yet, through the years, Sue's heart has grown cold toward her husband. She begins looking for a man whom she can respect and finds another man in another church whom she admires. Soon she is deeply in love with this other man. She announces that she is filing for divorce. She leaves the church and is unwilling to talk to any church leaders. She says she knows it is wrong, "but God will bring blessing out of wrong." She commits adultery with the other man. Sue is resolute about changing her mind. Closed to counsel, she pursues the divorce. But young children are involved and Sue is insistent that she have total custody of the children. What is John to do?

Is counterfiling for divorce a sin or his part?

Does he have an obligation to protect his children?

Does he let his wife have her way because he doesn't want to file for divorce since he believes it is unbiblical?

Answer

John is faced with a situation somewhat like that of the prophet Hosea. His wife has committed adultery and is resolute in her determination to end the marriage. I would encourage him to pray for his disobedient wife and to ask God to demonstrate the greatness of his grace and the power of redeeming love by bringing about a reconciliation. John cannot restore this marriage, but God can and *may* be pleased to do so. No marriage is beyond reconciliation until remarriage occurs (see Deut 24:1-4).

A tragedy such as this can make one bitter or better. In coping with this situation, I would encourage John to take this trial as from the Lord and use it as an opportunity to deepen his own spiritual life. For direction in dealing with his wife, I recommend that John read Ed Wheat's helpful little book, *How to Save Your Marriage Alone* (Zondervan, 1983).

Whatever the end result of this marital conflict, John can maintain his own integrity and follow biblical principles in dealing with a less than ideal situation. His best efforts may not save his marriage, but he can please God by avoiding bitterness and by living his own life according to scriptural teaching.

Is counterfiling for divorce a sin on John's part? The answer to this question depends on one's understanding of Paul's teaching on lawsuits (1 Cor 6:1-11). The biblical principle I glean from this text is that Christians should avoid bringing their disputes before unbelieving judges. I would recommend to John that alternatives to a countersuit be explored. Perhaps the settlement could be negotiated by the attorneys. Perhaps his spouse would consent to have the settlement mediated by a third party.

State laws vary and legal counsel would be necessary, but in many cases the only way for John to protect himself against an embittered wife is to file a countersuit as the basis for a negotiated settlement. I believe that 1 Corinthians 6:1-11 teaches the *avoidance* of court settlements rather than prohibiting them altogether. In some circumstances it may be best to be wronged and let the matter pass. Some situations involve more than financial loss and may require action. After all the alternatives have been explored and John is faced with wholesale exploitation by his wife, I do not believe counterfiling for divorce would constitute a sin on John's part. While I firmly believe that divorce is always wrong, it seems that John is forced into these circumstances by the actions of his wife and the peculiarities of the legal system.

Does John have an obligation to protect his children? Yes, a man's responsibility to his children does not end with the breakup of a marriage. As Paul says, "But if any one does not provide for his own, and especially for those of his household, he has denied the faith, and is worse than an unbeliever" (1 Tim 5:8 NASB). John's biblical responsibilities would include providing for his children, protecting and teaching them. Divorce makes these responsibilities more difficult, but the father would still bear a responsibility to do his best to fulfill them. Counterfiling for divorce may be necessary to gain custody of the children or at least share custody with the wife.

Does John let his wife have her way because he doesn't want to file for divorce since he believes it is unbiblical? As indicated above, I do not believe that John's view (that divorce is unbiblical) would prohibit him from taking legal steps to protect himself and his children against a wife who seeks the ruin of the family.

By way of summary, John is faced with the practical application of three basic biblical principles: Divorce is wrong; lawsuits should be avoided; a father should protect his children. In John's situation these principles are in tension. Recognizing that divorce is wrong and that lawsuits should be avoided, John could let his wife have her way. But this may jeopardize his children. While maintaining his views on the permanence of marriage and seeking to avoid a lawsuit, John may be forced by the legal system to counterfile for divorce in the interests of protecting his defenseless children. I would advise John to seek counsel from his pastor and church elders in making this decision. Their counsel, support and encouragement would be essential.

Notes

[1]J. Carl Laney, *The Divorce Myth* (Minneapolis: Bethany House Publishers, 1981).

[2]William Sanford LaSor, *The Dead Sea Scrolls and the New Testament* (Grand Rapids: Eerdmans Publishing Co., 1972), p. 27.

[3]Edwin M. Yamauchi, "Cultural Aspects of Marriage in the Ancient World," *Bibliotheca Sacra* 135 (July–September 1978):249.

[4]Renald E. Showers, *Lawfully Wedded* (Langhorne, Penn.: Philadelphia College of the Bible, 1983), p. 36.

[5]Lewis B. Smedes, "Controlling the Unpredictable: The Power of Promising," *Christianity Today,* January 21, 1983, p. 17.

[6]Roland de Vaux, *Ancient Israel: Social Institutions,* Vol. 1 (New York: McGraw-Hill Book Company, 1965), p. 35.

[7]Peter C. Craigie, *The Book of Deuteronomy,* New International Commentary on the Old Testament (Grand Rapids: Eerdmans Publishing Co., 1976), p. 305.

[8]James B. Pritchard, ed., *Ancient Near Eastern Texts,* 3rd ed. with supplement (Princeton, N.J.: Princeton University Press, 1969), p. 543.

[9]Craigie, *Deuteronomy,* p. 305.

[10]Gittin 9.3.

[11]The word *abomination (toebah)* is used of things detestable in either the

moral sense or general sense: foreign gods (Deut 32:16), unclean animals for food (Deut 14:3), homosexual relations (Lev 18:22). The term is used in Leviticus 18:26-30 with reference to numerous previously mentioned aberrations including incest, adultery, child sacrifice, homosexuality and bestiality.

[12]Laney, *The Divorce Myth*, p. 32.

[13]J. A. Thompson, *Deuteronomy* (Downers Grove: InterVarsity Press, 1974), p. 244.

[14]R. Yaron, "The Restitution of Marriage," *Journal of Jewish Studies* 17 (1966):1-11.

[15]Gordon J. Wenham, "The Restoration of Marriage Reconsidered," *Journal of Jewish Studies* 30 (1979):36-40.

[16]Ibid., p. 40.

[17]Gordon Wenham, "The Biblical View of Marriage and Divorce: Old Testament Teaching," *Third Way* 21 (Nov. 3, 1977):9.

[18]For further study see, J. Carl Laney, *Ezra-Nehemiah* (Chicago: Moody Press, 1982), p. 49-64.

[19]I previously argued that *yatsa* implied "divorce" since it is used in the divorce text of Deut 24:2 *(The Divorce Myth,* p. 38). On the basis of further study I discovered that in Ezra *yatsa* appears in a different form (Qal) than in the divorce text of Deut 24:2 (Hiphil). There it is used of the woman's departure from the house after she has received a divorce certificate and been "sent out." In neither Deut 24:2 or Ezra 10:3 is the translation or concept of "divorce" demanded.

[20]I am in debt to my student Jim Boyle whose paper "Biblical Principles on Marriage, Divorce & Remarriage," stimulated my thinking on this parallel.

[21]A. E. Cundall, "Ezra," in *The New Bible Commentary: Revised,* eds. D. Guthrie and J. A. Motyer (Grand Rapids: Eerdmans Publishing Company, 1970), p. 404.

[22]Eli Cashdad, "Malachi" in *The Twelve Prophets, The Soncino Books of the Bible,* ed. A. Cohen (London: The Soncino Press, 1948), p. 345.

[23]David E. Garland, "A Biblical View of Divorce" *Review and Expositor* 84 (Summer 1987):420.

[24]Walter C. Kaiser, Jr., *Malachi: God's Unchanging Love* (Grand Rapids: Baker Book House, 1984), p. 70.

[25]See Laney, *The Divorce Myth,* pp. 47-48.

[26]C. F. Keil, "Minor Prophets" in *Commentary On the Old Testament,* C. F. Keil and F. Delitzsch, vol. X (Grand Rapids: Eerdmans Publishing Co., 1982), p. 454.

[27]Kaiser, *Malachi: God's Unchanging Love,* pp. 73-74.

[28]Joyce Baldwin, *Haggai, Zechariah, Malachi* (Downers Grove: InterVarsity Press, 1972), p. 241.

[29]Josephus *Antiquities* 18. 109-111; Aidan Mahoney, "A New Look at the

Divorce Clauses in Matthew 5:32 and 19:9," *Catholic Biblical Quarterly* 30 (1968):33.

[30]*Gittin* 9:10.

[31]Robert H. Gundry, *Matthew: A Commentary on His Literary and Theological Art* (Grand Rapids: Eerdmans Publishing Co., 1982), p. 379.

[32]Craigie, *Deuteronomy*, p. 305.

[33]Gordon Wenham, "May Divorced Christians Remarry?" *(Churchman* 95 (1981):152-53. The single exception was Ambrosiaster (A.D. 375) who allowed remarriage for an "innocent" husband, but not an "innocent" wife.

[34]Mark Geldard, *Churchman* 92 (1978):134.

[35]Ibid., pp. 135-37.

[36]Joseph Jensen, "Does *porneia* Mean Fornication?" *Novum Testamentum* 20 (July 1978):180; Ben Witherington, "Matthew 5:32 and 19:9—Exception or Exceptional Situation?" *New Testament Studies* 31 (1985):571-76; F. J. Moloney, "Matthew 19, 3-12 and Celibacy: A Redactional and Form Critical Study," *Journal for the Study of the New Testament* 2 (January 1979):42-60.

[37]G. J. Wenham, *The Book of Leviticus,* New International Commentary on the Old Testament (Grand Rapids: Eerdmans Publishing Co., 1979), p. 255.

[38]R. K. Harrison, *Leviticus* (Downers Grove: InterVarsity Press, 1980), p. 186.

[39]H. Reisser, "Discipline: πορνευω," *New International Dictionary of New Testament Theology,* 3 vols., ed. Colin Brown (Grand Rapids: Zondervan, 1975-78), 1:499.

[40]F. F. Bruce, *Paul: Apostle of the Heart Set Free* (Grand Rapids: Eerdmans Publishing Co., 1977), p. 185; for a complete analysis, see Laney, *The Divorce Myth,* pp. 73-74.

[41]Joseph A. Fitzmyer, "The Matthean Divorce Texts and Some Palestinian Evidence," *Theological Studies* 37 (1976):213-21.

[42]*Testament of Judah* 13:6; *Testament of Reuben* 1:6.

[43]Josephus *Antiquities* 18. 109-119; 20. 145-147; Wars 2. 114-116.

[44]John Murray, *Divorce* (Philadelphia: Orthodox Presbyterian Church, 1953), pp. 36-43.

[45]W. A. Heth and G. J. Wenham, *Jesus and Divorce* (London: Hodder and Stoughton, 1984), pp. 113-16.

[46]W. A. Heth, "An Analysis and Critique of the Evangelical Protestant View of Divorce and Remarriage" (Th.M. Thesis, Dallas Theological Seminary, 1982), p. 30.

[47]Quentin Quesnell, " 'Made Themselves Eunuchs for the Kingdom of Heaven' (Mt. 19,12)," *Catholic Biblical Quarterly* 30 (July 1968):335-58; W. A. Heth, "Unmarried 'For the Sake of the Kingdom' (Matthew 19:12) in the Early Church" *Grace Theological Journal* 8.1 (1987):55-88; Gundry, *Matthew,* pp. 381-83.

[48]Josephus *Antiquities* 15. 259.

[49]H. E. Dana and Julius R. Mantey, *A Manual Grammar of the Greek New*

Testament (Toronto: The Macmillan Company, 1972), p. 184.

[50]The substance of this section appeared in my article, "Paul and the Permanence of Marriage in 1 Corinthians 7," *Journal of the Evangelical Theological Society* 25 (September 1982):283-93. Used by permission.

[51]When Paul gives directions on his own authority (v. 12), he says, *legō egō* ("I say") not *parangellō* ("I command").

[52]J. H. Moulton and G. Milligan, *The Vocabulary of the Greek New Testament* (Grand Rapids: Eerdmans Publishing Co., 1930), p. 696.

[53]Ibid., p. 97.

[54]Hans Conzelmann, *A Commentary on the First Epistle to the Corinthians,* trans. James W. Leitch (Philadelphia: Fortress Press, 1975), p. 120.

[55]Bruce, *Paul,* p. 167.

[56]Robert H. Stein, "Is It Lawful for a Man to Divorce His Wife?" *Journal of the Evangelical Theological Society* 22 (June 1979):118.

[57]Gordon D. Fee, *The First Epistle to the Corinthians,* New International Commentary of the New Testament (Grand Rapids: Eerdmans Publishing Co., 1987), p. 295.

[58]W. Harold Mare, "First Corinthians" in *The Expositor's Bible Commentary,* ed. Frank E. Gaebelein (Grand Rapids: Zondervan Publishing House, 1976), p. 229.

[59]Jay E. Adams, *Marriage, Divorce and Remarriage* (Phillipsburg, N.J.: Presbyterian and Reformed Publishing Company, 1980), p. 48.

[60]David L. Dungan, *The Sayings of Jesus in the Churches of Paul* (Philadelphia: Fortress Press, 1971), p. 97.

[61]Charles R. Swindoll, *Strike the Original Match* (Portland, Oreg.: Multnomah Press, 1980), pp. 145-46.

[62]G. Abbott-Smith, *A Manual Greek Lexicon of the New Testament,* s.v. "*douloō,*" p. 122.

[63]Ibid, s.v. "*deō,*" pp. 103-4.

[64]David Atkinson, *To Have and to Hold* (Grand Rapids: Eerdmans Publishing Co., 1979), p. 124.

[65]Swindoll, *Strike the Original Match,* p. 146.

[66]A. Robertson and A. Plummer, *A Critical and Exegetical Commentary on the First Epistle of St. Paul to the Corinthians* (Edinburgh: T. & T. Clark, 1911), p. 138.

[67]Dungan, *The Sayings of Jesus in the Churches of Paul,* p. 97.

[68]See Fee's helpful discussion, *First Corinthians,* pp. 302-5.

[69]Atkinson, *To Have and to Hold,* pp. 124-25.

[70]*The New Testament in Modern English,* trans. J. B. Philipps; so also Fee interprets the text, *First Corinthians,* p. 332.

[71]Mare, "First Corinthians," p. 237.

[72]For answers to the common objections and the implications for Christian leadership, see my book, *The Divorce Myth,* pp. 91-102; 103-14.

Response

William A. Heth

I want to begin by saying that I admire Carl Laney's ability to combine exegetical, pastoral and practical concerns in his essay. I wish my own chapter could have been as sensitive as his. He pursues a positive approach as he develops his own understanding of the relevant passages, always supporting his conclusions by references to the necessary lexical, grammatical and biblical/theological tools. He also quotes or refers to numerous commentaries, monographs and journal articles as he demonstrates that his is not a singular reading of the texts. Only rarely does Laney directly take issue with those who hold opposing views, and when he does he treats them fairly.

Readers of this volume will note that the chapters by Laney and myself complement one another. Our differences are minor. Our agreements are many. The first two chapters of this volume are more alike than either of the other two are with one another or with our own. Yet all four chapters desire to present answers from Scripture that will guide us in knowing God's specific will for our lives when marital breakdown occurs.

I am in complete agreement with the first two points Laney makes in his Introduction. First, he cautions that individual cases—however close they may come to devastating our emotional home—must be considered in the light of Scripture. Scripture is a revelation of God's character and will and should never be conformed to our personal preferences. I am sure that all the writers in this volume would agree on this point.

Second, I would like to echo the quotation that Laney takes from William Sanford LaSor, "We have nothing to fear from truth; only ignorance can hurt us." The size of this volume allows the contributors to present many of the strengths of their respective views. But each of our views have weaknesses, and we should be willing to discuss these as well. I sincerely hope that no one would consciously hide or obscure any evidence that undermines his or her own understanding of the biblical revelation related to this subject. I believe that only those who can make the best arguments for opposing viewpoints can best express their opinions with conviction.

Here for the first time under one cover InterVarsity makes it possible for the reader to hear four different views as each would want them to be presented. The reader may now evaluate them. Prior to the publication of Geoffrey Bromiley's *God and Marriage* in 1980 and Carl Laney's *The Divorce Myth* in 1981, evangelicals in this country had few, if any, scholarly alternatives to the view of Matthew 19:9 that permitted and sanctioned remarriage after divorce for adultery.

After our introductions, we both discuss the nature of marriage as it was designed by God at creation. Laney's approach appears to be the same as my own; we must first establish the meaning of the Genesis 2:24 paradigm of marriage in its Old Testament context before we truly hear Jesus' appeal to that passage as the basis for his teaching in the New. In short, Jesus derived whatever he taught about marriage, divorce and remarriage from Genesis 1 and 2. And if Paul is a faithful interpreter of Jesus—and we certainly believe that he is— then we must understand him along similar lines. Thus we need to be absolutely sure about the concepts taught in Genesis 2:24.

I agree with Laney that *leave* and *cleave* in Genesis 2:24 present the idea of marriage as a covenant between a man and a woman with God as the witness. But Laney goes beyond my somewhat dry treatment of the theological implications of these terms to give some very practical insights on what these concepts mean for marriages today (such as the problem of a husband or wife still being bound emotionally to the authority of their parents). In particular I liked his insight, "You or I might have used the word *love* in place of *cleave*" in Genesis 2:24 but that the concept of *cleave* in the Old Testament "would be less affected by changes in feelings and emotions." This is a needed reminder in a day in which personal peace and happiness have become gods to pursue in and of themselves. We also appear to be in basic agreement in our understanding that the reference to husband and wife becoming "one flesh" indicates that a new family or kinship unit begins with every marriage. I am still not sure, however, if Laney understands the kinship aspect of marriage in the specific way that I tend to think of it. Thus I can affirm with Laney that "marriage could be defined as God's act of joining a man and a woman in a permanent, covenanted, one-flesh relationship."

Laney's overall understanding of Deuteronomy 24:1-4—the key Old Testament passage in the divorce debate in Jesus' and our own day—is identical with my own. He says, "This passage does not institute or approve divorce, but merely treats it as a practice already known and existing." I commend Laney's willingness to change earlier conclusions in the light of new evidence. He no longer thinks that the Mosaic legislation was designed to discourage hasty divorce. This older view was based on the assumption that Moses himself instituted the practice of handing the divorced wife a certificate of divorce (v. 1); yet those who understand biblical case law agree that verses

1-3 reflect an ancient Near Eastern divorce procedure that existed long before Moses arrived on the scene. This practice did not originate with Moses or Yahweh. Laney correctly understands this important piece of evidence and how it relates to the contemporary debate.

What is the purpose of the legislation in verse 4? Laney accepts Wenham's view that the restoration of the first marriage is prohibited because it is viewed as a type of incest. I will suggest below that Wenham's application of the logic of the incest laws to the *circumstances* of this case is basically correct (that is, the restoration of the original union is prohibited if one's spouse has entered into a second marriage), but also that the specific case in Deuteronomy 24 is primarily concerned with banning another unjust practice. In the end, however, I agree with Laney's statement that "Deuteronomy 24:1-4 did not alter God's original plan for marriage. It simply provides recourse and direction where God's original plan for the permanence of marriage has not been followed."

I understand fully why Laney felt the need to discuss Ezra's marriage reform. I comment on this incident for the same reason. Some evangelicals argue for the right to divorce (and remarry?) by appealing to Ezra 9 and 10 as evidence that God does not consider all divorces wrong. A few mention that God even commands divorce in some circumstances. Laney and I both attempt to show that it is precarious to draw such conclusions from this particular passage.

When we come to the teaching of Jesus in Matthew 19:3-12, I must side with Laney in saying that a view of Matthew 19:9 that allows remarriage after divorce for immorality is contextually incongruent both with what precedes verse 9 and with what follows in verses 10-12. Furthermore, it is difficult to harmonize such an interpretation with Jesus' divorce sayings elsewhere in the Gospels. But what about Laney's "unlawful" or "incestuous marriages" view of the exception clause?

Laney adopts a view of the Matthean exception clauses which has virtually received consensus of opinion among critical exegetes within both Protestant and Catholic circles.[1] So Laney stands among a host of very respectable scholars even though the way he defends this view differs from the approach taken by some of the critical scholars. I think that the arguments he advances for his view may attract an even greater following among evangelicals, though I myself am still not ready to promote this particular "no remarriage" view of Matthew 19:9. Nevertheless, it stands high on my list as a probable reading of the text.

He concludes his arguments by saying that "God's plan for marriage does not include divorce except in the case of what would constitute an illegal, incestuous marriage." In terms of contemporary application this interpretation appears to amount to an absolute prohibition of divorce no matter what the circumstances. I do not know how strictly Laney would apply this prohibition, but I doubt that he would insist that a wife remain in a home where the husband beat her, or committed incest with the children or was promiscuously adulterous (that is, in which case his wife becomes just another one of his "flings.") My own view would not prohibit separation or legal divorce in these situations.

Laney argues that the eunuch saying in Matthew 19:12 "addresses the issue of remarriage for the one who has divorced for *porneia.*" I would agree that it applies to their situation, but that Jesus is thinking also of those who will marriage altogether because of the claims and interests of God's kingdom. Both will be able to live out their respective callings by God's grace.

I like very much the way Laney handles the question that remarriage after divorce poses for both his and my own view: "Is adultery once or continual?" Based on grammatical possibilities, the prohibition of Deuteronomy 24:1-4, Paul's statement in 1 Corinthians 7:5 and Jesus' prohibition of divorce, we should lean in the direction of viewing the action as singular at the time of remarriage.

Except for a few minor details, I agree with everything Laney says about the teaching of Paul in 1 Corinthians 7. It is amazing that evangelicals still attempt to appeal to the etymology of the words in verse 15 and verse 39 in their attempt to sanction remarriage to the deserted believer. I am thankful for the careful work of Gordon D. Fee on the status of the "notorious 'Pauline privilege.' " He gives four reasons that remarriage is not in view here, let alone sanctioned by verse 15, and adds: "All of this is not to say that Paul *disallows* remarriage in such cases; he simply does not speak to it at all. Thus this text offers little help for this very real contemporary concern."[2]

To conclude, it should be obvious that Laney and I think along the same lines. I am pleased with his contribution to this volume. Our differences stem only from the question of how to interpret the exception clause in Matthew 19:9, and, as a consequence, what this does or does not say about the permissibility of divorce without the right to remarry.

Notes

[1]Compare Ben Witherington, "Matthew 5.32 and 19.9—Exception or Exceptional Situation?" *New Testament Studies* 31 (1985):571-76. F. F. Bruce, R. P. Martin and C. C. Ryrie adopt this view as well.

[2]*The First Epistle to the Corinthians,* New International Commentary on the New Testament (Grand Rapids: Eerdmans, 1987), p. 303.

Response

Thomas R. Edgar

*I*n a time when our society as a whole is not interested in God's perspective on marriage, we should be thankful for someone who is earnest about God's view of marriage, divorce and remarriage, as Laney is. I totally agree with him that our position regarding divorce and remarriage should be based on Scripture and not on experience or our own ideas. Along with Laney, I also believe that God originally intended for marriages to be permanent, and that this is the desirable goal.

In addition I also feel that the scriptural evidence is against the concept that in a mixed marriage (believer and unbeliever) the believer should divorce the unbelieving spouse. I concur with Laney that Malachi 2:14 is intended to discourage divorce, at least the improper divorce discussed in the context. As he argues, the so-called betrothal view of Matthew 19:9 is incorrect, nor is an improper marriage a state of continuous adultery. His analysis and recommendations for the specific incident discussed in the case study seem to be correct.

However, several of these items of agreement would be considered true by all four writers in this work, and are, therefore, not crucial to the respective view. For example, most would claim to base their position regarding divorce on the Scriptures, yet there are several conflicting views. Therefore it is obvious that the areas of greatest concern are the areas of difference. These are also the areas where it is necessary to give some explanation for the differences.

Although I agree with Laney that our view of divorce and remarriage must be based on Scripture, the various differing views claim to be based on Scripture. There must be in some of these views either wrong interpretation or misplaced emphasis, or both. Any adequate analysis of Scripture on this subject must be based on all the passages. All the passages must be allowed to speak and must speak in harmony with all the others. To interpret some as if the others did not exist, and to then use the resulting interpretation as the basis to deny the explicit statements (exceptions) of those not originally taken into consideration is not really basing one's view on Scripture. It is instead a selection of passages which, taken by themselves, seem to fit the interpreter's presuppositions and then using these to get rid of those passages containing specific statements contrary to the interpreter's presuppositions.

I am referring to the use of passages such as Genesis 2:24 (which says nothing about divorce, remarriage, permanence of marriage, or for-or-against exceptions), Malachi 2:14; Mark 10:2-12; Luke 16:18; Romans 7:1-6 and 1 Corinthians 7:10-11, none of which denies the possibility of some exceptions, as a basis to conclude that since they give no exception Scripture allows no exception. This conclusion is then used to explain away the clearly stated exceptions in Matthew 5:31-32; 19:9 and to argue against the probable meaning of 1 Corinthians 7:10-11. This, it seems to me, is Laney's basic approach rather than an approach which harmonizes the voices of all the passages.

In other words, I disagree with the concept that a passage which does not give an exception may be considered as denying an exception clearly stated in another passage. This is contrary to any normal approach to Scripture on other subjects. It is also contrary to normal usage to conclude that every time a subject is mentioned a complete list of exceptions must always be stated or none exists.

Regarding individual passages, I do not agree that Genesis 2:24 indicates that marriage is a permanent relationship in the sense that it cannot be validly severed. The verse says nothing about divorce or remarriage, or permanence. Laney's argument based on the word *cleave* is placing more meaning on this word than it will bear. One of his own examples refers to a military alliance, something which no one would regard as indissoluble. This word is also used of clods of dirt cleaving together and of a girdle cleaving to one's loins. None of these are permanent or indissoluble. Laney's recourse to this argument is evidence that there is nothing in the verse to support the idea of permanence.

I also question his continued reference to Genesis 2:24 as God's intention for marriage, as if this implies indissolubility and rules out any valid exceptions. This verse describes actions before the Fall of humanity into sin. We could just as well argue that it was not God's original intention for humanity to sin, or to die, or for women to bear children in pain and so on. However, this does not mean we can ignore the fact that after the Fall, humanity needs a Savior or that death and sickness are realities. The ideal situation of humanity before the Fall cannot be used to rule out specific statements allowing exceptions for adultery and other sins which did not even exist before the Fall. Admittedly, Jesus refers to this verse in Matthew 19:3-12 as the starting point for discussion, but he does not treat it as ruling out all divorce. He qualifies its reference to the present sinful condition by stating that Moses allowed divorce and by giving an exception in Matthew 19:9 for a specific sin.

As I discuss in detail in my chapter (pp. 154-55), I also disagree that the term *one flesh* implies indissolubility, particularly since it is used in 1 Corinthians 6:16 to refer to relations with a prostitute. Laney's several statements that Deuteronomy 24:1–4 does not "condone" divorce seem intended to imply that it is against divorce (p. 21). In a code of laws, describing what is sin and what is not sin, to permit something without any negative comment is to condone it. It implies that it is not wrong.

Laney also argues that since the woman in Deuteronomy 24:1–4 is "defiled," this implies that her divorce was wrong (p. 22). However, the defilement is stated as the reason she cannot remarry her original husband. Since she is free to marry anyone else, this defilement does not exist with reference to them. This cannot be defilement per se, since it only exists with reference to her original husband. Laney's view that the "defilement" means adultery produces an unlikely situation in this passage. Since the remarriage to the original husband is called an "abomination" and the defilement is treated neutrally, this would mean that remarriage of a woman to her original husband is a much greater sin than adultery. He argues that divorce is always defiling since the Old Testament priest was prohibited from marriage to a divorced woman, thereby implying some spiritual stigma was attached to her (p. 24–25). This produces another awkward deduction since the priest was also prohibited from marriage to a widow. Does this mean that a spiritual stigma attaches to a widow; that becoming a widow is always wrong? The priest is not prohibited from marriage to these women because some stigma attaches to them, but because he is to have a "new" wife rather than a "preowned" one.

Laney's treatment of Matthew 19:3–12 seems slight, when we consider the fact that this is the primary passage teaching an exception. He states the common idea that *porneia* in Matthew 19:9 is not the normal word for "adultery," therefore, the exception is not adultery (p. 34). This seems to be based on the statements of lexicons, but a study of the words involved shows that it is a normal word for "adultery" by the woman.

I have also shown that the entire connection of Matthew 19:9 with Leviticus 18 (the incestuous marriage view) is without foundation, although Laney seems to prefer it (p. 35). Leviticus 18 is not referring to "incestuous marriage" but to incest. Laney refers to an article by Fitzmeyer to support his concept. Fitzmeyer's claim to have finally found evidence for such a meaning as "incestuous marriage," actually shows the dearth of evidence. Once his alleged evidence for such a meaning is studied, even that is seen to be doubtful. Not only is there no support for the argument that *porneia* means incestuous marriage, there is no evidence to connect Matthew 19:9 with Leviticus 18. Additionally, I have shown that the concept that the exception in Matthew 19:9 refers only to divorce and not to remarriage is grammatically impossible. Neither does Laney's argument from the order of the clauses hold up, since the exception is in the only place where it clearly is an exception allowing both divorce and remarriage (p. 37–38).

I disagree that it gives an accurate view based on Scripture to argue that Matthew 5:32 rules out all remarriage when it states "anyone who marries the divorced woman commits adultery" (p. 38). This relies on ignoring the beginning of the same verse which includes the exception. The verse states " 'anyone who divorces his wife, except for marital unfaithfulness causes her to become an adultress.'" This gives an entirely different and more accurate perspective to the clause Laney quotes. It in fact changes it to evidence for the exception allowing remarriage. It is also doubtful that Mark 10:10 requires that the statements of Jesus in Matthew 19:9 were made in the house. It is more likely that Jesus said all of the statements in Matthew 19:3–9 to the Pharisees, and then, as indicated in Matthew 19:10, the disciples asked their question "again" in the house.

I disagree with his idea that 1 Corinthians 7:10–11 does not allow for the exception. I have discussed this at length in my section. A much more probable view than Laney's for *hagiazō* in 1 Corinthians 7:13–14 is that rather than "witness," it means to be acceptable in God's sight. The argument that the passage implies that the marriage should be maintained for witness would be contrary to the clear permission to let him go. The above meaning for *hagiazō* best fits the passage and alleviates this apparent contradiction. Laney's discussion of *lelusai* in 1 Corinthians 7:27, based on the perfect tense, seems of little consequence, since the perfect tense can just as easily refer to someone "released" from a marriage and in the continuing state of one who has been released. The perfect makes no difference in the probability of the meanings. However, the fact that the verb *luō* is used of release from something (not just free) is of some consequence and is contrary to Laney's view.

In conclusion, I do not feel that most of Laney's arguments will stand up under examination. To argue that there is no exception to either divorce or remarriage it would seem more appropriate to give a detailed discussion of the passage apparently allowing exceptions, rather than arguing from passages which do not mention anything on this subject.

It is not mere coincidence that Laney's view closely agrees with that of the Roman Catholic Church. His definition of marriage as "God's act of joining a man and woman in a permanent, covenanted, one-flesh relationship" (p. 20) is very close to a sacramental view of marriage. This fact does not prove that his view is wrong. However, if we begin with this alleged "inherent nature" of marriage as indissoluble, and exegete all the verses in conformity with that concept, then the outcome can only be one way. As with most who hold this view, Laney's entire approach is structured and dependent on this alleged indissoluble nature of marriage. I do not think his arguments establish such a point sufficiently to force the exception clauses into a mold which is unnatural to them.

Response

Larry Richards

*I*t is certainly true that the "original creative intent and desired will of God is that marriage be permanent until death." It's true that the Law does not command divorce, and only allows it because of the hardness of people's hearts. There is not the slightest question that divorce involves sin—sin on the part of at least one, and more often on the part of both the divorcing husband and wife. At the very least the sin involved is failing to seek one's partner's good: failing to be sensitive, humble, forgiving, nurturing or caring. At the worst, the sin involved is brutality: physical or psychological battering, sexual abuse of sons and daughters, or blatant promiscuity. Anyone who does marriage counseling has more than once been forced to ask, how can people (and often "Christian" people) treat each other this way!

The answer of course is the one given by Jesus. The "hardness of your heart." No, not a hard-heartedness that leads a person to divorce despite God's revealed will. But a hard-heartedness that in the Old Testament describes persistent abuse of others (Deut 15:7) as well as obstinate rejection of God's will (Ps 95:8; 2 Chron 36:13). God did not command divorce. But in grace he permitted it. And, rightly understood, so does the New Testament. Both Jesus and Paul, as I've suggested in my section of this book, identify divorce and remarriage as falling short of God's ideal, and thus sin. But the passages in which Christ and the great apostle deal with this issue do not forbid either.

If I were to pinpoint the weaknesses in Laney's presentation, I would suggest three major failings: 1) A failure to grasp the nature of the one-flesh relationship of marriage; 2) a failure to grasp the rationale for Deuteronomy 24; and 3) a failure to apply Scripture's teaching on grace and forgiveness to the divorce/remarriage issue.

1. The nature of the one-flesh relationship. What does *one flesh* mean? I have suggested that the Hebrew *bāsār* ("flesh") focuses attention on human beings as persons who must live their lives as part of the physical universe. In this perspective

> the statement that a man and a woman in marriage become one flesh (Gen 2:24) affirms far more than the sexual union. That act of joining together is a symbol of the fact that the married couple are called by God to live in this world now as those who share every blessing and tragedy that life in the world may have for them.[1]

But the word *flesh* also draws attention to human frailty. As flesh we are mortal, weak and frail. This emphasis on frailty is seen in Psalm 78:39 as well as other passages. God in mercy "remembers that they were but flesh, a passing breeze that does not return." The stress on human frailty in *bāsār* is so clear that it has led Hans Walter Wolff to define it briefly as indicating "man in his infirmity."[2]

So the husband and wife who are called to share life together as one flesh, as one in their lifelong experience of existence in this world, do so as creatures of infirmity; mortal, weak and frail, subject together to flaws and failures, yet together objects of God's compassionate grace.

2. The rationale for Deuteronomy 24. Jesus put it succinctly. Moses permitted divorce because their hearts were hard. The flesh was weak. A husband or a wife rejects God's call to oneness and with a heart hardened toward his or her partner turns what was intended to be a nurturing, positive relationship into a harsh, destructive one. In such cases, is it God's will that a couple stay together anyway? Does God expect the battered wife to remain, waiting helplessly for the next outburst of fury? Does God expect the victim of constant verbal abuse from a spouse who can only prop him or herself up by cutting down the partner, to continue being diminished and demeaned? I don't say that in such cases one must, or even should, divorce. But when God permitted divorce for victims of hard hearts, how can we today deny Christians that option?

3. Applying Scripture's teachings on grace and forgiveness to divorce and remarriage. What troubles me most, of course, is Laney's failure to sense what the psalmist saw so clearly. God has grace for us in our sin and in our failures. Psalm 78 is a historic psalm: it traces the persistent rebellion of Israel against God, not once but dozens of times. Yet God held back his wrath, reminding himself of human weakness. Not only that, the Lord "chose David his servant" and gave David to his people as their shepherd (78:70-71).

Admittedly divorce and remarriage fall tragically short of God's ideal and are unquestionably the product of sin. I can agree wholeheartedly with Laney's call for one indissoluble union and his clear identification of divorce as sin. But is there forgiveness of those who divorce? Is there grace enough to permit remarriage? From what I read in his chapter, I wonder. In my good brother's universe of rigid rule by law, I suspect Peter, who disowned his Lord, would have been discarded on the junk heap of history. And Jonah would have been digested by the whale.

How glad I am to live in God's universe! How gracious God has proven to be! Time and again we fall short. Yet time and again he reaches down to us in grace. He forgives. And he sets us on our feet to try again.

Notes

[1]Larry Richards, *Expository Dictionary of Bible Words* (Grand Rapids: Zondervan, 1985), p. 283.
[2]Hans Walter Wolff, *Anthropology of the Old Testament* (Minneapolis, Minn.: Fortress, 1981), p. 26.

2
DIVORCE, BUT NO REMARRIAGE

Divorce, but No Remarriage

William A. Heth

*E*ven though marital separation or legal divorce may be advisable under some circumstances, Jesus taught that his disciples should not remarry after divorce.[1] This would be contrary to the nature of marriage as God designed it in his creation and a violation of the seventh commandment: "You shall not commit adultery" (Deut 5:18 NIV). If separation or legal divorce occurs, it should be done with the sincere hope and aim that reconciliation would be possible eventually. The New Testament allows Christians to remarry after divorce only in the event that the marriage has been dissolved through the death of one of the partners (see Rom 7:2-3; 1 Cor 7:39).[2]

This chapter will follow the history of marriage as outlined by our Lord in Matthew 19:3-12 (see also Mk 10:2-12). A reading of this passage reveals that Jesus divides the history of marriage into three periods. The first period, relatively brief in duration, saw marriage in its ideal form in Paradise (Mt 19:4-5; Mk 10:6-8). The second period coincided with the outworking of God's kingdom under the Mosaic Covenant: it was a time of compromise and concession to human sinfulness. Human "hardness of heart" (Mt 19:7-8; Mk 10:4-5) made use of the open-ended ancient Near Eastern practice of divorce (Deut 24:1). Men also legitimized and tolerated the ancient Near Eastern social institution of polygamy. Yet when Jesus came, he introduced a third period in the history of marriage, the one in which we all now live. It began when Jesus spoke the words in Matthew 19:6 and Mark 10:9: "Therefore what God has joined together, let man not separate" (NIV).

In this third and decisive era, Jesus not only redefines the popular conception of divorce by reintroducing the Father's creation standard for marriage from the first period, he also introduces the new possibility that some may forgo marriage altogether. These people sense in a unique way the necessity of advancing the claims and interests of God's kingdom, for they "have renounced marriage because of the kingdom of heaven" (Mt 19:12 NIV).[3]

Genesis 1-2: Marriage in Its Creational Design

In Matthew 19 and Mark 10 Jesus refers to the first two chapters of Genesis for the basis of his own teaching on divorce and remarriage. This is where we should begin as well. All commentators agree that Genesis 2:18-25 is a narrative expansion of the creation of humankind and our role in creation as related in 1:26-28. Genesis 2:18-25, however, focuses on the relationship of men *and* women in God's creation. There seems to be little doubt that the "male" and the "female" of Genesis 1:27 refer specifically to Adam and Eve, whose marriage relationship is detailed in Genesis 2:24. At least one writer attempts to argue that the marriage of Adam and Eve is unlike other marriages in history since only Eve was created out of Adam.[4] If this is so, then Genesis 2 says nothing about other marriages. Furthermore, if we were to adopt this line of argument, then we would have to say that Jesus' appeal to Genesis 2:24 in his debate with the Pharisees is misleading and without force. It is clear, however, that Jesus applies the Genesis 2:24 concepts to all marriages. The marriage of Adam and Eve is thus the pattern for all marriages within the human race. To understand the concepts found in Genesis 2:24 is to understand the nature of the marriage relationship itself. To understand this relationship is to understand the basis for Jesus' teaching on divorce and remarriage.

"For this cause a man shall *forsake* his father and his mother, and *shall cleave*[5] to his wife; and they shall become *one flesh*" (Gen 2:24 NIV, emphasis mine). Two important concepts about marriage are taught in this verse. The first concerns the words *forsake* (traditionally translated "leave") and *cleave*, and the second concerns the nature of the new "one-flesh unit" that is predicated upon the consummation of the marriage through sexual union.[6] A careful understanding of both of these concepts will lead to an appreciation of the nature and permanence of the marriage relationship.

Marriage as a Covenant. The first thing that must be noticed is that the words *forsake* (or *leave*) and *cleave* embody covenant terminology.[7] When they are used of interpersonal relationships—person to person, or God to human—they have clear covenant significance.[8] The term *forsake*, here and many other places in the Old Testament (see Deut 28:20; 31:16; Ruth 2:11; Jer 1:16; Hos 4:10), refers to the shift of an individual's devotion and loyalty from one person or group to another.

The word *cleave* is especially prominent as a technical term in the covenant terminology of Deuteronomy (10:20; 11:22; 13:4; 30:20; see also Josh 22:5; 23:8; Ruth 1:14-16). Earl Kalland notes that in verses which speak of the Israelites cleaving to the Lord in affection and loyalty, "parallel words and phrases that describe this proper attitude to the Lord are: fear, serve, love, obey, swear by his name, walk in his ways, and keep his commandments."[9] In short, the use of *cleave* in Genesis 2:24 has no specific sexual significance,[10] but points to a covenant relationship modeled after God's covenant with Israel in the Old Testament (see Ezek 16:8, 60; Mal 2:10-16). It refers to "a situation of very personal concern, fidelity and involvement."[11] Thus human marriage in its creational design serves as a pedagogical metaphor of God's love for his elect.

The permanence of marriage is fundamentally a theological issue, rooted in the divine-human relationship to which marriage stands as an antitype (see Eph 5:31-32). At least one theological consideration ought to be drawn from the parallel between Israel's unfaithfulness to her covenant with God and a spouse's unfaithfulness to a marriage covenant. Even though Israel repeatedly violated her covenant with Yahweh, there is no indication that this dissolved or nullified the covenant relationship (see Lev 26:44-45; Judg 2:1-3; Is 50:1; Jer 3:8, 12).

This maintenance of the covenant in the face of flagrant violations of it is fleshed out in Hosea's marriage to, and broken relationship with, Gomer (Hos 1-3). Hosea 2:2 is not a divorce formula, but in this context (compare 2:5 with 2:13) means "We are no longer living together as husband and wife."[12] F. I. Andersen and D. N. Freedman further note that Hosea 1:9 is *not* an announcement by God of the dissolution of the covenant comparable to divorce.

The covenant nowhere makes provision for such an eventuality. Covenant-breaking on the part of Israel (unilateral withdrawal) calls for severe punishment. Israel cannot opt out by no longer acknowledging Yahweh. The punishment is not an expression of a broken relationship. On the contrary, it is enforced within the relationship; punishment maintains the covenant.[13]

The love, commitment and loyalty that are part and parcel of the marriage covenant can no doubt be violated by human sin. Yet the terms *forsake* and *cleave* should tell us that the essence of the marriage covenant is commitment to the covenant partner whatever it may cost us personally. Genesis 2:24, however, does not end with its comments about "forsaking" and "cleaving." The biblical description of this relationship goes beyond the discussion of marriage as a covenant. It also defines marriage as a kinship relationship as denoted by the concept of "one flesh."[14]

Marriage Results in Permanent Kinship Ties. We are able to appreciate even more Jesus' teaching about divorce and remarriage when we grasp the meaning of the second and equally important point about the nature of the marital union. This idea is indicated by the final statement: "they will become one flesh." This phrase does not refer primarily to the sexual union of the man and his wife, nor does it refer to the child who would be the fruit of their relationship. The word *flesh (bāsār)* is capable of carrying a number of different nuances, and so it must always be considered in each individual context to appreciate its significance. The meaning of "flesh" in Genesis 2:24 carries the same nuance as it does in the more concrete statement in Genesis 2:23: "The man said, 'This is now bone of my bones and *flesh* of my *flesh;* she shall be called "woman," for she was taken out of man' " (NIV). To be someone's "bone and flesh" is a common expression used in the Old Testament to denote kinship. This "formula of relationship" also appears in Genesis 29:14; Judges 9:1-2 (see also vv. 3, 18); 2 Samuel 5:1; 19:12-13 (see also 1 Chron 2:13-17). In each case it indicates a permanent relationship of kinship.[15] This is what the abbreviated "one flesh" signifies in Genesis 2:24 (see also Gen. 37:27).

A man and woman become married when they pledge their loyalty to one another (covenant) and consummate their marriage. The biblical picture of marriage appears to indicate that both elements—covenant and consummation—are necessary to form a genuine marriage. One without the other is insufficient (see 1 Cor 6:16).

Something unique and "creational" takes place when husband and wife consummate their marriage covenant: they become closely related ("one flesh"). In Matthew 19:6 and Mark 10:9 Jesus' interpretation of Genesis 1:27 and 2:24 implies that God himself is involved in creating this new family unit. Thus Jesus explains that marriage involves three persons: a man, a woman, and the One who in the beginning created mankind as male and female.

Marriage as Companionship? Unfortunately some evangelical counselors have only paid lip service to Genesis 2:24, jumping to other passages for a definition of marriage that is more palatable to twentieth-century counselees. Jay Adams, for example, teaches that "*Companionship* . . . is the essence of marriage" and develops this idea from Genesis 2:18: "The Lord God said, 'It is not good for the man to be alone. I will make a helper suitable for him.'" He therefore defines divorce as

> the repudiation and breaking of that covenant (or agreement) in which both parties promised to provide companionship (in all its ramifications) for one another. A divorce is, in effect, a declaration that these promises are no longer expected, required or permitted.[16]

On this reading of Genesis 2:18, Adams understands man's "aloneness" in the sense of "loneliness" (so also S. Ellisen and J. MacArthur).[17] Stephen Clark aptly notes that this way of reading Genesis means that a "man needs a companion, a woman to talk to and share his life with, someone to give him ego support. In this view, the real companion for a man is one woman with whom he can be especially intimate and share his 'real self.' "[18]

The problem with Adams's interpretation of Genesis 2:18 is that he reads the ancient biblical text with modern-day psychologically tinted glasses. Clark provides the necessary corrective when he says, "Such interpretations proceed from a modern view of companionship marriage that was undoubtedly foreign to the author of Genesis 2, as well as to the writers of the New Testament."[19]

Man's "aloneness" in the context of Genesis 1 and 2 does not refer to his need for self-actualizing companionship, but to his need for assistance in the accomplishment of the tasks that God has given the human race. Man's "aloneness" in Genesis 2:18 is not his "loneliness" but his "helplessness," his inability, apart from the woman, to carry out God's creation directives to perpetuate and multiply the race and to cultivate and govern the earth (Gen 1:26-28).

Any notion of companionship here should be restricted to mutual assistance in the broad sense, namely, living together and helping one another as a married team (see Eccles 4:9-11; Prov 31:10-31).[20] As Gerhard von Rad points out, the description of the woman as "a helper fit for him" is not a romantic evaluation of the woman.[21] Rather it points to man's "helplessness," his need for someone who complements him and shares his nature—someone not like the animals. Marriage certainly involves companionship, but the essence of marriage is not companionship in the modern sense of the term.

The Mosaic Covenant: Concession and Compromise[22]

From the day that "God himself, like a father of the bride, [brought] the woman to the man,"[23] God's standards for the marriage relationship have been and always will be the same this side of heaven (see Mt 22:30; Mk 12:25; Lk 20:34-36). Jesus affirmed this notion in his debate with the Pharisees when he directed them away from their Deuteronomy 24:1 "proof text" and pointed them back to the creation accounts: "Moses permitted you to divorce your wives because your hearts were hard. But it was not this way from the beginning" (Mt 19:8 NIV).

We need to remember that within the Mosaic Law (the second period in the history of marriage) we find aspects of Israelite marriage and divorce practice that appear to contradict the ordinance of marriage in the creation accounts (the first period of human marriage). C. J. H. Wright points out that even though Israel was called to be a holy nation, "They did not live in a hermetically sealed isolation from the rest of humanity. . . . So there are countless points of common culture, social norms and conventions, shared by Israel and her contemporaries."[24] Israel's faith produced various responses to these practices of the neighboring nations. We find outright rejection and prohibition of some customs while others are tolerated and regulated. Finally, some practices are accepted and even affirmed, but are invested with the new theological content of Israel's faith. The various sexual regulations in the Pentateuch teach us about God's perspective of the marital relationship and how seriously he views any attempt to violate the sanctity of it.

Leviticus 18:6-18. The Genesis 2:24 idea that the "one flesh" terminology primarily refers to the establishment of a new family, or kinship unit, is further elucidated in the biblical legislation concerning certain forbidden unions (Lev 18:6-18; 20:11-12, 14, 17, 19-21; Deut 22:30; 27:20, 22-23). The various prohibitions in Leviticus 18 "embrace six relationships of consanguinity (verses 7, 9, 10, 11, 12, 13), and eight of affinity (verses 8, 14, 15, 16, 17, 18). These are representative cases, of course, and do not exhaust all the possible illicit combinations."[25] A long debate has continued as to whether or not these regulations focus on potential marriage partners or on casual sexual relations outside of the marriage bond. But as R. K. Harrison notes, "A careful reading of these verses makes it apparent that both situations were envisaged by the legislation."[26]

The incest legislation is not only predicated on relationships of consanguinity (that is, vertical blood lines between parents and children) but also on relationships based on affinity (that is, horizontal "blood" or kinship relationships established by marriage).[27] The opening refrain in Leviticus 18:6-18 directs, "No one is to approach any close [literally, "blood"] relative to have sexual relations [literally, "to uncover nakedness"]. I am the LORD" (v. 6 NIV). In this verse, "Blood relative" or "close relative" is actually "flesh of his flesh" (see Gen 2:23).[28] These regulations, therefore, interpret relationships of affinity (connection by marriage) in terms of the Genesis 2:24 principle that a man and his wife are "one flesh," that is, kin or blood relations.[29] This is the clear implication of Leviticus 18:7-8:

> You shall not uncover the nakedness of your father, which is the nakedness of your mother; she is your mother, you shall not uncover her nakedness. You shall not uncover the nakedness of your father's wife [that is, stepmother]; it is your father's nakedness" (RSV).

We are familiar with the idea that our own children are an extension of ourselves. But we may be confused by the biblical notion that a wife's nakedness is her husband's nakedness and vice versa (vv. 7-8, 16).[30] "In other words, marriage, or more precisely marital intercourse, makes the man and wife as closely related as parents and children."[31] These pentateuchal laws understand that the wife's father, mother, brother and sister *become, by marriage,* the father, mother, brother and sister of the man whom she marries, and vice versa for the husband where his wife's close relatives are concerned. Extended relationships come into being through the marriage of two formerly unrelated people.

Perhaps one specific example will help to conceptualize the biblical kinship view of marriage. Leviticus 18:8, quoted above, prohibits a son from having relations with or marrying[32] his stepmother. A familiarity with the range of biblical laws relating to sexual offenses reveals that regulations like those in Leviticus 18:6-18 prohibit sexual liaisons with close relatives who are living, *as well as* sexual relations with, or marriage to, a spouse's close relatives after the death or divorce of someone who forms a link in the relationships. Unlike the prohibition of adultery (Ex 20:14; Lev 18:20), which applies to sexual liaisons with someone who is not a relative when that person's marriage is still intact, the focus of the incest laws is on sexual relations with, or marriage to, a spouse's close relatives even after the marriage that created those extended relationships has ended through divorce or the death of one of the partners.[33]

In the case of Leviticus 18:8, note that there is no direct or literal blood relationship between the father's son and his stepmother. Nevertheless the union is forbidden because the father's marriage to this woman has brought his son into a close relationship with his stepmother. The literal flesh-and-blood father now forms a link in the relationship between his son and the son's stepmother as a result of marrying her. This is the very situation the arrogant Corinthians were tolerating, and which Paul condemns in 1 Corinthians 5:1-5 (see also Amos 2:7). Paul's reaction to this situation shows the moral relevance of the Old Testament incest laws for the church today.

Curiously, W. C. Kaiser, an Old Testament specialist, now adopts the position of H. W. Hoehner, a New Testament specialist, when Hoehner claims that the Old Testament kinship texts that apply to actual blood relatives (Gen 29:14; Judg 9:1-2; 2 Sam 5:1; 19:12-13) cannot apply to the husband-and-wife relationship.[34] But Hoehner imposes his own view of kinship on the biblical texts. The same metaphors that denote literal blood relatives are the very ones used in Genesis 2:23-24 to specify the nature of a man's relationship to his wife. This means that the Old Testament blurs the concepts of consanguinity with affinity.[35] Therefore, to say that the Old Testament sees a different one-fleshness between spouses from that between actual blood relatives is to distort the biblical viewpoint. The biblical view is consistent. It does not make the fine distinctions Hoehner makes in his attempt to invalidate the significant implications for divorce and remarriage suggested by the biblical kinship view of marriage. As George Bush states in his commentary on Leviticus 18:

> [W]e ourselves know of no more interesting view of the marriage union, than that it creates to each of the parties a new circle of endeared relatives, bound together by ties which are never henceforth to be sundered. . . .
>
> It is also to be remarked, that the view now suggested of the nearness and sanctity of the marriage relation, would tend more powerfully perhaps than any other to counteract those lax and lawless sentiments in regard to that institution, which are unhappily at all times too prevalent among men, and which generate a dangerous facility in the procurement of divorces.[36]

I am not attempting to argue from the Leviticus 18 regulations—nor does the Old Testament anywhere imply this (and the NT teaches the opposite [Mt 22:23-30; 1 Cor 7:35])—that *the "kinship" aspect of the marriage bond* continues after the death of one of the partners, as if marriage is for time and eternity. However, this legislation does view *the circle of relationships established by marriage* to endure beyond the *death* of the person who forms a link in the relationship. If these extended relationships formed by marriage last beyond the death of someone who forms a link in those relationships, it follows that those relationships are not invalidated by divorce either. Sexual relations, and any marriage in which such relations occur, between the living husband or wife with any of their relatives by marriage are prohibited by the biblical legislation concerning forbidden unions.

The only exception to these prohibited relationships—given in view of the great importance the Old Testament and the ancient Near East placed upon heirs and offspring to prevent the extinction of the family name—is found in the law of the levirate in Deuteronomy 25:5-10, and the analogous custom of sororate marriage allowed by Leviticus 18:18.[37] These "exceptions" resolve conflicting Old Testament principles: the obligation to perpetuate the family conflicts with the principle of not marrying one's sister-in-law.[38]

The Mosaic legislation in Leviticus 18—of moral relevance today—makes it clear that legal divorce does not dissolve "one flesh" nor the extended relationships that arise through a consummated marriage covenant.

Deuteronomy 24:1-4. Many evangelicals believe that Jesus permitted innocent spouses to remarry after divorce without being guilty of adultery if the divorce resulted from the immorality of the partner (Mt 5:32; 19:9). They find support for this view in their understanding of how the certificate of divorce operates in Deuteronomy 24:1-4. John Murray, for example, argues that "the dissolution permitted or tolerated under the Mosaic economy had the effect of dissolving the marriage bond."[39] Guy Duty wants to argue the same point when he claims that the Hebrew word for "divorce" in the "certificate of divorce" signifies "a cutting off." He claims it refers to the "absolute dissolution" of the marriage.[40] These authors then conclude that remarriage after a proper divorce (such as in Mt 5:32 and 19:9) does not constitute adultery. If the marriage is dissolved, then no tie to the former spouse remains against whom one would commit this offense.

These kinds of inferences, however, confuse more than they help to clarify the biblical teaching on divorce and remarriage. Neither the divorce procedure that was practiced by Israel nor the purely lexical meaning of a single word in Deuteronomy 24:1 can establish the claim that the nature of a "biblical" divorce is that it completely dissolves the marriage bond. It is one thing to speak of an *extrinsic* or legal dissolution of the marital *love* relationship, but quite another to speak of an *intrinsic* or constitutional dissolution of the marital *kinship* relationship.

The Pharisees also felt that the mere certificate of divorce was enough to dissolve the relationship. But as R. Westbrook notes with reference to Jesus' commentary (Mt 5:32) on this Pharisaical practice (Mt 5:31), "Jesus is here denying the efficacy of the bill of divorce to dissolve the old marriage (or rather, the husband's ability to dissolve and use the bill as evidence thereof), thus allowing the wife the freedom to remarry."[41] Therefore, if the divorces in the Mosaic economy did *not* actually result in "the dissolution of the marriage bond," and we adopt Murray's and Duty's reasoning, it follows that the "divorce" Jesus talked about likewise did *not* dissolve the marriage bond. J. D. M. Derrett accurately points out that, "Where the Jewish law went wrong was in the failure to perceive that the one flesh persisted after divorce."[42]

Deuteronomy 24:1-4 is the Old Testament passage most often discussed by those who attempt to legitimize remarriage after divorce for sexual unfaithfulness. Unfortunately, the appeal to Deuteronomy 24 as a commentary on Jesus' teaching violates the intended purpose of that passage in its Old Testament context. It also reads far more significance into it than is actually present.[43] Stated briefly, this restoration-of-a-former-marriage regulation (v. 4) says that a divorced woman who has contracted a second marriage may never subsequently be taken back by her first husband.

Prior to 1986, five major interpretations of the legislation found in Deuteronomy 24:1-4 were discussed in the relevant literature.[44] Each new discussion of the passage sought to point out the weaknesses of the preceding ones. I summarized and critiqued five of these in

Jesus and Divorce[45] and opted at that time for the fifth. The five interpretations can be summarized as follows: (1) when the law considers the return of the wife to her original husband after her marriage to another, it describes the wife as "defiled," and this suggests that the second marriage is viewed as adulterous (Philo, S. R. Driver, C. F. Keil, P. C. Craigie); (2) the law's intent was to discourage hasty divorce by forever prohibiting the man who divorced his wife from taking her back; thus the husband ought to think twice before initiating such an irrevocable separation (R. H. Charles, J. Murray, R. C. Stedman); (3) the law reflects the Israelite view that a man must not have sexual intercourse with his wife after she has had it with another man (A. Isaksson, J. D. M. Derrett); (4) the law views the second marriage as perfectly legal and is designed, like other pieces of incest legislation in the Old Testament, to protect and stabilize the second marriage by prohibiting the restoration of the first (R. Yaron); and (5) the law draws upon the theological logic of the Leviticus 18 incest laws and views the restoration of the first one-flesh relationship after the establishment of a second as a type of incest: the woman who now forms a link in the relationship between the two men has made them like brothers, and to reunite with one's former husband would be like a man marrying his sister (G. J. Wenham, W. A. Heth).

The most recent solution to the reason behind the prohibition of the restoration of marriage in Deuteronomy 24:1–4 comes from R. Westbrook. Westbrook seems to have pointed the way to a more comprehensive understanding of this problematic passage when he notes that all the views up to this point have failed to consider a crucial element in the circumstances (vv. 1–3) of the case that receives its ruling in verse four: namely, the difference that is noted in the dissolution of the first and second marriages prior to the attempt by the first husband to return to his wife.

In the former, the husband finds "some indecency" in his wife and divorces her; in the latter he "dislikes" her and divorces her, or in the alternative, dies. There must therefore exist some underlying factor which is on the one hand common to divorce for "dislike" and death, and on the other distinguishes these two types of dissolution from divorce for "indecency". That factor, we submit, lies in the property aspect of marriage—more exactly, in the financial consequences of its dissolution.[46]

Westbrook notes that the Bible contains no direct evidence on this aspect of marriage—and there is certainly no necessity to require this kind of evidence to validate Westbrook's solution—but the common ancient Near Eastern practice and evidence from postbiblical Jewish sources is sufficient to establish the existence of a continuous legal tradition that informs our understanding of the ruling on the particular case in view in Deuteronomy 24.

Two legal principles emerge from all of the available evidence.[47] First, if the wife is guilty of socially recognized misconduct, either in the sphere of her financial or household duties, or because of sexual misconduct short of adultery,[48] her husband is justified in divorcing her without any financial consequences to himself. This principle applies to the first husband's divorce mentioned in Deuteronomy 24:1, the divorce for "some indecency." Second, it is recognized that when a marriage is legally dissolved, whether by divorce or by death, the wife is entitled to a financial settlement. At the very least her dowry would be restored, but usually the husband also had to pay something to her out of his own pocket. This principle applies to the second husband's divorce mentioned in Deuteronomy 24:3, the divorce for "dislike" (literally, "hate").

Westbrook notes that the legal distinction between these two kinds of divorces also emerges in the divorce formulas found in the various ancient Near Eastern law codes. Whenever the divorce is not legally justified by the presence of "some indecency," the word "hate" is added to the normal divorce formula and refers not to the divorce itself (for which there is another technical term), but to a purely subjective divorce in which the husband will be financially penalized.[49] This combination of "hate [NIV 'dislike'] and divorce" is found not only in Deuteronomy 24:3 but also in Malachi 2:16.

Now the stage is set for understanding why the first husband in the Deuteronomy 24 passage is forbidden to return to the wife he divorced for "some indecency."

The first husband has divorced his wife on the grounds of her "indecency" and has therefore escaped the normal financial consequences—he paid her no divorce-money and most probably kept her dowry. The woman nonetheless managed to find another husband, and that marriage has ended in circumstances which leave her well provided for: her dowry (if she had received a second one from her family), possibly marital gifts from the second husband, plus divorce money or the widow's allowance. Now that she is a wealthy widow or divorcée, the first husband forgets his original objections and seeks to remarry her.

The effect would be that the first husband profits twice: firstly by rejecting his wife and then by accepting her. It is a flagrant case of unjust enrichment which the law intervenes to prevent. The prohibition on remarriage is based on what in modern law would be called estoppel. This is the rule whereby a person who has profited by asserting a particular set of facts cannot profit a second time by conceding that the facts were otherwise. He is bound by his original assertion, whether it is objectively the truth or not.[50]

Westbrook explains that this legal principle (estoppel) is expressed by the phrase "after she has been defiled." The form of the Hebrew verb expresses causation and would best be translated as "she has been caused to be unclean." The point is not whether or not the wife is in fact unclean, but that the first husband has asserted that she was unclean. "Having profited from the claim that she was unfit to be his wife, he can not now act as if she were fit to marry him because circumstances have made her a more profitable match."[51]

I find Westbrook's solution the most satisfactory to date. It also fits nicely with S. A. Kaufman's brilliant analysis of the structure of the Deuteronomic law.[52] The case in Deuteronomy 24:1-4 falls within the 23:20—24:7 section which expands the eighth commandment: "Thou shall not steal." Wenham's and my understanding of the biblical kinship view of marriage—based as it is on the Genesis 2:24 teaching that husband and wife become "one flesh"—is not called into question, and our application of the logic of the incest laws to the prohibition of Deuteronomy 24:4 coheres with the details of the case and the ruling given, but may not be the primary focus of the legislation in that passage.

Based on the new information Westbrook has provided, what may be said in summary about the significance of Deuteronomy 24:1-4 for the contemporary divorce debate among evangelicals? Hoehner claims, along with Murray and Duty, that the certificate of divorce "indicates that there was a dissolving of marriage relationships of such significance that Moses decreed that the first marriage could not be reconsummated—that is, that it was permanently dissolved."[53] I had claimed in my earlier publications that the most probable explanation for prohibiting the restoration of the original marriage was because the logic of the incest laws viewed the restoration of that relationship as a type of incest. Even though forbidding incestuous-type unions may not be the chief focus of the legislation here, it would seem that in light of the logic of the incest laws one should discourage the "restoration of marriage to a divorced partner after one of the partners has consummated a second marriage."[54] Westbrook's information invalidates, however, the conclusions of Hoehner, Murray, Duty and others. The use of the certificate of divorce in no way "indicates that there was a dissolving of marriage relationships of such significance that Moses decreed that the first marriage could not be reconsummated—that is, that it was permanently dissolved," as Hoehner claims. The certificate of divorce was part of the ancient Near Eastern legal practice. It had legal consequences in that period of the history of marriage, but its use in the Old Testament tells us nothing of its "power" to dissolve a marriage.[55]

If Deuteronomy 24 tells us nothing about the ability of the certificate of divorce to dissolve the relationship, it also tells us nothing about the permanence of the marriage relationship.[56] The biblical kinship view of marriage nevertheless suggests that just as parents cannot "cut off" their children from being their own flesh and blood, no matter how disreputable or immoral they may be, so a man cannot "divorce" or sever the kinship relationship with his wife, who is his own flesh and blood (Gen 2:23-24; Lev 18:7-8) through the covenant and consummation of marriage.

Ezra 9 and 10. A failure to interpret Ezra's marriage reform in the context of the Mosaic Covenant along with a superficial reading of Ezra 9—10 has led some evangelical leaders to appeal to this passage in order to justify remarriage after divorce in 1 Corinthians 7:15. Thus we need to examine briefly the nature of Ezra's marriage reform and what implications it may have, if any, on our understanding of Paul's teaching that a Christian is "not bound" to a non-Christian spouse when the unbeliever wants out of the marriage.

Israel was to play a unique role in God's plan to bring blessing to all the peoples of the earth. They were to be distinct, set apart from the other nations and their pagan religious practices. The maintenance of a true relationship between Yahweh and his people could only be achieved through purity of race. Thus it is significant that, when the prophet of God addresses the problem of intermarriage in Malachi 2:13-16, the rejection of divorce is accompanied by an emphasis on marriage to one wife for the purpose of raising godly children (see Lev. 11:44; Is 6:13). Israel's history is a testimony to the fact that intermarriage led to idolatry and compromise (Judg 3:1-6; 1 Kings 11:1-6; 16:31-33; Ezra 9—10).

When Ezra arrived in Jerusalem, having journeyed from Babylon (c. 458 B.C.), he was informed about a serious problem: the people of Israel, including the priests and the Levites, had not separated themselves from the peoples of the land and from their abominations. Ezra 9:2 states that this nonseparation consisted in "taking" daughters of the land for themselves and their sons "so that the holy race has intermingled (*'ārab,* "have fellowship") with the peoples of the lands" (NASB). This is described as "unfaithfulness." Ezra is so overcome with grief that he tears his garment and sits down appalled.

In a prayer of confession he says, "Shall we again break your commands and *intermarry* [*ḥtn*—see also Deut 7:3] with the peoples who commit such detestable practices? Would you not be angry enough with us to destroy us, leaving us no remnant or survivor?" (Ezra 9:14 NIV). In the past these very sins had caused God to give them into the hands of their enemies, and Ezra feared for the future of Israel's existence if such sins were repeated. In view of the situation, Shecaniah makes a proposal, and it is accepted and carried out: "Now let us make a covenant before our God to *send away [yāṣā']* all these women and their children, in accordance with the counsel of my lord and of those who fear the commands of our God. Let it be done according to the Law" (Ezra 10:3 NIV).[57]

The situation described in Ezra 9—10 is often set forth as the classic example of one in which the lesser of two evils had to be chosen: divorce is a lesser evil than the destruction of the Jewish people. This can only be said, however, if Ezra looked on these connections as real marriages. All the evidence indicates that he did not.

As early as 1890, George Rawlinson observed:

> It is quite clear that [Ezra] read the Law as absolutely prohibitive of mixed marriages (Ezra ix. 10–14)—*i.e.,* as not only forbidding their inception, but their continuance. Strictly speaking, he probably looked upon them as unreal marriages, and so as no better than ordinary illicit connections. For the evils which flow from such unions, those who make them, and not those who break them, are responsible.[58]

In Ezra's eyes this was not a question of breaking up legitimate marriages but of nullifying those which, in the eyes of the Mosaic Law, had been prohibited. H. G. M. Williamson notes that the Mosaic Law

> recognized the particular danger that affinity by marriage with the indigenous population of Canaan would almost certainly lead to religious apostasy or syncretism; cf. Exod 34:11–16; Deut 7:1–4; 20:10–18. Such marriages were therefore expressly forbidden, and it is of interest that even the patriarchs are portrayed as being aware of this danger (Gen 24; 28:1–9).[59]

Thus in a very real sense these "marriages" had been illegally contracted. They were unlawful marriages from their inception, and Ezra could take the action he did in light of the threat such unions posed to the nation of Israel. God had established a relationship with his people via the Mosaic Covenant, and the Israelites were to abide by the stipulations of this covenant.

The fact that Ezra regarded these marriage unions as somehow irregular is further suggested by the two Hebrew words Ezra chooses to describe them *(nāsā'* and *yāšaḇ)*. Though Ezra knows of and uses the usual Hebrew verb for "to marry" *(lāqaḥ* in 2:61), he uses other terms when he says that the men "took" *(nāsā'* in 9:2, 12; 10:44) some of the daughters of the land, or "gave a dwelling to" *(yāšaḇ* in 10:2, 10, 14, 17–18) "foreign women." The former verb is used elsewhere in the Old Testament of "to take as a wife" (Ruth 1:4; 2 Chron 11:31; 13:21; 24:3; Neh 13:25), and in each of these references foreign women, multiple wives and/or concubines is the object. The latter term is used only in Ezra and Nehemiah (13:24, 27), and the accusative is always foreign women.[60] The "divorce" terminology employed by Ezra argues for a similar conclusion.[61]

Ezra "was a scribe skilled in the law of Moses" (Ezra 7:6). He

studied, practiced and taught it in Israel (v. 10). Yet he employs out-
of-the-ordinary terminology to describe the "marrying" ("taking") and
the "divorcing" ("sending away") of these women. Ezra's prayer
seems to indicate further that "intermarriage" had not yet actually
taken place (compare Ezra 9:2 with 9:14). How could these Israelites
have made a covenant with God (Ezra 10:3) to put away legal "wives"
if it is true that Scripture portrays marriage as a covenant made
between husband and wife in the presence of God?[62] Ezra's actions
are usually looked on as cruel and harsh. Yet the most serious cases
of unlawful unions could be punished by the death of both parties,
just like adulterers (Lev 20:10). Numbers 25:6-15 records the case of
an Israelite who took a foreign wife and was summarily executed. It
could be a significant act of kindness that Ezra only demanded the
"divorce" of the foreigners, not their execution.

When the men of Israel put away the foreign women in obedience
to the law, they most likely remarried Israelite women. We have
already noted that remarriage was regarded as perfectly "legal" under
the Mosaic Covenant even though, strictly speaking, Ezra probably
did not regard the prior unions as legitimate marriages and may have
viewed the divorcing as comparable to annulment. When this situation of "divorce" and remarriage is viewed in light of its Old Covenant context, it becomes difficult to make any direct application to
Paul's teaching in 1 Corinthians 7:15 under the New Covenant. In fact,
Paul commands Christian spouses *not* to divorce or separate from
non-Christian mates (1 Cor 7:12-14). This is in keeping with Jesus'
restoration of marriage to its creation standards in the third period
in the history of marriage. As a creation ordinance marriage is binding on all, irrespective of one's faith or the lack thereof. Under the New
Covenant the fact that a spouse is a Christian or a non-Christian has
little effect on Jesus' (and thus Paul's) teaching about the permanence
of marriage. Ezra's marriage reform tells us nothing about the permissibility of remarriage for the deserted believer in 1 Corinthians
7:15.

Conclusions from the Second Period of Marriage. I would like to
conclude this brief overview of the period of concession and compromise in the history of marriage with some comments from
Wright's study of the place of Old Testament ethics today. Wright, in

his survey of how Israel's faith related to, and interacted with, the ancient Near Eastern world, notes that polygamy and divorce, along with slavery, "were tolerated within Israel, without explicit divine command or sanction, but with a developing theological critique which regarded them as falling short of God's highest standards."[63] There is an instructive difference, however, between the Old Testament view of polygamy and the Old Testament view of divorce. As Wright explains,

> [divorce] falls much further short of God's ideal than seems to have been the case with polygamy. On divorce there is the uncompromising attack of Malachi 2:13–16, culminating in the blunt denunciation: " 'I hate divorce,' says the Lord God of Israel." Nothing as sharp as this, or with such powerful theological argument, is directed at polygamy. Presumably this is because, whereas polygamy is a kind of "expansion" of the ordinance of marriage beyond the monogamous limit intended by God, divorce is a severing destruction of it. It is a "covering oneself with violence", as Malachi puts it. Polygamy multiplies relationships where God intended a single relationship; but divorce destroys, or presupposes the destruction of, relationships.[64]

The Restoration of the Creation Standard: New Testament Teaching

It is impossible to deny, after a reading of the Gospels, that Jesus demanded the unconditional allegiance of those who chose to follow him (see Mt 5:29–30; 10:32–36; Lk 9:57–62; 14:25–33; 18:24–30; Jn 15:13). He went so far as to forewarn prospective disciples that there would be a high cost involved in responding positively to his preaching of the good news of the kingdom of God: disciples would be expected to submit themselves to the ethics of that kingdom. Those who claim to be Jesus' followers must therefore accept the new elements of the present rule of God that Jesus inaugurated. In this kingdom, God's rule is both gracious and demanding. This is just as true of Jesus' high standards for marriage as it is for other aspects of Christian faith and practice.

Our Lord's teaching about divorce and remarriage in this third and decisive period in the history of human marriage astounded his closest followers. They responded as if his standards for the permanence of marriage were too difficult to bear: "If this is the situation between a husband and wife, it is better not to marry" (Mt 19:10). Nevertheless, Jesus encouraged them and let them know that God's sustaining grace was available to them in the realm of marriage too (see Mt 19:9-12, 26).

The teaching of the New Testament on divorce and remarriage may be summarized in the following statements. The first statement is central to the New Testament teaching as a whole and reflects Jesus' understanding of Genesis 1:27 and 2:24: God's design for marriage within the human race.

1. God intends that marriage be a lifelong relationship. "What God has joined together, let no man separate" (Mk 10:2-9; Mt 19:3-8).

2. Married couples should not separate or divorce (1 Cor 7:10; see also Mk 10:9; Mt 19:6).

3. In cases of separation or divorce, those involved must remain single or be reconciled (1 Cor 7:11).

4. Remarriage after divorce constitutes adultery (Mt 5:32; Mk 10:11-12; Lk 16:18).

5. Divorce itself is a kind of adultery and leads the woman to commit adultery if she remarries, except in the case of unchastity (Mt 5:32 in the context of vv. 27-32: violations of the seventh commandment).

6. "Anyone who divorces his wife, except for marital unfaithfulness, and marries another woman commits adultery" (Mt 19:9).

7. The Christian spouse who is deserted by an unbeliever is "not under bondage" (1 Cor 7:15).

Statements 1 through 4 present a unified picture of the permanence of the marriage union. Nowhere in the Gospels nor in Paul do we find a clear and unambiguous mandate for remarriage after divorce, though statements 6 and 7 may come closest. Two other relatively straightforward passages from Paul not listed above agree particularly well with statement 4, that remarriage to another before the death of a former spouse constitutes adultery. In Romans 7:2-3, Paul plainly states that remarriage before the death of one's spouse is adultery. In 1 Corinthians 7:39 Paul addresses the situation of a Christian widow: she may remarry when her spouse has died (see 1 Cor

7:8-9), and the person she remarries must be a believer.

Only statements 5 thru 7 appear to conflict with statements 1-4. However, further consideration of statement 5 should reveal that there is really no conflict. If lust is seen as a breach of the seventh commandment, "adultery in the heart" (Mt 5:27-30), it is not surprising to find divorce condemned in similar terms (Mt 5:31-32). The way that these two antitheses are arranged under the topic of the seventh commandment indicate that both "lust" and "divorce"—when the divorce is not for unchastity—violate the spirit of the seventh commandment, "Do not commit adultery" (v. 27).

Remember that in the Jewish marriage customs of Jesus' day the bill of divorce, once delivered, guaranteed the freedom of the woman to remarry (Mt 5:31). So when Jesus says that the man who divorces his wife makes her commit adultery he is saying two things. First, Jesus is saying that the bill of divorce does not do what the Jews thought it did: it does not dissolve the marriage union. Second—and there is complete consensus on this point—Jesus' statement ("makes her commit adultery") points a finger at the divorcing husband and makes him morally responsible for making his wife and her second husband commit adultery against him.[65]

But what is the meaning of the "except for marital unfaithfulness" clause in this context of sins that violates the spirit of the seventh commandment? The answer to this question is not nearly as complicated as some of the popular works on divorce and remarriage have made it. The "except for marital unfaithfulness" clause does not need to mean any more than the fact that divorcing an unchaste wife would not *make* her an adulteress, for she has *made herself* an adulteress, adultery being the most common type of sexual offense covered by the term *porneia* (rendered by the NIV as "marital unfaithfulness").[66]

The exception clause in Matthew 5:32 is simply a matter-of-fact recognition that if the wife has already committed adultery, her husband cannot be held guilty of driving her into it by divorcing her. *She* is the one who will be held guilty of violating the seventh commandment in this situation, not he. Jesus says nothing in the first part of Matthew 5:32 about remarriage after divorce for sexual immorality. But immediately following, we find Jesus' absolute and unqualified conditional statement that "whoever marries a divorced woman commits adultery" (Mt 5:32 NASB). This addition, along with the omission of the exception clause in the Lukan parallel (Lk 16:18), strongly suggests that Jesus never intended to sanction remarriage after divorce for marital unfaithfulness.

This leaves only statements 6 and 7: Matthew 19:9 and 1 Corinthians 7:15. Scholarly and sincere Christian leaders are divided over the propriety of remarriage after divorce under the particular circumstances which these two passages mention. Some interpret them as permitting divorce or separation but not remarriage, while others understand them to say that Christians may divorce and remarry without being guilty of committing the sin of adultery. In what follows I will set forth the most important reasons for believing that even though separation or legal divorce may be advisable under certain difficult circumstances—not necessarily limited to sexual misconduct—neither Matthew 19:9 nor 1 Corinthians 7:15 sanction remarriage after divorce under the particular circumstances that are in view.

Matthew 19:9

Jesus replied, "Moses permitted you to divorce your wives because your hearts were hard. But it was not this way from the beginning. I tell you that anyone who divorces his wife, except for marital unfaithfulness, and marries another woman commits adultery" (Mt 19:8-9 NIV).

There are six major reasons why I do not believe that Jesus' authoritative pronouncement in Matthew 19:9 was ever intended to single out "marital unfaithfulness" or some other sexual sin as the one exception to his absolute prohibition of remarriage after divorce. In surveying these reasons I believe it can be shown that Jesus viewed remarriage after divorce, for whatever reason, as both a violation of the seventh commandment and contrary to God's creation design for marriage. I will begin with the least important arguments and move to what I believe are the most weighty.

1. *The historical perspective argument.*[67] When I began my own serious study of Jesus' divorce sayings in the summer of 1980, it did not take long before I realized that the vast majority of nonevangel-

ical scholars almost unanimously rejected the interpretation of Matthew 19:9 that most of my seminary professors held with unquestionable certitude. Those scholars who did interpret the problematic exceptions in Matthew 5:32 *and* Matthew 19:9 as allowing divorce *and* remarriage in the case of "unchastity" would also be sure to state, like T. W. Manson does: "I assume that it is as certain as anything can be in N.T. criticism that the qualifications *parektos logou porneias* and *me epi porneia* (Mt. v. 32; xix. 9) are not part of the genuine teaching of Jesus on this point."[68]

I began to suspect that evangelical Protestants had adopted not a scriptural, but a traditional understanding of the biblical teaching on divorce and remarriage. One writer goes so far as to warn Protestants who are often eager to repudiate tradition in favor of "Scripture alone" of unwittingly subjecting themselves to a self-deception.

> For their interpretation is, for the most part unconsciously, conditioned to a large extent by the Christian education and environment from which they come—that is, by the tradition (here used in the customary meaning of the word) of their particular denomination. A great part of the differences in exegesis among them is to be explained by different doctrinal presuppositions.[69]

Thus I believe an appreciation of when and where the Protestant exegesis of the divorce texts arose in the history of the church helps to explain the discrepancy that exists today between the lack of firm scriptural support for this view and the widespread influence it holds.

The first reason I do not believe that Matthew 19:9 should be interpreted as permitting remarriage after divorce in the event of marital unfaithfulness is that this idea was foreign to the early church. The modern notion of divorce as a "dissolution" of the marital relationship with the possibility of remarriage afterwards was unheard of in the early Christian centuries. "The lack of evidence for divorce (in this modern sense) and remarriage in the first five centuries is the more striking in view of the fact that throughout this period both Jewish and pagan law *did* permit divorce and remarriage."[70] The most probable explanation for this elevated view of the solidarity of the marriage union and the early Christian maintenance of it in the face of the laxity within secular marriage law is that this teaching went back to Jesus himself.

The most comprehensive study of the earliest Christian writers' understanding of the New Testament teaching on divorce and remarriage was written by Henri Crouzel and published in 1971. Crouzel contends that in the first five centuries all Greek and Latin writers except one agree that remarriage following divorce for any reason is adulterous. These early Christian interpreters held that spouses were bound to the marriage until the death of one of them. When a marriage partner was guilty of unchastity, usually understood to mean adultery, the other was expected to separate but did not have the right to remarry. Even in the case of 1 Corinthians 7:15—the so-called Pauline privilege that later Catholic teaching claimed to sanction the practice of permitting remarriage to a believer deserted by an unbeliever—the early church fathers maintained that the deserted Christian did not have the right to remarry.

The patristic or early Christian writers' interpretation of the divorce texts remained the standard view of the church in the West until the early sixteenth century when Erasmus suggested a different interpretation that was adopted by Luther and other Protestants. Erasmus was a theologian who sought "to solve an ethical problem within Church and society by finding a solution based on Scripture and centered in Christ."[71] His interpretation of the divorce texts was not an academic exercise,[72] and the reason for Erasmus's new approach was no doubt influenced by the Catholic concept of marriage as a sacrament that transmits grace.

Erasmus reasoned that if no salvation was possible outside the doors of the Catholic Church, then what would be the fate of the many thousands unhappily coupled together? Would not both parties perish? He felt that if they were divorced and able to marry someone else they could be saved. Charity, Erasmus reasoned, "sometimes does what it legally is not able to do, and it is justified in doing so."[73]

The Protestant theologians latched on to Erasmus's interpretation of the divorce texts and defended them from the moment they became known. This Erasmian/early Protestant view later became enshrined in the Westminster Confession of Faith in 1648. Sections 5 and 6 of Chapter 24 communicate the results of the Protestant exegesis:

Section V.—Adultery or fornication committed after a contract,

being detected before marriage, giveth just occasion to the innocent party to dissolve that contract [Matt. 1:18-20]. In the case of
adultery after marriage, it is lawful for the innocent party to sue
out a divorce [Matt. 5:31-32], and, after the divorce, to marry another, as if the offending party were dead [Matt. 19:9; Rom. 7:2-
3].

Section VI.—Although the corruption of man be such as is apt
to study arguments, unduly to put asunder those whom God hath
joined together in marriage; yet nothing but adultery, or such wilful
desertion as can no way be remedied by the Church or civil mag-
istrate, is cause sufficient of dissolving the bond of marriage [Matt.
19:8-9; 1 Cor 7:15; Matt. 19:6]: wherein a public and orderly course
of proceeding is to be observed, and the persons concerned in it
not left to their own wills and discretion in their own case [Deut.
24:1-4].

There can be no question that the Westminster Confession has been
influential in the establishment of certain beliefs and practices within
the Protestant tradition ever since its emergence in 1648. The question must be asked, therefore, if that document's understanding of the
divorce texts, and the Protestant exegesis that undergirds it, is perhaps not more reactionary than it is scriptural, in view of its Erasmian
origin and the historical situation that produced it.

I do not think that the fathers were infallible by any means, nor do
I agree with all the details of their exegesis of the divorce texts.
Nevertheless, their unanimity on the subject of divorce and remarriage is remarkable. It is one thing for the interpretation of a verse
of Scripture to change with the passing of time, but it is another thing
for an important aspect of Christian marital practice to change. To
quote Tony Lane, a lecturer in Christian doctrine at London Bible
College:

If Jesus did allow remarriage, presumably it happened. How did it
then cease to happen, despite the fact that his teaching was
known, leaving no trace either of a period when it happened or of
any controversy.

Such a theory is no more plausible than a theory that the "Lord"s
day" was originally a Friday and that it changed to Sunday without
leaving any trace of the change and without any controversy over

the change. Those who have been involved in church leadership know that beliefs can change gradually and subtly; changes in practice are much harder to bring about.[74]

Thus the view of the early church stands as an important witness to an interpretation of Jesus' divorce sayings as not allowing remarriage after divorce for marital unfaithfulness.

Virtually every one of the modern-day arguments for permitting remarriage after divorce for immorality can be found in Erasmus. The only major difference between Erasmus and the exegetical tradition he started—and this is a significant one—concerns the *basis* in Matthew 19:9 for permitting the "innocent" party to remarry. Erasmus appealed to charity and the importance of marriage as a sacrament that aids in the salvation of those who contract marriage. The Protestant basis for allowing innocent spouses to remarry, however, has changed with time. The inadequacies of the earlier arguments gave rise to new ones in the ongoing attempt to support the earliest Protestant interpretation of Jesus' divorce sayings. These changing arguments lead to the second and third reasons that I do not believe the exception clause in Matthew 19:9 was ever intended to sanction the right to remarry in the event of sexual immorality. But first I will give a brief overview of the changing Protestant basis for permitting remarriage after divorce due to marital unfaithfulness.

Luther and others felt that since the adulterer in the Old Testament was stoned, the adulterer in their day should be considered "as if . . . dead," a hermeneutical concept endorsed by the Westminster Confession (Chap. 24, § 5). Of course, this is a legal fiction, and evangelicals no longer appeal to it as a major argument for allowing the innocent party to remarry. Furthermore, adultery was not the only sin in the Old Testament that carried a maximum penalty of death.

In 1921 R. H. Charles gave a more sophisticated basis for this legal fiction approach when he claimed that the penalty of death by stoning for adultery could not be carried out by the Jews in Jesus' day, and so divorce for adultery (with remarriage permitted) replaced it.[75] But Charles also introduced a new argument in support of the Protestant exegesis that remains influential to this day. Based on 1 Corinthians 6:15-17, Charles argued that extramarital sexual relations destroy the one body formed by marriage, thereby dissolving the marriage tie that unites a man or woman to his or her spouse.[76] Charles argued not only that sexual sins dissolved the husband and wife relationship, but that it also severed one's relationship with Christ.

John Murray also appealed to 1 Corinthians 6:15-17 to support his argument that adultery gives grounds for the dissolution of the marriage bond.[77] But Murray's main arguments for allowing the innocent party to remarry involve his understanding of the Mosaic "dissolution divorce" (which we have seen is untenable) and his understanding of the syntax or word order of Matthew 19:9. Murray argues that the exception clause qualifies both halves of Jesus' double conditional statement: IF a person divorces . . . and IF a person remarries, THEN that person commits adultery. On this understanding, divorce followed by remarriage—if the divorce was occasioned by marital unfaithfulness—does not constitute adultery because the exception excludes this situation from the principal statement: "he or she commits adultery." The idea that sexual sins dissolve the marriage bond and the view that the exception clause modifies both halves of Jesus' double conditional remark (which specifies how and when someone commits adultery) are the two main pillars supporting the Erasmian view as it is defended today.

2. Sexual sins do not dissolve the marriage bond. Charles's argument that extramarital sexual sins result in a dissolution of the marriage bond still persists among those who would permit remarriage today. D. A. Carson and others argue that if sexual relations are so important in establishing the marital relationship (see Gen 2:24) third-party sexual violations of that relationship involve a *de facto* exception on which that marriage may (but does not need to be) dissolved and remarriage permitted to the innocent party.[78] The tradition to permit remarriage is the same, but two aspects of Charles's argument have been changed: the appeal to 1 Corinthians 6:15-17 is often missing and Charles's claim that extramarital sexual sins sever one's relationship with Christ has been abandoned.

First, it seems odd to say, as some evangelical writers now claim, that the *de facto* exception of sexual sin *permits* but does not *necessitate* divorce (and remarriage). Sexual sin is either a *de facto* exception to the permanence of marriage, or it is not. If sexual sin only permits divorce (and remarriage), but does not necessitate divorce and the right to remarry, on what basis can it be argued that the original one-flesh relationship has been obliterated, thus eradicating the relationship with the former spouse? If the marriage bond has not been dissolved or obliterated entirely, but only defiled in some way, then how can it be said that Jesus permitted remarriage to another when the God-joined one-flesh union remains between the original couple? But if sexual sin dissolves the marriage, and the one spouse is willing to forgive and be reconciled to the other, should not the consummation of a new marriage covenant (that is, wedding ceremony) with the same person again take place if they are to be joined in marriage? These are some of the questions that must be answered if one insists that Jesus permits divorce and remarriage in the case of sexual sin.

Second, and far more important, since marriage is not constituted solely on the basis of sexual union, it seems inconsistent to say that it is dissolved solely on the basis of sexual infidelity. The comments of P. P. Levertoff and H. L. Goudge on this very point are worth quoting in full.

> The view that adultery dissolves the marriage bond not only de-
> grades the conception of marriage by making its physical side the
> dominant consideration; it involves two absurdities. First, a man
> may cease to be married and yet be unaware of the fact. Secondly,
> it makes adultery, or the pretence of having committed it, the one
> way to get rid of a marriage which has become distasteful, and so
> it puts a premium on adultery. If marriage is to be dissoluble at
> all, it should be also dissoluble upon other grounds than this, as
> sensible opponents of the Christian law recognize. The suffering
> which an unhappy marriage involves is not in the least confined
> to that caused by unfaithfulness.[79]

Though these words were written in 1928, the point made in the final line of the quote is all the more pertinent in view of a 1985 *Journal of Psychology and Theology* article entitled "The Place of Wife Battering in Considering Divorce."[80] The author seeks to justify grounds for divorce in cases of wife battering by showing that the detrimental effects of wife battering on the interpersonal elements necessary for full marital intimacy (trust, security and freedom) are more pervasive than those brought on by adultery. The author then proposes that if battering can be found to violate the marital relationship to the same, or greater, degree than adultery does, then wife battering deserves recognition as an acceptable reason for divorce in keeping with the teaching of Matthew 19:9. These kinds of considerations cause problems for the traditional Protestant view of permitting divorce and remarriage only in the event of "marital unfaithfulness," but they help to clarify my argument that there are other reasons that would warrant separation or legal divorce, but never remarriage.

It is one thing to advise separation or legal divorce when one's marriage partner is unrepentant and involved in numerous immoral relationships (see 1 Cor 5:11), or when the lives of the wife or the children are endangered; but it is quite another to suggest that remarriage is a live option based on the teaching of Matthew 19:9. There is a large gap that must be jumped between the idea that marital unfaithfulness or anything comparable results in a disruption of the marital love relationship (which may or may not be possible to forgive *and* resume), and the further idea that the offended partner is now free to enter in to another marital union.

Another misuse of the sexual-sin idea in the exception clause should also be pointed out. I find it utterly arbitrary to argue, as do MacArthur, Swindoll and others, that the term *unchastity* in Matthew 19:9 refers to a *lifestyle* of immoral sexual behavior, then claim that Matthew 19:9 supports the permission for the spouse to remarry.[81] The exception clause was uttered in the context of Jewish marital laws and first-century social mores which looked upon a wife's unfaithfulness as making the continuation of marriage as impossible (see Mt 1:18-19). For Jesus' Jewish hearers *one* instance of *porneia* was enough to put an end to the marriage.

I am not arguing that evangelicals should adopt first-century Jewish attitudes about ending a marriage when marital unfaithfulness occurs. I am protesting the imprecise interpretation and hence misapplication of Matthew 19:9 that stands behind the popular understanding of Jesus' teaching. This popular teaching claims that his saying sanctions remarriage after divorce in certain extreme cases. The fact that popular evangelical preachers want to read the "unrepentant immoral lifestyle" idea into *porneia* shows that they know Jesus would require the forgiveness of seventy times seven and marital reconciliation for one or two acts of sexual unfaithfulness (Mt 18:21-35).

I find that most evangelicals are attempting to understand the meaning of the exception clause in Matthew 19:9 in the light of Protestant tradition and twentieth-century marriage laws. We should rather take the time to understand *how* Jesus would convey his new teaching *within* the context of first-century Jewish marriage laws and the debate between the followers of Hillel and Shammai over permissible grounds for divorce, *while keeping in mind* that Jesus restores the creation standards for marriage. E. Lövestam's understanding of the function of the exception clause—one that neither sanctions divorce for immorality nor permits remarriage should this kind of separation occur—fits these requirements.

> According to Jewish marital laws the wife could cause the breakup of a marriage by being unfaithful and the man had no say in the matter. If the wife was unfaithful, it was thus she and not the man who was responsible for the divorce. When the teachings in question are intended for people with this background, they relieve the man in this case of the responsibility for the divorce and its consequences. The wife bears it. That is what the exceptive clause means.[82]

So Jesus is not saying that "unchastity" *(porneia)* is the only ground for separating from a spouse. He is simply taking note of a situation that his disciples would encounter in the face of Jewish marriage customs that did not permit but *demanded* the divorce of an unfaithful, adulterous wife. However, if someone were to divorce a spouse for a single act of marital unfaithfulness today—and I think most evangelicals would agree with me on this point—I believe Jesus would call that person hard-hearted. If our understanding of the roots of Jesus' teaching in the Old Testament is correct, Jesus recognized that unrepentant human hard-heartedness may well destroy the marital love relationship, but he absolutely prohibited remarriage in view of the solidarity of the marital kinship relationship.

3. Murray's syntactical argument. If we cannot take seriously the claim that sexual sin is a genuine exception to Jesus' teaching on the indissolubility of marriage this side of death, what can be said of the second pillar of the Erasmian superstructure; namely, the argument from the syntax or word order of Matthew 19:9? Jesus said, "I tell you that anyone who divorces his wife, *except for marital unfaithfulness,* and marries another woman commits adultery."

John Murray attempted to argue that the exception clause in Matthew 19:9 applies to both the act of divorcing as well as to the act of remarrying, even though the particular position it now occupies connects it most intimately with the act of divorcing only.[83] On Murray's understanding, not only may someone divorce an unfaithful spouse without being guilty of violating Christ's prohibition of divorce ("What God has joined together, let man not separate"), but he or she may also marry again without being guilty of the sin of adultery.

Virtually every evangelical who understands Matthew 19:9 in this way either repeats or appeals to Murray's discussion of the word order of Matthew 19:9.[84] I have taken up and responded point-by-point to each of Murray's arguments in *Jesus and Divorce.*[85] In that study I concluded that Murray's arguments were not only inconclusive, but that on more than one occasion he assumes what he wants to prove and then proceeds to build a case. Murray insists in no uncertain terms that the coordination of divorce *and* remarriage in Matthew 19:9 must not be broken if the sentence as a whole is to make sense. I argued that his insistence was part of his own construct for interpreting the passage, one which he imposed upon the text, and not one that emerges from the text itself. Divorces *do* take place without remarriage following. These are sequential actions that do not have to follow one another. Indeed, remarriage after any divorce should not be pursued if Jesus taught that the one-flesh bond of marriage endures this side of the death of one of the spouses.

In his recent commentary on *Matthew,*[86] Carson merely repeats the thrust of Murray's argument when he says that

if the remarriage clause is excluded, the thought becomes nonsensical: "Anyone who divorces his wife, except for *porneia,* commits adultery"—surely untrue unless he remarries. The except clause must therefore be understood to govern the entire protasis. We may paraphrase as follows: "Anyone who divorces his wife and marries another woman commits adultery—though this principle does not hold in the case of *porneia."*[87]

But why do Carson and Murray build an argument for the Erasmian, or early Protestant, exegesis by leaving out "and marries another" after connecting the exception clause solely to "divorce?" It is their omission of "and marries another woman" that results in a nonsensical statement, not the fact that the exception clause most probably qualifies only the divorce action. This appeal to a part of the sentence instead of the whole complex is unwarranted. Furthermore, it is quite clear that in Matthew 5:27-32 divorce is seen as a breach of the seventh commandment, that is, to divorce *is* tantamount to committing adultery.

We have already noted that the early Christian writers understood the "divorce" which Jesus seems to permit for unchastity as mere separation from bed and board, and not the "dissolution" of the marriage. These early interpreters of the Greek New Testament had a built-in cultural, social and linguistic grid that served them in their reading and interpretation of the Gospels—and Matthew's was the most popular in the early church. As far as I am aware, the early Greek-speaking fathers never discuss or debate the question of what the exception clause qualifies. This is a modern debate that began with Murray. It is one of the two most recent arguments put forward in defense of what I would call an improbable interpretation of Matthew 19:9.

The fathers' teaching on divorce and remarriage suggests that they understood the exception clause as a simple limitation of the divorce action only. This means that Matthew 19:9 was read as follows: "Anyone who divorces his wife—unless he divorces her for marital unfaithfulness—and marries another woman, commits adultery." On this reading it is clear that Matthew 19:9 contains two conditional statements, one that is qualified and one that is unqualified or absolute: (1) A man may not divorce his wife *unless* she is guilty of adultery, and (2) Whoever marries another woman after divorcing his wife commits adultery. Or to paraphrase the idea another way: "Divorcing for reasons other than marital unfaithfulness is forbidden, and remarriage after every divorce is adulterous."[88]

Even though the Gospels contain no precise parallel to the grammatical structure of Matthew 19:9, with two verbs and an exception in one protasis, G. J. Wenham has added further support for our no remarriage view by showing that other conditional relative clauses in Matthew realize the same deep semantic structure as the one the early church apparently found in Matthew 19:9: a double condition with the exception applying to only one verb in the protasis.[89] That the exception qualifies only the divorce action is further suggested by the precise question posed by the Pharisees: "What reason justifies divorce?" The phrase "for any and every reason" that accompanies their test question in Matthew 19:3 anticipates the answer "except for marital unfaithfulness" in verse 9, and both are peculiar to Matthew's Gospel. Thus any attempt to justify remarriage after a divorce for marital unfaithfulness based on Murray's understanding of Matthew 19:9 rests on shaky ground.

4. The context following Matthew 19:9.[90] There is a growing conviction among scholars of various theological persuasions that the verses immediately following Matthew 19:9 are best understood as an extension and confirmation of Jesus' teaching on the indissolubility of marriage in verses 4-9. This makes it very difficult to interpret Matthew 19:9 in a way that allows remarriage after divorce for *porneia*.[91] The text of Jesus' pronouncement in verse 9 and the private discussion with the disciples that it generates is included here so the full force of this argument may be appreciated.

> "And I say to you: whoever divorces his wife, except for unchastity, and marries another, commits adultery." The disciples said to him, "If such is the case of a man with his wife, it is not expedient to marry." But he said to them, "Not all men can receive this saying, but only those to whom it is given. For there are eunuchs who have been so from birth, and there are eunuchs who have been made eunuchs by men, and there are eunuchs who have made themselves eunuchs for the sake of the kingdom of heaven. He who is able to receive this, let him receive it." (Mt 19:9-12 RSV).

In order to understand how verses 10-12 strengthen and extend the preceding discussion on the permanence of marriage, it is crucial to note that verse 11 does *not* refer to two classes of disciples among the followers of Jesus. Matthew's Gospel paints a picture of faithful disciples as those who have been given insight into the divine revelation mediated through Jesus. The ones who do not accept this revelation are those unbelievers outside the circle of the followers of Jesus. Matthew 13:11, the closest conceptual and linguistic parallel to Matthew 19:11,[92] explains this aspect of Matthean theology: "To you [faithful disciples] it has been given to know the secrets of the kingdom of heaven, but to them [that is, the unbelieving outsiders] it has not been given" (RSV). Therefore, Matthew 19:11 does *not* refer to two classes of faithful disciples, some who have been given the gift of celibacy and some who have not; rather it speaks of the true disciples of Jesus who have been granted insight into Jesus' teaching as opposed to the Pharisees and unbelievers who have not been granted insight into Jesus' teaching (and therefore will not accept his high standards for marriage).

The antecedent to "this precept" in verse 11 is not the disciples' words in verse 10—"It is better not to marry"—but Jesus' precept in verse 9,[93] his hard saying on divorce and remarriage which the Pharisees and unbelievers will not accept. The argument which Jesus begins in verse 11 is designed to show the disciples that they have acted like unbelievers when they so strongly object to Jesus' teaching about the permanence of marriage. Jesus will help them understand that he does not ask his disciples to do the impossible. They will be granted the ability to accept and abide by his teaching on the indissolubility of marriage.

Thus Matthew 19:9-12 should be understood as follows: Jesus creates a problem for the disciples when he makes his forceful pronouncement on the indissolubility of marriage in verse 9, the concluding statement from the whole debate that had transpired between Jesus and the Pharisees in verses 3-8. Divorce for marital unfaithfulness may be conceded in view of the prevailing social mores, but there must be no remarriage lest adultery be committed. The disciples then react in unbelief at the thought of a life of singleness apart from marital relations: if a man cannot get out of a marriage so as to marry another, it is probably better not to marry at all (v. 10). Jesus then responds by saying that his standards on divorce and remarriage are indeed difficult to understand and to live by. Nevertheless, God gives true disciples the ability to understand and live by Christ's teaching. Furthermore, God will give faithful disciples the grace they need if they should face a divorce they cannot prevent (v. 11).

Then in verse 12 (compare with 19:26, "With man this is impossible, but with God all things are possible") Jesus explains ("For") why what he has been saying about indissoluble marriage should not be too difficult for them to bear. By means of the eunuch saying Jesus says that not only is continence in the face of a broken marriage possible (by God's grace)—for consider those who never marry because they are born eunuchs or are made eunuchs and these men live apart from marital relations unaided by the grace of God—but there are even some who have renounced the possibility of marriage altogether because of the claims and interests of God's kingdom. These have a special gift or calling from God.

After introducing the possibility that some may choose not to marry because they have been seized by the kingdom of God and its claims upon their lives, Jesus finally concludes with a call to faith: "The one who can accept this should accept it." This call is directed to two groups of people: (1) those disciples who might be so inclined—as Paul apparently found himself to be (see 1 Cor. 7:7-8, 25-26, 28, 29-35, 40)—to forgo marriage because of the claims and interests of God's kingdom (the new possibility Jesus just introduced in v. 12), and (2) those followers who find it difficult to accept and live by Jesus' teaching on the lifelong permanence of marriage (Jesus' redefinition of divorce in vv. 4-9). Whereas Jewish custom declared, "Behold, thou art permitted to any man" after the bill of divorce was given (*m. Git.* 9.3), Matthew 19:10-12 radically counters such a notion by solidifying Jesus' teaching that true disciples do not remarry after divorce for any reason, lest they should commit adultery.

5. The Synoptic parallels: Luke 16:18 and Mark 10:2-12. One of the major reasons I do not believe Matthew 5:32 and Matthew 19:9 should be read as permitting divorce *and* remarriage when marital unfaithfulness occurs is based upon the record of Jesus' divorce sayings in the Gospels of Luke and Mark. Everything that Luke has to say about Jesus' teaching on the subject is found in Luke 16:18: "Anyone who divorces his wife and marries another woman commits adultery, and the man who marries a divorced woman commits adultery" (NIV). In Mark 10:11-12 Jesus says, "Anyone who divorces his wife and marries another woman commits adultery against her. And if she divorces her husband and marries another man, she commits adultery" (NIV).

Notice that in both Mark and Luke the one who "divorces *and* remarries" commits adultery. There is absolutely nothing in the divorce sayings in Mark or Luke which suggest that Jesus permitted divorce *and* remarriage (that is, remarriage after divorce) for one exception or another. Both Mark and Luke do, however, leave open the possibility that Jesus might have conceded the possibility of a separation or legal divorce that was *not* followed by remarriage.

Notice also that the latter part of Luke 16:18, like that of Matthew 5:32, tells the reader that the legal procedure of divorce does not really work. The Jewish or Roman divorce legalities do not dissolve the marriage union: that is why a second marriage is called adultery. Jesus views marriage as more than a bilateral covenant between two mutually consenting individuals. His explanation of the significance of Genesis 1:27 and 2:24 in Matthew 19:6 and Mark 10:9, "Therefore what God has joined together, let no man separate," uses the third-person negative imperative and clearly shows that God himself, and not only the husband and the wife, is involved in the formation of this marital unity. The unity of marriage therefore cannot be obliterated by some magical power inherent in the sphere of law. Finally, notice that Luke 16:18, like Matthew 5:32, would even view a single man's marriage to a divorced woman as an act of adultery, a violation of the seventh commandment.

Those who say that Jesus allows remarriage after divorce assume what they want to prove when they claim that Mark and Luke would no doubt recognize the right to divorce and remarry in the event of sexual immorality. This is the way Erasmians harmonize their understanding of Matthew 19:9 with the other Gospel divorce texts that do not even hint of the permission they want to find in Matthew. That these early accounts of the words and works of Jesus initially circulated separately is admitted by all. Even if the readers of Luke's or Mark's Gospel did have access to Matthew, it is presumptuous to claim that the "remarriage permitted" interpretation of Matthew 19:9 was assumed by the early church though never expressly stated. We have already argued that there is no hint of such an interpretation in the early church outside the New Testament. Thus it is amazing that Erasmians still persist in claiming that this eisegetical end-run is the most likely means of harmonizing the Gospel divorce texts.[94]

6. Paul's understanding of the Lord's teaching. Not only is there no hint of the "remarriage permitted" understanding of Matthew 19:9 in Mark or in Luke, or in the early church outside the New Testament, there is nothing in Paul that would suggest we ought to adopt the Erasmian understanding of Matthew 19:9. When Paul, who claims to be passing on what the Lord taught on this subject, talks about what the believer should do if separation or divorce occurs, he instructs the Corinthians—in the name of the Lord—to remain unmarried or else be reconciled (1 Cor 7:10-11). There is no mention or hint of a sexual-sin-exception that permits remarriage. And when Paul does specifically discuss the "right" to remarry he always mentions the matter of the death of one of the spouses in the same context (1 Cor 7:39; see also Rom 7:2-3). Thus, where Paul *does* speak clearly on the permissibility of remarriage after divorce, we find in the same context a remark about the death of one of the spouses as well.

In short, these are the reasons that I do not believe Matthew 19:9 sanctions remarriage after divorce for unchastity. It appears to me that modern-day proponents of the remarriage-permitted view of Matthew 19:9 read their particular interpretation of that verse into every other passage dealing with divorce that appears in the New Testament. When texts which contradict the modern-day Erasmian or early Protestant view stare us in the face, we should not make such a strained effort to deprive them of all their significance by more or less sophisticated subtleties, arguments from silence or interpretations which have no support in the passage and which make it say the opposite of what it clearly states.

First Corinthians 7:15

If Jesus in Matthew 19:9 did not allow remarriage after divorce for the reason of marital unfaithfulness, how should we respond to the claim that Paul in 1 Corinthians 7:15 recognizes a second ground for remarriage after divorce: the desertion of a believer by an unbeliever? Many of the Reformers, including Calvin and Beza, brought the permission for remarriage in 1 Corinthians 7:15 in line with Jesus' saying in Matthew 19:9. They were persuaded that adultery was the only reason for divorce and remarriage recognized by Jesus. They reasoned that when a non-Christian husband abandoned the Christian he would marry another woman, which amounts to adultery. Some modern-day defenders of the Erasmian view also adopt this line of reasoning. Most, however, argue that Paul admits of another exception to the general rule of the indissolubility of marriage when he says: "But if the unbeliever leaves, let him do so. A believing man or woman is not bound in such circumstances; God has called us to live in peace" (1 Cor 7:15 NIV). I can find at least seven reasons why verse 15 should not be construed to permit remarriage to the deserted Christian.

Once again, the first argument against reading a permission for remarriage into 1 Corinthians 7:15 is the argument from church history. Ambrosiaster, a Latin father who wrote between A.D. 366 and 383, was the only writer in the first five centuries to allow remarriage to a believer deserted by an unbeliever.

Second, the lexical argument offered by many defenders of the two-reasons-for-divorce-and-remarriage view is tortuous. Charles, for example, argues that the word for "is not under bondage" in verse 15 has the same meaning as the word for "free" in 1 Corinthians 7:39 and Romans 7:2-3. Note the NASB translation of these verses and the relevant words:

> Yet if the unbelieving one leaves, let him leave; the brother or the sister *is not under bondage [douloō]* in such cases, but God has called us to peace. (1 Cor 7:15)
>
> A wife is *bound (deō)* as long as her husband lives; but if her husband is dead, she is *free (eleutheros)* to be married to whom she wishes, only in the Lord. (1 Cor 7:39)
>
> For the married woman *is bound (deō)* by law to her husband while he is living; but if her husband dies, she is released from the law concerning the husband. So then if, while her husband is living, she is joined to another man, she shall be called an adulteress; but if her husband dies, she is free *(eleutheros)* from the law, so that she is not an adulteress, though she is joined to another man. (Rom 7:2-3)

Charles's argument appears to involve an attempt to extend the legal-fiction exegesis of the Westminster Confession (the offending party should be treated *as if dead*) to the situation of the deserter, who, like the adulterer in the case of Matthew 19:9, is classified as an "offending party." It is obvious, however, that whereas 1 Corinthians 7:15 deals with a situation of *divorce* where both spouses are still alive, the other two passages envision a situation of *death* which Paul clearly says "frees" a person to remarry.

Paul also consistently uses different terms in these disparate contexts. When Paul is speaking about the biblical-legal aspect of being "bound" to one's partner in marriage (or bound by a promise of marriage to one's betrothed as in 1 Cor 7:27),[95] he uses the verb *deō* (Rom 7:2; 1 Cor 7:39). But he uses a different verb when he refers to the kind of duty or subjection *(douloō)* the believer is freed from in 1 Corinthians 7:15. Never does Paul use *douloō* with reference to that biblical-legal aspect of marriage which, in Paul's theology, can only be broken by the death of one of the partners.[96]

The third and perhaps most important reason Paul never intended 1 Corinthians 7:15 to be understood as freeing the believer up for remarriage is the nature of marriage itself. As a creation ordinance, marriage is binding on all humankind, Christian and non-Christian alike. Paul knows the binding nature of creation directives because he appeals to them in support of his teaching elsewhere (1 Cor 11:2-16; Eph 5:22-33; 1 Tim 2:12-15). Thus, if Paul did not permit one Christian divorced by another Christian to remarry (1 Cor 7:11), why should he permit a Christian divorced by a non-Christian to remarry?

I am persuaded that Paul shared Jesus' understanding of the Genesis 1:27 and 2:24 basis for marriage. The parallel that Paul draws between the unity the church has with Christ and the unity the husband has with his wife (Eph 5:31-32) suggests that Paul was not unfamiliar with the one-flesh basis for marriage which is so foundational to the teaching of Jesus. Markus Barth has observed in his commentary on Ephesians that the concept of "one flesh" is related to other Pauline ideas. "Just as the vss. 2:15, 16, 18 speak of two groups of persons that become 'a single new man' in 'one single body' through 'one single Spirit,' so the OT and Pauline formula 'one flesh' describes the amazing result of the union of 'two,' even of a man and a woman, in 'one.' Certainly their sexual relationship is in mind, but not only this expression and means of union."[97]

Fourth, the whole argument of 1 Corinthians 7:10-16 centers around Paul's strict adherence to the Lord's command that a believer should not separate *(chōrizō)* or divorce *(aphiēmi)*. The question we should ask, then, is what does it mean to be "not bound" in this context? Lövestam's analysis is again appealing.

> This freedom from bonds is related to the foregoing *chorizestho* "let him separate" and means that the Christian is not obliged to prevent the breaking-up of a mixed marriage with all the means at his disposal, if the unbeliever does not consent to carry on their life together but "separates". The Christians in Corinth and elsewhere should be whole-heartedly faithful to God and his radical will in the matter of marriage and divorce. But in a case like this they find themselves in the situation not through choice, the responsibility falling on the unbelieving partner.[98]

Paul's statement that the believer is "not bound" in such cases has the same function that the exception clause does in Matthew 19:9: it relieves the innocent party of the guilt of violating Christ's command not to divorce. In the case of Matthew 19:9 the woman who commits adultery is held responsible for the breakup of the marriage, while in 1 Corinthians 7:15 Paul exempts the Christian from the responsibility for the divorce which an unbelieving mate brings about. Nothing is said one way or the other about the possibility of remarriage for the believer.

Fifth, Paul uses the same word for "divorce" *(chōrizō)* in verse 15 as he does in verse 11 (along with *aphiēmi)*. Though Paul uses secular divorce terminology, he makes it clear that he wants his readers to understand that the kind of divorce or separation he is talking about does not include permission to remarry. He does this by the addition of the qualification should divorce and/or separation occur: "Let [them] remain unmarried or else be reconciled" (v. 11). J. A. Bengel picks up on this detail when he speaks about the believer's freedom in verse 15 from feeling that they somehow had to change the desire of their mate to be divorced, yet adds "but with that exception, *let her remain unmarried, ver.* 11."[99]

Sixth, D. L. Dungan draws attention to the "similarity" between "let her remain unmarried *or be reconciled*" (v. 11) with the general hopeful outlook in verse 16 that not divorce but conversion occur."[100] The NEB translation of verse 16 helps make Dungan's point: "Think of it: as a wife you may be your husband's salvation; as a husband you may be your wife's salvation." This implies that the hope of conversion is good and suggests that verse 16 looks back to verses 12-13, both of which conclude with a prohibition of divorce.

It is interesting that the early church fathers connected verse 16 with the distant verse 13. I believe the NEB rendering of verse 16 is more accurate than some others because lexical usage (of interrogative *ei*) allows for it and contextual congruency favors it. Thus verse 16 seems to provide a reason for Paul's remarks in verses 12-15 as a whole. Why should believers live harmoniously with their unbelieving mates either in marriage or in separation? Because they may very well be the channel through which God brings their unbelieving partner to faith.

Finally, the principle which Paul reinforces in verses 17-24, immediately following this question of desertion, is further evidence that Paul did not permit the deserted believer to change his or her status. J. A. Fischer argues for the unity of 1 Corinthians 7:8-16, but notes that "within this pericope 1 Cor 7:8-16 is a specific application of a more generic teaching in 1 Cor 7:17-24."[101]

At least three times in verses 17-24 Paul states the equivalent of "Let each person remain in that condition in which he was called." The argument of this passage is that believers should remain in the same situation in life in which they were when they became Christians because what Christ demands of his "slaves" is sole obedience to him and not a shared allegiance to other masters. Does this passage not help to answer the question, "What if I was divorced before I became a Christian? May I remarry now that I am 'in Christ'?" I would have to say that the answer to this question is a difficult no.

Some would appeal to 2 Corinthians 5:17, "the old has gone, the new has come!" in support of the contention that pre-Christian divorce is somehow different, and all of that is changed once a person becomes a believer. But 2 Corinthians 5:17 really does not convey this idea, and in reality teaches that the believer, as a new creation in Christ, now has the divine resources necessary to obey the ethical standards required of Christian disciples.

In the light of these seven points I feel that the burden of proof lies with those who would argue that Paul permits the deserted Christian to remarry. In saying that "a man or woman is not bound," Paul simply allows the Christian to agree to the non-Christian's insistent demand for divorce. The responsibility for the breakup of this marriage lies on the unbeliever's head. Paul is not thereby suggesting that the Christian divorcée may remarry. This would be antithetical to the covenant and kinship aspects of marriage found in the Genesis 2:24 basis for Jesus' teaching that anyone who remarries after divorce commits adultery.

Conclusion

Most evangelicals would declare that marriage is to be a permanent, lifelong relationship. If problems arise that lead to separation or divorce, every attempt possible ought to be made by the spouses to forgive one another and restore the relationship. This may take weeks, months or even years of prayer, patience and perseverance. Two aspects of the New Testament teaching on marriage and divorce commend this general approach to marital breakdown.

First, based on the teaching of the Lord on the subject of divorce, Paul knows of only two alternatives that he can authoritatively set before the divorced or divorcing Corinthian Christians: remain unmarried or else be reconciled (1 Cor 7:11). Separated or divorced Christians should avoid any thought or action that would hinder the possibility of restoration. In particular, this means not dating or forming intimate friendships with a member of the opposite sex.[102]

The second consideration that would commend forgiveness and reconciliation in the event of marital breakdown is the New Testament teaching of redemption. The death of Christ has implications for lifelong Christian marriages because Christ took upon himself the cost of human unfaithfulness. His great sacrifice has broken the power of sin and made forgiveness possible. In Bromiley's words: "Living with *divine* reconciliation as a constant fact in human life means living with *mutual* reconciliation as a constant fact. This makes indissoluble union a practical and attainable goal even for sinners."[103]

But what if reconciliation is impossible, primarily because one's spouse has already remarried? Jesus told his followers to lay up treasures for themselves in heaven, "for where your treasure is, there your heart will be also" (Mt 6:21 NIV). In a very real sense our affection for and devotion to the Lord is the biggest part of the answer to this problem. David said in Psalm 19:7-8: "The law of the LORD is perfect, reviving the soul. The statutes of the LORD are trustworthy, making wise the simple. The precepts of the Lord are right, giving joy to the heart. The commands of the LORD are radiant, giving light to the eyes" (NIV). Do we really believe that God is infinitely good, that he will withhold no good gift from his children when he knows their situation, and yet points to a life of singleness as the path of greatest fulfillment and highest blessing (see Mt 7:11; 19:10-12, 26; Lk 11:13; 1 Cor 7:11, 32-35; Ps 19:7-14)? If Jesus calls remarriage adultery, and if reconciliation is seemingly impossible, then the path of God's highest blessing must lie in the direction of pursuing a single life.[104]

I am sometimes asked, "Where does God's grace enter the picture of your no-remarriage position? Do you expect divorcées to remain single the rest of their lives?" To which I reply, "Does God give grace for Christians to sin?" I cannot think of any instance in Scripture where God gives grace to do that which is contrary to his will. In fact, Paul expresses horror at the thought: "Shall we go on sinning so that grace may increase? By no means! We died to sin; how can we live in it any longer?" (Rom 6:1-2 NIV). Thus if the Scriptures teach that marriage is only dissolved when one of the covenant kinship partners dies, then remarriage prior to the death of one of the partners involves the grave sin of adultry. So the question "Where does God's grace enter into your no-remarriage view?" is really framed on the assumption of a view of the marriage relationship other than the one I find portrayed throughout the Scriptures. God's grace is indeed magnified in my no-remarriage understanding of this subject because God's grace is abundantly bestowed on those disciples who desire to be faithful to their Lord's teachings, no matter how difficult they seem to be. In our weakness, God infuses us with the strength of his grace. The church, too, as an instrument of redemption, must be ready when necessary to financially support or help in any way possible the separated or divorced as they seek to honor Christ by obeying him.

Jeremiah may well be looked on as a role model for those who would live in obedience to God's call when it is contrary to their own personal longings. Though it was no choice of his own, Jeremiah was compelled to remain single and forgo married life as part of his function as a prophet of God to disobedient Israel (Jer 16:1-9).

That he abstained from marriage and children was a powerful sign that the end of Judah was at hand. People would die in the land before many days were past. Jeremiah, who never had wife or children, was as those would be who had married and had produced children but would lose them all in the calamity that would befall Judah.[105]

The total picture that emerges from vv. 1-9 is that Jeremiah was to be deprived of many of the normal activities of his fellows, marriage, family, and participation in the joys and sorrows of their common life. He was someone apart from his fellows. The strangeness of such isolation no doubt provoked many questions and provided Jeremiah with the opportunity to declare his word of judgment to a sinful and covenant-breaking people. His own separateness was a powerful testimony to the separateness of Yahweh as his people turned away from him.[106]

Jeremiah's call to singleness illustrates the prophetic value of a life lived in obedience to God. The consequences of his obedience for his own personal life appear to be entirely negative, but it must be remembered that he patterned his life according to the call of God. He was a willing instrument that the Lord used to convey his message to a people that had turned their backs on God. And there must have been satisfaction and fulfillment in this, namely, that in spite of his pain and deprivation he could know that he had been a faithful servant of his Lord's plan, in a very real sense the glove on God's hand. For Jeremiah says, "When your words came, I ate them; they were my joy and my heart's delight, for I bear your name, O LORD God Almighty" (15:16 NIV; see also Ezek 2:8—3:3).

Case Study

Jack is a respected man in the church. His children are grown and have successful marriages. His wife left him fifteen years ago to marry another man. Jack would like to have a wife again. Sarah is a widow. Her husband died in an auto wreck twelve years ago. All her children are grown. She has two sons in college. Jack and Sarah have become friends, attracted to each other by their personal walks with God. Both Jack and Sarah are involved in discipling young believers. For two years Jack and Sarah have been friends. But recently their friendship seems to be blossoming into a wholesome love that would sustain a marriage. Their children are delighted at the prospects of them getting married. They see that they are suited for each other in temperament and spiritual maturity. Their children and church friends encourage them to get married. Both Jack and Sarah are excited about ending the loneliness with which they have lived for years.

Answer

How does one respond to the desire for remarriage that comes from people like Jack, whose wife left him fifteen years ago to marry another man, and Sarah, a widow of twelve years? Though not everyone in the divorced or widowed singleness categories wants to marry again, it would probably be safe to say that most people in Jack and Sarah's situation would pursue the opportunity to marry and end their loneliness. Their Christian maturity is evidenced by the fact that they were attracted to each by the other's close personal walk with God, and their suitability for one another is reinforced by the favorable attitudes of their children and church friends toward the successful outcome of their marriage. Jack's and Sarah's desires are perfectly natural and their intentions are no doubt noble.

But in this, as in any situation, the question must be asked: Will these perfectly natural desires lead Jack and Sarah into a marriage that will glorify God and be blessed by him, or will their remarriage lead them to sin against their Lord and his church? To put the question another way: Can something that seems so right and natural to Jack and Sarah and their church still violate God's will? It ought to go without saying, of course, that just because Jack and Sarah, their children, and all their church friends "feel so right" about this remarriage does not mean that it should take place. The rightness or wrongness of remarriage for Jack and Sarah must ultimately be determined by the teaching of Scripture. Nevertheless, I want to preface the way I would handle Jack and Sarah's situation by mentioning one concern that I have about this particular scenario.

There are always dangers in treating a particular case of remarriage like this one. When we put Jack and Sarah's marital histories together with their spiritual maturity, the age and favorable response of their adult children and the encouragement of their friends at church, their case becomes exceptional. For instance, the death of one's father or mother does not make a new spouse easy to accept even for adult children. Not only is Jack and Sarah's situation unparalleled in the overwhelming majority of divorce and remarriage cases in the church today, but pastors tell me that most of the requests for divorce and remarriage they encounter do not even fall under the adultery and desertion exceptions allowed by the most popular evangelical view. Thus in view of the old legal maxim that "hard cases make bad laws," we are walking on thin and slippery ice if we attempt to base our standards for Christian marital conduct on the exceptional cases. Furthermore, there is always the danger of allowing our decisions in the exceptional cases to overrun their banks and flood the houses that we live in every day. We must be loving and compassionate as we apply our understanding of the biblical teaching to every case of marital breakdown that we encounter. But we should not allow our overall approach to divorce and remarriage center on the case of the unfortunate person or this or that particular situation.

There is no question in my mind that as a widow Sarah is free to remarry. I rejoice at this possibility for her and others in her situation. Nevertheless, Paul himself strongly encourages widowers and widows to remain single if they are able to exercise sexual self-control (1 Cor 7:8-9, 39-40). Even though Paul's advice sounds odd and restrictive to me today, I am challenged to "hear him out," to step back from the contemporary society and the evangelical subculture that I live in, and to examine my feelings about this issue and see if they are biblically informed or not. May God give us the grace to do this in every area of our Christian lives.

I am personally convinced that Paul himself was a widower. (Note his "as I have remained" example in the context of 1 Cor 7:8 and the similar language in v. 40 along with his personal note about the happiness or blessedness that Paul feels will abide with the choice for singleness.) I am also persuaded that Paul gives three very good reasons in 1 Corinthians 7 for commending this course of action. Paul encourages singleness (1) because of the trials, tribulations and afflictions that come with being "new creatures" who still must live within a largely unredeemed world (v. 26); (2) the shortening of the time preceding Christ's return and therefore the urgency of doing the Lord's work in this last hour (v. 29); and (3) because of the simple fact that the married state brings with it very natural and legitimate cares and concerns for the things of the world (vv. 32-35). All of Paul's reasons relate in some way to his life objective of advancing the claims and interests of God's kingdom here and now. I believe that Paul chose to remain unmarried because of the claims and interests of the kingdom of God (see Mt 19:12).

Thus if Sarah has the natural ability or the grace to remain continent in singleness, one of Sarah's primary considerations in whether or not to remarry would be the potential impact remarriage would have on her devotion to the Lord and how this would affect the impact of her discipleship ministry with young believers. We seldom think along these lines today, but I believe that for Jesus, Paul and other early Christians, availability and freedom for ministry with eternity in view were important Christian commodities.

Jack's situation, of course, is more complicated. I believe that every Christian is responsible before God to make his or her own decisions on matters of Christian conduct. Thus, I would never presume to dictate to any believer what he or she must do, nor would I attempt to hide the fact that many people disagree with my own interpretation of the biblical data on divorce and remarriage. A pastor's role is that of a shepherd and a teacher. The pastor guides and informs and speaks from personal convictions, but never decides for the counselee or hides opposing viewpoints. One's understanding about the nature and permanence of the marriage bond must arise out of his or her own prayerful, personal study of the Old and New Testament passages pertaining to this subject. The Christian should place his or her own observations and personal Bible study notes next to the advice he or she receives from pastors and counselors and what is read in books. I will respect, though I may disagree with (to varying degrees depending on the situation), the decision one makes to remarry. And if my convictions about the biblical teaching conflict with a church member's decision to remarry, then I am sure that person would never ask me to violate my own conscience (Rom 14:23) and perform a wedding that I felt was contrary to the will of God.

If Jack's wife had not remarried, Jack's prayers and actions would be focused continually on the hope of reconciliation that Paul points to in his directive to divorcées in 1 Corinthians 7:11: "Let them remain unmarried or else be reconciled." But Jack's wife has remarried, and reconciliation is now impossible. Is Jack free to remarry or not? If I could know for certain that Paul's directive to remain single in 1 Corinthians 7:11 applied only insofar as reconciliation is possible, and if 1 Corinthians 7:39 and Romans 7:2-3 were absent from Paul's letters, I might say that there is nothing in Paul to prevent Jack from marrying Sarah. Nevertheless, I question the former restriction of Paul's meaning in 1 Corinthians 7:11, and the passages which specifically say that only death ends a marriage are present in Paul.

Ephesians 5:22-33 argues indirectly for the lifelong permanence of the marriage union irrespective of violations that seem to destroy that relationship. The same Genesis 2:24 passage that Jesus appeals to for the unity in "one flesh" of husband and wife, Paul appeals to as a picture of Christ's oneness with his church. Just as Christ gave himself as a self-sacrifice for his church, so the husband's self-sacrifice in nourishing and caring for his wife is an acting out of what Jesus is for the members of his church. In short, the husband's love for his wife is an enactment of the Christian message. When Jack took his first wife "for better or for worse, for richer or for poorer," he committed himself to a life that would be completely sacrificial as Christ's was. A husband's sacrificial love on behalf of his wife may even mean that he has to throw away his life for her if she proves to be unfaithful. If reconciliation is impossible, Christians must trust in an infinitely good God who will withhold no good gift from them (Mt 7:11; Lk 11:13), who knows their situation, and yet points to a life of singleness as the path of greatest fulfillment and highest blessing (see Mt 10:10-12, 26; 1 Cor 7:11, 32-35; Ps 19:7-14).

Notes

[1]An essay of this size cannot possibly deal with all of the reasons I would like to offer for my own view. Therefore, I refer the reader to: "The Meaning of Divorce in Matthew 19:3-9," *Churchman* 98 (1984):136-52; W. A. Heth and G. J. Wenham, *Jesus and Divorce* (London: Hodder & Stoughton, 1984; Nashville: Thomas Nelson, 1985); and "Divorce and Remarriage," in *Apply-*

ing the Scriptures: Papers from ICBI Summit III, ed. K. S. Kantzer (Grand Rapids: Zondervan, 1987), pp. 219-39. See also the broad overview by C. C. Ryrie, "Biblical Teaching on Divorce and Remarriage," *Grace Theological Journal* 3 (1982):177-92.

²A brief but helpful unpublished paper by John Piper, "Divorce and Remarriage: A Position Paper" (July 21, 1986), explains his reasons for coming to a similar no-remarriage conclusion. Piper wrote it for members of his church (Bethlehem Baptist Church, Minneapolis, MN 55415) as a biblical rationale for why he feels constrained to make the decisions he does with regard to performing or not performing certain marriages and what sort of church discipline seems appropriate in regard to divorce and remarriage.

³See the unpublished work (available through University Micro films, Ann Arbor, MI) by Wm. A. Heth, "Matthew's 'Eunuch Saying' (19:12) and Its Relationship to Paul's Teaching on Singleness in 1 Corinthians 7" (Th.D. dissertation, Dallas Theological Seminary, 1986).

⁴So H. W. Hoehner, "A Response to Divorce and Remarriage," in *Applying the Scriptures,* ed. K. S. Kantzer (Grand Rapids: Zondervan, 1987), p. 241.

⁵The NIV's "be united" is overly suggestive of the sexual aspect of the action. In reality the covenant aspect of marriage is in view in the terms *leave* and *cleave.*

⁶This is the same statement on the connection between sexual union and the nature of the one-flesh relationship that appears in my ICBI paper ("Divorce and Remarriage," in *Applying the Scriptures,* p. 222). It has been misquoted and distorted more than once since then; see the responses of H. W. Hoehner and R. Stedman in *Applying the Scriptures,* and W. C. Kaiser, "Divorce in Malachi 2:10-16," *Criswell Theological Review* 2 (1987):83.

⁷I have developed these ideas in greater detail in "Divorce and Remarriage," in *Applying the Scriptures,* pp. 222-24.

⁸See G. Wallis, *"dāḇaq,"* Theological Dictionary of the Old Testament, eds. G. J. Botterweck and H. Ringgren, trans. J. T. Willis, G. Bromiley and D. E. Greene (Grand Rapids: Eerdmans, 1974-), 3 (1978):80-81; K. L. Schmidt, "κολλάω, προσκολλάω," *Theological Dictionary of the New Testament,* eds. G. Kittel and G. Friedrich, trans. and ed. G. W. Bromiley, 10 vols. (Grand Rapids: Eerdmans, 1964-76), 3 (1965):822-23; and W. Brueggemann, "Of the Same Flesh and Bone (Gn 2,23a)," *Catholic Biblical Quarterly* 32 (1970):532-42, esp. p. 540.

⁹E. S. Kalland, "dāḇaq," in *Theological Wordbook of the Old Testament,* 2 vols., ed. R. L. Harris (Chicago: Moody, 1980), 1:178.

¹⁰Hoehner offers no support when he says that "to suggest that there is no sexual significance in the term 'cleave' seems to ignore this context" (p. 241). In making this statement he goes against all the major lexical tools that discuss this term. Even the use of "cleave" in Genesis 34:3, where Schechem is said to have loved Dinah and clave to her (NIV: "His heart was

drawn to Dinah"), is not a reference to sexual relations, for this aspect of their "relationship" was described in the preceding verse where it says that "he took her and violated her" (so Wallis, *"dāḇaq"*).

[11]C. Westermann, *Genesis 1-11,* trans. J. J. Scullion (Minneapolis: Augsburg, 1984), p. 234.

[12]F. I. Andersen and D. N. Freedman, *Hosea,* Anchor Bible (Garden City, N.J.: Doubleday, 1980), p. 220.

[13]Ibid., p. 221.

[14]See Brown-Driver-Briggs, "בשׂר," 4, p. 142; F. Baumgärtel, *"σαρχ" TDNT* 7 (1971):106; and N. P. Bratsiotis, *"bāsār," TDOT* 2 (1977):327-28.

[15]See W. Reiser, "Die Verwandtschaftsformel in Gen. 2, 23," *Theologische Zeitschrift* 16 (1960):1-4.

[16]J. Adams, *Marriage, Divorce and Remarriage in the Bible* (Phillipsburg, N.J.: Presbyterian & Reformed, 1980), pp. 8, 32. See also E. Dobson, "What Is Marriage?" *Fundamentalist Journal,* Sept. 1985, pp. 40-41.

[17]S. A. Ellisen, *Divorce and Remarriage in the Church* (Grand Rapids: Zondervan, 1977), pp. 28, 69-70; J. MacArthur, *The Family* (Chicago: Moody, 1982), p. 54; and J. B. Hurley, *Man and Woman in Biblical Perspective* (Grand Rapids: Zondervan, 1981), pp. 31-32.

[18]S. B. Clark, *Man and Woman in Christ* (Ann Arbor, Mich.: Servant Books, 1980), p. 21.

[19]Ibid.

[20]See Westermann, *Genesis 1-11,* pp. 227, 232.

[21]G. von Rad, *Genesis,* rev. ed., original trans. by J. H. Marks, Old Testament Library (Philadelphia: Westminster, 1972), p. 82.

[22]See W. Eichrodt, *Theology of the Old Testament,* trans. J. A. Baker, 2 vols., Old Testament Library (Philadelphia: Westminster, 1961-7), 2:322-26.

[23]von Rad, *Genesis,* p. 84.

[24]C. J. H. Wright, *An Eye for An Eye: The Place of Old Testament Ethics Today* (Downers Grove, Ill.: InterVarsity, 1983), p. 174.

[25]R. K. Harrison, *Leviticus,* Tyndale Old Testament Commentary (Downers Grove, Ill.: InterVarsity, 1980), p. 186.

[26]Ibid. See also E. Neufeld, *Ancient Hebrew Marriage Laws* (London: Longmans, Green and Co., 1944), p. 192.

[27]See George Bush, *Notes, Critical and Practical, on the Book of Leviticus* (New York: Newman & Ivison, 1852; reprint ed., Minneapolis: Klock & Klock Christian Publishers, 1981), pp. 171-98; G. J. Wenham, *The Book of Leviticus,* New International Commentary on the Old Testament (Grand Rapids: Eerdmans, 1979), p. 255; and Harrison, *Leviticus.* Philo leads into his exposition of the Mosaic incest laws after making the statement: "Intermarriages with outsiders create new kinships not a wit inferior to blood-relationships" *(Special Laws* 3. 25).

[28]In addition to the references in n. 15, see also Brown-Driver-Briggs, "שׁאֵר,"

2 (p. 985); "לָקַח", 4e (p. 543); "קָרַב" 1a (p. 897); and "גָּלָה," 1a under Piel (p. 163).

[29]See Bush, *Notes/Leviticus,* pp. 172–75; Neufeld, *Ancient Hebrew Marriage Laws,* pp. 191–93; Wenham, *The Book of Leviticus,* p. 253; and Harrison, p. 186. Also note W. C. Kaiser, Jr., *Toward Old Testament Ethics* (Grand Rapids: Zondervan, 1983), pp. 115–16, 181–82, 190–91, 202–3.

[30]This idea is totally obscured by the NIV translation of these verses.

[31]Wenham, *The Book of Leviticus,* p. 255.

[32]See Deut. 22:30 and A. Phillips, "Uncovering the Father's Skirt," *Vetus Testamentum* 30 (1980):38–43.

[33]See Bush, *Notes/Leviticus,* pp. 174–79; Neufeld, *Ancient Hebrew Marriage Laws,* pp. 193–94; D. R. Mace, *Hebrew Marriage: A Sociological Study* (New York: Philosophical Library, 1953), p. 161; and Wenham, *The Book of Leviticus,* pp. 253–58. R. Stedman ("A Response to Divorce and Remarriage," in *Applying the Scriptures,* p. 249) emotionally argues that "there is no hint in the passage [i.e., Lev 18:6–18] that these prohibitions envision a death or a divorce. This seems to be an arbitrary interpretation which [Heth] brings in without warrant." The readers can check the authorities I cite for themselves. By reading Stedman one can determine whether he has properly considered the text's total possibilities or has adequately defended his views on this. Kaiser ("Divorce in Malachi 2:10–16," p. 83) picks up on this aspect of Stedman's response and agrees with him, I believe, incorrectly.

[34]Hoehner, p. 241. Kaiser ("Divorce in Malachi 2:10–16," p. 83) follows Hoehner's lead, but in so doing he appears to abandon the more weighty OT authorities he follows in his *Toward Old Testament Ethics* (pp. 114–17, 181–82, 185–86, 190–92, 202–3). Kaiser himself has a footnote to his concluding discussion of "one flesh" in Gen. 2:24 that reads, " 'Bone of my bones,' with the idea of becoming part of the family, one's blood relatives [sic] is also found in Gen. 29:14; 37:27; Judg. 9:2; 2 Sam. 5:1; 19:12–13 and 1 Chron. 11:1" (p. 182, n. 2). These are the very passages I cite for the kinship meaning of "one flesh" in Gen. 2:24. Yet Kaiser says in his "Divorce in Malachi 2:10–16" article of these very same OT references, "none of the texts that Heth cites prove that 'one flesh' is equivalent to blood relatives." Kaiser has misunderstood me because I never say they *are* "the equivalent to blood relatives." Kaiser apparently has Hoehner's ICBI response paper in front of him (see above n. 9) and is citing Hoehner's version of my understanding of the biblical texts. It is inappropriate that Kaiser refers to Hoehner's incorrect presentation of my views as views that I myself hold. It would seem that Kaiser is too dependent on second- and third-hand sources.

[35]Bush, *Notes/Leviticus,* pp. 173–75. It is also interesting to note that the punishments for incestuous relations with relatives are just as strict as that required for incestuous relations with consanguines (Lev 20:11, 12).

[36]Ibid., p. 175.

[37]See Wenham, *The Book of Leviticus,* pp. 257-58. Traditionally Leviticus 18:18 has been understood as the last in the list of incest laws found in Leviticus 18:6-18. For the view that verse 18 explicitly forbids polygamy and implicitly forbids divorce, see A. Tosato, "The Law of Leviticus 18:18: A Reexamination," *Catholic Biblical Quarterly* 46 (1984):199-214. Tosato makes special mention of the fact that closest to his proposal is Murray's view that Leviticus 18:18 condemns bigamy in general ("Appendix B: Additional Note on Leviticus 18: 16, 18" in *Principles of Conduct* [Grand Rapids: Eerdmans, 1957], pp. 250-56).

[38]Note that in Deuteronomy 13:6-11 family solidarity conflicts with the higher principle of "no idolatry," and the closest of family members may be put to death if they tempt other family members to follow other gods.

[39]J. Murray, *Divorce* (Phillipsburg, N.J.: Presbyterian & Reformed, [1961], p. 41). See Guy Duty, *Divorce and Remarriage* (Minneapolis: Bethany, 1967), pp. 32-44; and Hoehner, "A Response to Divorce and Remarriage," p. 244.

[40]Duty, *Divorce and Remarriage,* pp. 39 and 40.

[41]R. Westbrook, "The Prohibition on Restoration of Marriage in Deuteronomy 24:1-4," in *Studies in the Bible: 1986,* ed. S. Japhet, Scripta Hierosolymitana 31 (Jerusalem: Magnes Press at Hebrew University, 1986), p. 389, n. 4.

[42]J. D. M. Derrett, *Law in the New Testament* (London: Darton, Longman & Todd, 1970), p. 377. See A. Isaksson, *Marriage and Ministry in the New Temple,* trans. N. Tomkinson with J. Gray, ASNU 24 (Lund: Gleerup, 1965), p. 126.

[43]See further Heth, "Divorce and Remarriage," pp. 227-30.

[44]See R. Yaron, "The Restoration of Marriage," *Journal of Jewish Studies* 17 (1966):1-11; G. J. Wenham, "The Restoration of Marriage Reconsidered," *Journal of Jewish Studies* 30 (1979): 36-40; Isaksson, *Marriage and Ministry,* pp. 21-25; Derrett, *Law in the New Testament,* pp. 376-77; and now Westbrook, "The Prohibition on Restoration of Marriage," pp. 387-405.

[45]Heth and Wenham, *Jesus and Divorce,* pp. 89-90, 106-10.

[46]Westbrook, "The Prohibition on Restoration of Marriage," p. 393.

[47]I have reversed the order in which Westbrook discusses these principles in order to bring them in line with the sequence of the circumstances noted in Deuteronomy 24:1-3.

[48]Westbrook (p. 399) knows of only one modern scholar who thinks that the "some indecency" means actual adultery: A. Toeg, "Does Deuteronomy 24,1-4 Incorporate a General Law on Divorce? *Diné Israel* 2 (1970):v-xxiv, at p. vii. Westbrook also notes that Toeg's argument is even more questionable because he thinks the clause is an interpolation. I have found one other modern author who argues that the "some indecency" is a reference to adultery: Y. Zakovitch, "The Woman's Rights in the Biblical Law of Divorce," in *The Jewish Law Annual* 4, ed. B. S. Jackson (Leiden: Brill, 1981),

pp. 28–46. Zakovitch prefers this view over the view numbers one and four surveyed above. But the "some indecency" *('erwat dābār)* in Deuteronomy 24:1 cannot be "adultery" for two reasons: (1) the law punishes adultery by death, not by divorce (Lev 20:10; Deut 22:22), and (2) the only other place where these two words appear together is Deuteronomy 23:15, and a sexual connotation is out of the question in that context.

[49]Westbrook, "The Prohibition on Restoration of Marriage," pp. 401–2.

[50]Ibid., p. 404.

[51]Ibid.

[52]S. A. Kaufmann, "The Structure of the Deuteronomic Law," *Maarav* 1/2 (1978–79):105–58.

[53]Hoehner, "A Response to Divorce and Remarriage," p. 244.

[54]Heth and Wenham, *Jesus and Divorce,* p. 201.

[55]The Pharisees who debated with Jesus in Matthew 19 and Mark 10 held the same view of the efficacious power of the certificate of divorce to dissolve marriages that many evangelicals want to claim for it today.

[56]I had formerly argued that Deuteronomy 24:1–4 "seems to imply that to seek a divorce is to try to break a relationship with one's wife that in reality cannot be broken" (Heth and Wenham, *Jesus and Divorce,* p. 110). Though I still believe this concept is valid based on the kinship aspect of marriage, I would no longer attempt to argue the point based on the Deuteronomy 24 passage.

[57]W. R. Eichhorst ("Ezra's Ethics on Intermarriage and Divorce," *Grace Journal* 10:3 [1969]:23) thinks that Ezra also required the men to send away these women "according to the law" (10:3) found in Deuteronomy 24:1–4. But this not only misunderstands Deuteronomy 24:1–4, it fails to see that "the law" according to which the Israelites should "put away" their women refers to that law in 9:1–2, 10–12 and 14 which Ezra was confessing: "Shall we again break Thy commandments and intermarry with the people who commit these abominations?" The law in view is Deuteronomy 7:3 and Exodus 34:16, not Deuteronomy 24:1–4.

[58]G. Rawlinson, *Ezra and Nehemiah: Their Lives and Times* (New York: Randolph, 1890), p. 42.

[59]H. G. M. Williamson, *Ezra, Nehemiah,* Word Biblical Commentary (Waco, Tex.: Word, 1985), p. 130. See F. C. Fensham, *The Books of Ezra and Nehemiah,* New International Commentary on the Old Testament (Grand Rapids: Eerdmans, 1982), pp. 124–25.

[60]The LXX uses *kathizō* (to sit down, settle, live) to translate this word, and *kathizō* is never used to translate any of the other "usual" words for marriage (i.e., *lāqaḥ, ba'al,* or *nāsā').*

[61]See Heth and Wenham, *Jesus and Divorce,* p. 243, n. 29.

[62]"No extant law required divorce in such cases, so *Shechaniah* proposes a way out, a *hope* by a *covenant,* suggesting by the words he uses for *married*

and *foreign women* that these had not been true marriages" *(The Oxford Annotated Bible with the Apocrypha,* ed. H. G. May and B. M. Metzger [New York: Oxford Univ. Press, 1965], p. 584 n. at Ezra 10:2).

[63]Wright, *An Eye for An Eye,* pp. 175-76.

[64]Ibid., p. 178.

[65]See R. H. Gundry, *Matthew: A Commentary on His Literary and Theological Art* (Grand Rapids: Eerdmans, 1982), pp. 90-91.

[66]There is a good possibility that the word *porneia* in Matthew 5:32 and 19:9 refers to "pre-marital" unfaithfulness during the Jewish betrothal period (see Mt 1:18-19; Jn 8:41). Isaksson (pp. 116-48) preferred this view over six others. This interpretation is usually ridiculed or regarded as impossible by most evangelicals (Murray, *Divorce,* p. 34, n. 4). It is argued that "our Lord is not applying his rule to an unconsummated marriage, but to the one who is divorcing his wife (Mt 19:3; see also vv. 6, 8, 9)" (Kaiser, "Divorce in Malachi," p. 82). But this kind of response does more to demonstrate one's misunderstanding of the arguments for the betrothal view of the exception clause than it does to show the improbability of this view. If the betrothal view is correct, then there is no need for the debate over the syntax of Matthew 19:9: it would not be an issue.

[67]For the details of this argument see Heth and Wenham, *Jesus and Divorce,* pp. 19-44, 73-99.

[68]T. W. Manson, *The Teaching of Jesus,* 2nd ed. (Cambridge: University Press, 1935), p. 200, n. 5.

[69]E. Flesseman-van Leer, *Tradition and Scripture in the Early Church,* Theologische Bibliotheek 26 (Assen, Netherlands: Van Gorcum, 1954), p. 9.

[70]J. J. Hughes, review of *L'église primitive face au divorce du premier au cinquième siècle,* Théologique historique 13 (Paris: Beauchesne, 1971), in *Journal of Ecclesiastical History* 24 (1973):61.

[71]V. N. Olsen, *The New Testament Logia on Divorce: A Study of Their Interpretation from Erasmus to Milton,* Beiträge zur Geschichte der biblischen Exegese 10 (Tübingen: J. C. B. Mohr [Paul Siebeck], 1971), p. 12.

[72]Ibid., p. 19.

[73]Ibid., p. 22.

[74]Tony Lane, "Till When Us Do Part? Divorce Part 1," *Today,* Sept. 1986, p. 37.

[75]R. H. Charles, *The Teaching of the New Testament on Divorce* (London: Wms. & Norgate, 1921), pp. 3-34. See Hurley, *Man and Woman,* pp. 102-4, and C. Brown, "Separate, Divide," *The New International Dictionary of New Testament Theology,* ed. C. Brown, 3 vols. (Grand Rapids: Zondervan, 1975-78), 3 (1978):538, 540-41.

[76]See Charles, *Teaching,* pp. 32, 62-71; Ellisen, *Divorce and Remarriage,* p. 52; and Brown, "Separate, Divide," 3:535, 539. Charles is convinced that 1 Corinthians 6:13-17 is the central text in which Paul deals with "the legitimacy

or illegitimacy of divorce on the ground of unchastity" (p. 62), and Brown follows the argument of Charles.

[77]Murray, *Divorce,* p. 43.

[78]D. A. Carson, "Matthew," in *The Expositor's Bible Commentary,* ed. F. E. Gaebelein (Grand Rapids: Zondervan, 1984), 8:417, and Ellisen, *Divorce and Remarriage,* p. 58.

[79]P. P. Levertoff and H. L. Goudge, "The Gospel according to St. Matthew," in *A New Commentary on Holy Scripture,* ed. C. Gore, H. L. Goudge, A. Guillaume (New York: Macmillan, 1928), p. 174.

[80]See G. P. Liaboe, "The Place of Wife Battering in Considering Divorce," *Journal of Psychology and Theology* 13 (1985):129-38.

[81]Both MacArthur *(The Family,* pp. 107-28) and C. Swindoll *(Divorce* [Portland, Oreg.: Multnomah, 1981], p. 15) would tend to see in *porneia* a sustained form of adulterous behavior.

[82]E. Lövestam, "Divorce and Remarriage in the New Testament," in *The Jewish Law Annual,* vol. 4, ed. B. S. Jackson (Leiden: Brill, 1981), p. 61. The same analysis is found in F. Hauck and S. Schulz, "πόρνη κτλ.," Theological Dictionary of the New Testament, 6 (1968):592. See also K. Stendahl, "Matthew," *Peake's Commentary on the Bible,* ed. M. Black and H. H. Rowley (Thomas Nelson, 1962), § 679g, and B. Vawter, "Divorce and the New Testament," *Catholic Biblical Quarterly* 39 (1977):531, n. 4.

[83]Both Murray *(Divorce,* p. 39) and Carson ("Matthew," p. 416) are aware of this point.

[84]See D. Atkinson, *To Have and to Hold: The Marriage Covenant and the Discipline of Divorce* (London: Collins, 1979), p. 132, n. 78; Adams, *Marriage, Divorce and Remarriage,* pp. 51-53; D. Guthrie, *New Testament Theology* (Downers Grove, Ill.: InterVarsity, 1981), pp. 949-50 and n. 154; Hurley, *Man and Woman,* p. 103, n. 13; and others.

[85]Heth and Wenham, *Jesus and Divorce,* pp. 90-93, 113-20.

[86]Carson's discussion of Jesus' teaching on divorce and remarriage is now being heralded as one of the best modern defenses of the Erasmian or Protestant view of Jesus' teaching on divorce and remarriage. See R. T. France, *Trinity Journal* 6 NS (Spring 1985):109-10, and Craig L. Blomberg, "The Legitimacy and Limits of Harmonization," in *Hermeneutics, Authority, and Canon* (ed. D. A. Carson and John D. Woodbridge; Grand Rapids: Zondervan, 1986), p. 150.

[87]Carson, "Matthew," p. 416.

[88]Even this way of paraphrasing Matthew 19:9 is imprecise and cannot reflect the considerations I raise in *Jesus and Divorce,* pp. 123-26, 128, 168, 183-84, 189.

[89]G. J. Wenham, "The Syntax of Matthew 19.9," *Journal for the Study of the New Testament* 28 (1986):17-23.

[90]See Heth and Wenham, *Jesus and Divorce,* pp. 53-68, 128-29, and W. A.

Heth, "Unmarried 'for the sake of the kingdom' (Matthew 19:12) in the Early Church," *Grace Theological Journal* 8 (1987):55–88.

[91]See Chap. 4, "Matthew 19:10–12: Meaning and Function" in Heth, "Matthew's 'Eunuch Saying' (19:12)," pp. 139–98 (see n. 4 above).

[92]1 Corinthians 7:7 should not be used to help illuminate Matthew 19:11. First Corinthians 7:7 is talking about the diversity of gifts possessed by a single group of people: Christians. Matthew 19:11, however, envisions two disparate groups of individuals: unbelievers who respond negatively to Jesus' teaching as opposed to faithful disciples who (should) respond positively and welcome his teaching.

[93]See Levertoff and Goudge, "The Gospel according to St. Matthew," p. 175; P. Ketter, " 'Nicht alle fassen dieses Wort': Bemerkungen zu Mt 19,10–12," *Pastor Bonus* 49 (1938–39):319; P. Bonnard, *L'évangile selon Saint Matthieu,* Commentaire du Nouveau Testament 1 (Paris: Delachaux et Niestlé, 1963), p. 284; T. V. Fleming, "Christ and Divorce," *Theological Studies* 24 (1963):113; H. Baltensweiler, *Die Ehe im Neuen Testament,* Abhandlungen zur Theologie des Alten und Neuen Testaments 52 (Zürich/Stuttgart: Zwingli, 1967), p. 112; and T. Matura, "Le célibat dans le Nouveau Testament d'après l'exégèse récente," *Nouvelle Revue Théologique* 97 (1975): 493. Carson ("Mathew," p. 419) gives the wrong volume number (107) for Matura's article.

[94]Blomberg, "Legitimacy," p. 150.

[95]For a defense of the engaged-couple view of 1 Corinthians 7:25–38, see Heth and Wenham, *Jesus and Divorce,* pp. 144–48.

[96]Hoehner (p. 245) commits a similar lexical error when he appeals to "the analogous language in 7:39" to argue that the most natural sense for the meaning of " 'to be bound' . . . is that the believing partner is not bound to the marriage covenant and is free to remarry."

[97]M. Barth, *Ephesians,* Anchor Bible, 2 vols. (Garden City, N.Y.: Doubleday, 1974), pp. 640–41.

[98]Lövestam, "Divorce and Remarriage," p. 65. See A. Robertson and A. Plummer, *A Critical and Exegetical Commentary on the First Epistle of St Paul to the Corinthians,* 2nd ed., International Critical Commentary (Edinburgh: T. & T. Clark, 1911), p. 143.

[99]J. A. Bengel, *New Testament Word Studies,* trans. C. T. Lewis and M. R. Vincent, 2 vols., 1864; reprint ed., Grand Rapids: Kregel, 1971), 2:210.

[100]D. L. Dungan, *The Sayings of Jesus in the Churches of Paul* (Philadelphia: Fortress, 1971), p. 97.

[101]J. A. Fischer, "1 Cor. 7:8–24—Marriage and Divorce," *Biblical Research* 23 (1978):27.

[102]A. Bustanoby, "Can Men and Women Be Just Friends?" *Fundamentalist Journal* 5:18 (Sept. 1986):44–46.

[103]Geoffrey Bromiley, *God and Marriage* (Grand Rapids: Eerdmans, 1980), p.

47.

[104]I applaud the brief but insightful article by Julia Duin, "We Must Learn to Celebrate Celibacy," *Christianity Today,* March 21, 1986, p. 13.

[105]J. A. Thompson, *The Book of Jeremiah,* New International Commentary on the Old Testament (Grand Rapids: Eerdmans, 1980), p. 404.

[106]Ibid., p. 407.

Response

J. Carl Laney

*I*t was in 1981, shortly after the publication of my book, The Divorce Myth, that I became acquainted with the writings of William A. Heth. I have followed his many writings and publications ever since with a good deal of interest. We have had the opportunity to become acquainted as we have shared our research through letters, phone calls and conversations at theological society meetings. I appreciate this brother and sense a real kindred spirit with him in our mutual concern for the issue of divorce and remarriage.

What impresses me about Bill's work is his commitment as an evangelical to the rigorous demands of scholarly research. This is evidenced by the numerous books and articles cited in his writings. His book *Jesus and Divorce* contains the most complete bibliography on divorce and remarriage presently available. The present document (containing 107 notes) reflects careful interaction with other scholars and experts in the field. This illustrates the fact that Bill Heth is not just interested in presenting his own opinion, but in weighing his views against the research of others and working towards a more precise understanding of the truth.

I am also impressed with Bill's willingness to modify his views on the basis of further study and the research of others. This is evident in his present treatment of Deuteronomy 24:1-4 (pp. 81-84) in which he takes into account the insightful work of R. Westbrook. Having published a book in which he states a different opinion, Heth now writes, "I find Westbrook's solution the most satisfactory to date." This humility and teachable attitude serves us well in the ongoing pursuit of truth.

I have also grown to appreciate Bill's keen exegetical insights in dealing with the subject of divorce and remarriage. Far from being content to rehearse the opinions of others, Bill's own research and exegesis bring fresh insight into the divorce and remarriage debate. I have appreciated his work on Leviticus 18:6-18, a text which prohibits incestuous relationships, both illicit and marital. Together with his colleague Gordon Wenham, he has shown that these laws reflect the fact that extended relationships come into being through the marriage of two formerly unrelated people (p. 75). Marital intercourse makes a man and wife as closely related as parents and children. This is a tremendous insight in seeking to understand the prohibition of Deuteronomy 24:4. Similarly, Heth furthers our understanding of Deuteronomy 24:1-4 and Ezra 9—10. These contributions are stimulating and helpful.

Bill's treatment of the New Testament teaching on divorce and remarriage is very clear and understandable. I appreciate the seven statements which summarize the New Testament teaching on divorce and remarriage (p. 92). I agree with Heth that "nowhere in the Gospels nor in Paul do we find a clear and unambiguous mandate for remarriage after divorce" (p. 93).

It is generally assumed by those dealing with the subject of divorce and remarriage that legitimate divorce means that the marriage is terminated and that remarriage is permitted. This was certainly the opinion of the Jews of Jesus' day. Heth points out on the basis of Matthew 5:31 that the certificate of divorce does not do what the Jews thought it did. It does not dissolve the marriage union. That is why divorce and remarriage constitutes adultery. This simple observation is the key to understanding the principle of the indissolubility of marriage. It seems that from God's point of view, marriage ends with death, not divorce. If adultery ends a marriage, then there are a lot of people whose marriages have terminated (due to illicit activity), and they do not even know it.

I appreciate Bill's clear and straightforward presentation of the six major reasons why Matthew 19:9 does not allow for remarriage after divorce. The historical perspective he provides is most instructive (pp. 94-99). Based on the work of Henri Crouzel, Heth points out that the modern notion of divorce as a "dissolution" of the marital relationship with the possibility of remarriage was unheard of in the early church.

It is surprising to learn that the traditional Protestant viewpoint can be traced to Erasmus and his sacramental view of marriage. Yet, whereas Erasmus appealed to the principle of "charity" as a basis for remarriage, Protestants have sought to defend his opinion exegetically. The popular concept of divorce replacing stoning as the penalty for adultery is traced by Heth to the 1921 work of R. H. Charles. All this is to say that the Protestant evangelical viewpoint is a relatively modern tradition. It is not that being modern is wrong. One just wonders if there is a legitimate exegetical basis for abandoning our line of continuity with the early church on the matter of divorce and remarriage.

I also appreciate Heth's clear and convincing arguments that sexual sins do not dissolve the marriage bond (pp. 99-102). I agree with his point that "since marriage is not constituted solely on the basis of sexual union, it seems inconsistent to say that it is dissolved solely on the basis of sexual infidelity" (p. 103).

Heth presents a very helpful treatment of Murray's argument that the syntax of Matthew 19:9 applies the exception clause to both the act of divorce and the act of remarriage (pp. 102-105). Although presented in his book *Jesus and Divorce,* I believe he has refined the presentation and provided greater clarity. Many modern comment-ators have simply followed Murray's arguments without critically ex-amining them. Heth examines them, compares them to the thinking of the early church fathers and proposes that the exception applies to the act of divorce, not the remarriage. Although Murray insisted on linking divorce and remarriage in Matthew 19:9, the early church did not. Although divorce and remarriage are sequential, they do not necessarily follow one another.

The application of the context following Matthew 19:9 is quite significant (pp. 105-107). Heth points out that verse 11 does not refer to two classes of disciples among the followers of Jesus—some who have the gift of celibacy and others who do not. Rather, Jesus is referring to true disciples in contrast with unbelievers.

Heth provides new insight into the last words of Jesus in Matthew 19:12, "The one who can accept this should accept it." This call is directed to two groups—those who might be so inclined (like Paul, 1 Cor 7:40) and those who find these teachings difficult. Yet God's grace is sufficient to enable his people to meet difficulties and over-come them.

Heth's work on the Synoptic parallels is helpful (pp. 107-108). It is unfortunate that the rather clear and precise statements of Luke 16:18 and Mark 10:1-12 receive so little attention among those who argue the legitimacy of divorce and remarriage.

Bringing the Pauline writings into the discussion (pp. 109-114), Heth demonstrates rather convincingly that the Apostle gives no hint or mention of a sexual sin exception which permits remarriage. When Paul does speak of the right of remarriage, he always mentions the death of the partner (1 Cor 7:39, Rom 7:2-3). I agree with Heth that 2 Corinthians 5:17 does not teach that a new believer has a right to a new marriage, but that the new believer has the new covenant resources to obey the ethical standards required of disciples.

In the person of Paul we have a first-century interpreter of the words of Jesus. Nowhere in his discussion on marriage and divorce does he directly mention an exception to the permanence of marriage. We would do well to bring our own exegesis in line with Paul's first-century insights as a commentator, theologian and apostle.

In conclusion, I must say that I am in agreement with Bill Heth on nearly every point of his presentation. Furthermore, I am persuaded that we are saying essentially the same thing on the subject of divorce and remarriage. According to Heth, God clearly intended for marriage to be lifelong, and divorce and remarriage is a violation of his creation design. I say Amen.

Response

Thomas R. Edgar

*H*eth is to be commended for his obvious desire to defend marriages and reduce the alarming number of divorces in our present culture. He is also to be commended for his desire to argue from Scripture rather than experience. Despite his strong stand against divorce and remarriage, in the case study he is aware of the difficulties facing the people involved and handles their situations in a gracious manner.

In contrast to many, I also agree with his view that a person divorced before salvation is not free on that account to remarry where it is otherwise prohibited. If it is wrong for a believer to remarry who was divorced after salvation, I would think it is equally wrong for a believer to remarry who was divorced before salvation.

As the nature of the discussion requires, however, it is the areas of difference which must receive the stress in this response. I find it very difficult to write a brief response to Heth's chapter, since I not only disagree with his overall approach, but I also disagree with most of the details, interpretations and logical connections he makes in his lengthy chapter. In my chapter I refute at some length many of his points; however, I will include some of it in this response for those who may not make a comparison.

I disagree with his basic method, which is to quote some writer's comment and then seemingly to assume that this is evidence and proceed in his argument as if it were undoubtedly so. In some cases he quotes a very questionable statement without any defense of the same and proceeds on his discussion with this as his basis. An example (which I will later discuss further) is his use of Westbrook's highly unlikely view as a basis for argument. Heth gives no indication that various writers have different opinions on the same subject and, therefore, apart from some evidence, one writer's view is offset by another's. Since there are writers for each of the positions, one receives the impression that Heth quotes those who state the view that best accords with his presuppositions and proceeds as if it were fact. I do not agree that quotation of others' opinions is adequate basis for argument. They must be proven by exegetical arguments.

Overall, Heth gives very little direct exegetical evidence in this lengthy statement of his view. He states that divorce and remarriage are basically theological issues (p. 75). I do not think this is the proper perspective. Theology can only arise from an exegesis and harmonizing of all the passages on a given subject. The disagreements are not on a theological basis (except for the Roman Catholic position) but on the meaning of specific passages. Therefore, the issue is basically an exegetical one. Heth is consistent with this perspective in that his approach is basically theological. He assumes the inherent indissolubility of marriage which he supports by several tenuous interpretations of certain Old Testament passages. With this as his "theological" perspective he then interprets all the passages in accordance with this presumed indissolubility of marriage. In contrast I attempt to exegete each passage as it stands and then combine them into a harmonic whole.

To cite a more specific point of disagreement, Heth argues, as Laney does, that the word *cleave* in Genesis 2:24 implies permanence (pp. 74–75). However, since this word is used to refer to clods of dirt "cleaving together" and to a girdle "cleaving to one's loins" it obviously cannot prove permanence. He also argues on the basis of the word *covenant* that this implies permanence (pp. 76–77). However, covenants are not necessarily permanent, nor is this word used in Genesis 2:24. There is nothing in Genesis 2:24 that states marriage is permanent. In fact Christ's statement, referring to Genesis 2:24, "What God has joined together let not man separate" (Mt 19:6) implies just the opposite of permanence, that it can be broken. The basic problem, however, is that if marriage were permanent it is not because of the legal or human aspects, but because God declares it so. Yet Heth seems to never consider the completely logical conclusion that if marriage were permanent due to God's action, then the same God can also decree when it can be dissolved. In other words, all the argument on permanence cannot overrule the clear statement in Matthew 19:9 allowing the exception. The crux of one's position on divorce and remarriage is not on alleged implications from verses not discussing divorce, but from explicit statements from verses specifically dealing with the issue. Heth, as well as others, majors on uncertain implications and uses these as a foundation to nullify the explicit passages. There is little question that the foundation of his entire approach is the concept that marriage is permanent, indissoluble.

I have shown in my chapter that the entire discussion regarding one flesh—the connection with Leviticus chapter 18, the "marital kinship" view and the "incestuous marriage" view—is without any basis. The fact that 1 Corinthians 6:16 specifically quotes Genesis 2:24 and says that sexual relationship with a prostitute is one flesh, rules out "permanence" as the meaning for one flesh, unless the relationship with a prostitute is permanent. Nor is it likely that this expression means the person involved is now related to the prostitute's family. Nor does it rule out, in the case of a single person, marriage to someone other than the prostitute. But, if one flesh does not carry these connotations in 1 Corinthians 6:16, then neither does it in Genesis 2:24 which Paul quotes.

Heth's argument regarding levirate and surrogate marriage in Leviticus chapter 18 as "exceptions" resolving conflicting Old Testament principles is necessary to uphold his marital kinship view (p. 80). However, it is much more natural to realize that unlike a blood relationship the marital kinship ends upon death of the spouse so that one is free, for example, to marry her sister (Lev 18:18). Therefore, the marital kinship is not comparable to the permanence of a blood relationship. It is interesting that in order to defend his "marital kinship" view Heth has no problem regarding these as "exceptions," but he cannot seem to conceive of any "exceptions" to his idea of the permanence of marriage.

I also disagree with Heth's apparent belief that the Mosaic Law does not conform with, and even contradicts, God's intention for marriage (p. 79). He often argues as if the Mosaic Law is merely an adaptation to Near Eastern culture, or is only Moses' ideas. This is an attempt to play down those verses allowing divorce. The Law was given by God, and is described as holy, righteous and good. Therefore, it does not contradict God. It is much more likely that rather than contradict God's intentions, it is contradicting Heth's interpretation of God's intentions. Heth often mentions Jesus' reference to God's original intention in Matthew 19:5-6 as if that were the end of Jesus' statement, and as if God's original description of marriage before the Fall of humanity is definitive for the time after the Fall. But Jesus goes on to state that Moses (God, in the final analysis) did permit divorce, and then Jesus refers to his own concept which includes the exception. I have demonstrated in my discussion of this issue that Jesus' ideal for the post-Fall world includes the exception. Therefore, God's original intention in Genesis 2:24 is not the final word on the issue. Jesus merely refers to the pre-Fall situation as the starting point for his discussion, not the definitive statement. To argue that a pre-Fall intention of marriage rules out any changes after the Fall, as Heth implies, would logically mean that God's pre-Fall intention for humanity to be sinless rules out a need for any adjustment to the Fall—the need for a Savior.

Heth's argument based on a quotation from Westbrook is amazing in its overlooking of the obvious (p. 83). Why is it assumed (for assumption can be the only basis) that in Deuteronomy 24:1-4 the divorce from the second husband must be for a significantly different reason than the divorce from the first? There is no reason to assume this from the passage. It is more in line with the passage to assume that the reasons are not significantly different, and, therefore, that there is some thread of similarity between the reasons "indecency, dislike and death" in this passage. They are all common reasons for breaking of marriages. To assume that "dislike and death" are in a different category from "indecency" and from this to conclude that the Deuteronomy 24:1-4 passage is to preclude the original husband from profiting twice from the woman's dowry is certainly not an obvious conclusion. Yet Heth accepts this incongruous opinion as evidence and claims that it destroys the opposing views.

It is certainly strange to regard this passage as referring to the wife's dowry, when there is no implication to that effect. Since the reason she is not to marry the original husband is because "she is defiled," this interpretation would require that "she is defiled" somehow refers to the husband's profit from her dowry. This view apparently regards the remarriage to the original spouse as acceptable but for the aspect of undue profit from the dowry. Therefore, this would mean that the Lord, rather than allowing an otherwise acceptable reconciliation of the original marriage, is more concerned that the husband not have undue financial profit. We must remember that Deuteronomy 24:1-4 is God's Word and expresses his thinking. Is the Lord more concerned about such financial situations, which are obviously not illegal, than reconciliation of marriages? Why does Heth accept this seemingly improbable interpretation? He states that at least one reason that he accepts it is because it helps his view. This is not a sufficient or valid reason.

His example from Numbers 25:6–15, which describes the Israelite who took a foreign wife and was summarily executed, is hardly evidence (as Heth claims) for Ezra's action as kindness. Heth regards as kindness the fact that Ezra only demanded the "divorce of the foreign wives, not their execution." It should be obvious that this deduction does not follow since the instance in Numbers 25 would require the execution of the Israelites as well, rather than the foreign wives only, and therefore is hardly an act of kindness toward the wives.

Heth argues that "nowhere in the Gospels nor in Paul do we find a clear and unambiguous mandate for remarriage after divorce" (p. 92). I disagree. Matthew 19:9 is a clear and unambiguous mandate for remarriage after divorce in the case of the exception. The verse, if taken as it stands, is perfectly clear. The problem is not in the verse, but in the refusal to accept its clear, unambiguous testimony. On the other hand, it can be accurately stated that nowhere do we find a clear and unambiguous mandate that there are no allowable exceptions to divorce which allow remarriage.

As far as Heth's argument from the New Testament passages, his summary of the New Testament teaching on divorce into seven statements is not best explained by his view, as he claims (p. 92). On the contrary, if the exception in Matthew 19:9 is regarded, as it claims to be, as an exception to the rule, then the best explanation is that the passages not stating an exception are stating the general rule, and the specific exceptions are allowable exceptions to that rule. We cannot avoid the exception of Matthew 5:31–32, as Heth attempts to do (p. 93), by stating the verse as if the exception is not there and ignoring the obvious similarity to the exception in Matthew 19:9. It may be a grammatical *possibility* to argue, as Heth does, that Jesus is only describing *who* makes the woman an adulteress. However, is this the point of the passage?

The following clause indicates it is not the point, but the point is that the woman is an adulteress because the previous marriage is still valid. Heth's view would ignore the fact that the man's actions are improper and would, therefore, also prohibit his remarriage. It would merely stress whether the husband or wife caused her to be an adulteress. This is improbable. Matthew 5:31–32, in any case, still means that one who divorces because of *porneia* does not make his wife an adulteress; that is, he does nothing wrong. He does not commit the wrong of the previous clause which describes the one who divorces his wife improperly.

Heth's argument from the "historical perspective" (p. 94) is irrelevant as evidence for the correct view. It seems more of an attempt to claim that those who allow for remarriage do so for ulterior motives. I do not question Heth's motives since right or wrong they are not evidence; only his arguments are evidence. The church fathers were wrong so often, even regarding justification by faith, that his appeal to them (p. 96) carries little weight. Is Heth's argument from the Westminster Confession (pp. 96–97) implying that it is Erasmian in its outlook? Are we to conclude that due to "the Erasmian origin" and "historical situation of the exegesis" undergirding it, the Westminster Confession is false, or is it only inaccurate on one subject, divorce? This argument is also irrelevant, since I for one, as well as others, do not use this document to control or even to influence my views or my exegesis.

Heth's discussion about the syntax of Matthew 19:9 (pp. 102–3) and his comments about Murray's argument (pp. 102–4) would lead us to believe that the view that remarriage is allowable in the case of the exception is some novel idea introduced only lately into the discussion. He fails to realize that this is not some novel idea, but a statement of the exegetical and syntactical facts which have always existed in the verse. Are we to really believe, as Heth states, that no one debated this position until John Murray wrote his commentary in 1961? This seems particularly inconsistent for someone who argues that this view is from Erasmus. Does Heth mean that there was no debate in Erasmus' time? This is contrary to historical fact.

Should we conclude that in the first thousand years of the church no one argued this point? Murray is often quoted not because others copied him, but because he is one of the few writers who discuss the syntax of Matthew 19:9.

Heth's argument that unless divorce is required it cannot be argued that the one-flesh relationship has been broken due to sexual sin, fails to take into account that although relationship with a prostitute is "one flesh" it is not marriage unless a certain legal ceremony is carried out. In the same way sexual sin breaks the marriage bond, but the marriage is not actually dissolved until a certain legal procedure (divorce) is carried out. Does anyone argue that the marriage itself is actually dissolved the instant one enters into sexual unfaithfulness? I think that my discussion of the syntax shows that Heth's view of Matthew 19:9 is incorrect. It is grammatically impossible to claim that Matthew 19:9 does not allow remarriage in the case of the exception.

Heth's discussion of Matthew 5:27–32 does not recognize that this section discusses divorce and adultery as two separate issues, not as one basic issue as he assumes (pp. 107–8). This is clear from the antithetical statements in verses 21–22, 27–28, 31–32. The argument that this passage teaches that divorce alone is adultery (p. 108), is incorrect. The passage assumes the remarriage of the wife. Otherwise the verse would read that "everyone who divorces his wife commits adultery." The man would be the individual guilty of adultery, but the verse does not say this. The next line makes it clear that marriage is necessary, "he who marries the divorced woman commits adultery" (Mt 5:32).

I have shown in my chapter that Heth's division of Matthew 19:9 into the two conditional statements which he deduces, is grammatically impossible, that the argument based on the disciples reactions is invalid and that the use of Mark 10:2–12 and Luke 16:18 as a control over Matthew 19:9 can only be on an implicit assumption that Matthew is wrong (pp. 107–8). I also think that I have refuted his argument on 1 Corinthians 7:10–15.

In summary, the most outstanding aspect of Heth's discussion is a lack of exegetical evidence and a reliance on quoted opinions of others. However, we must not be too hard on Heth for this approach. In my opinion, there is little exegetical evidence for this view. It depends entirely, as does Laney's view, on an alleged indissolubility of marriage. This is an allegation that cannot be demonstrated. One verse alone, 1 Corinthians 6:16, is enough to call in question Heth's main argument, based on the expression *one flesh,* for the permanence (indissolubility) of marriage. Apart from this alleged indissolubility, however, his view cannot stand.

Response

Larry Richards

I *appreciate Heth's scholarly study of divorce and remarriage. It is* appropriate in exploring an area which touches so many lives to examine issues with great care and throughness. And certainly he has done that. Yet his refutation of the various opinions he surveys reminds us that there *are* a variety of opinions on this issue. The church does not speak with one voice on interpreting New Testament passages on divorce and remarriage. It is possible to examine the data and reach Heth's conclusions. But it is also possible for Christians to examine the same data—and reach very different conclusions indeed.

One of the difficulties we have in exploring Scripture is that we are all subject to a defect Heth points out in those who disagree with his interpretations. Harold Hoehner "imposes his own view" on Scripture "in his attempt to invalidate the significant implications for divorce and remarriage suggested by the biblical kinship view of marriage" (p. 81). John Murray "on more than one occasion assumes what he wants to prove and then proceeds to build a case" (p. 103). I mention this, not to accuse Heth, whom I find careful and fair in his exposition, but simply to note that the perspective with which we come to a particular verse of passage necessarily has an impact on our understanding of it. Certainly each of us, not just Hoehner, Murray, Heth— or I myself—are vulnerable to this flaw.

For my part, I observe one or two assumptions made by Heth that lead him to "impose his own view" on certain passages and also lead him to "assume what he wants to prove." These two assumptions are (1) that Christ in Matthew 19:3-12 does in fact introduce a "new period" in the history of marriage and (2) that a second marriage automatically involves adultery.

1. Did Jesus institute a "new period" in the history of marriage and divorce? The answer hinges in large part on our understanding of what is happening in Matthew 19. I have explained in my section of this book that, in the context of Matthew 18—20's exploration of "greatness" (compare Mt 18:1, 4; 20:25-28), the passage is not primarily dealing with divorce at all. In the flow of that passage Jesus is confronted by the Pharisees, who assume that keeping the Law is the way to achieve spiritual greatness. Christ refers to the well-known divine ideal and then explains the permission granted in Deuteronomy 24 to divorce *despite* it. That permission is evidence within the law that law is a lowered standard, showing God's compassion and willingness to accommodate his standards to humanity's weakness. Thus, law, a lowered standard, can hardly be the means to spiritual superiority the Pharisees assumed it to be.

It is in this context that we must interpret Matthew 19—not in the context assumed by Heth of Jesus' imposition of a higher law than that found in the Old Testament. In this context, we avoid the error of assuming that God has a different ideal will for his people of different historic eras. And in this context, several of the sayings on which Heth's interpretation depends are seen to mean something very different than he understands. "What God has joined together, let man not separate" (Mt 19:6) is a rejection of the implicit claim of the Pharisees of the right to serve as an ecclesiastical court in divorce cases. The explanation that Moses permitted divorce because their hearts were hard (Mt 19:8) is the crucial evidence that law is an accommodation God makes to sinful human beings; a "step down" from his ideal. That saying also is an expression of Christ's continuing compassion for human beings who, through their own or their partner's sin, find their marriage a caricature of the supportive relationship God's ideal envisions.

Neither the disciples nor the Pharisees grasped the impact of what Christ had said. But this is nothing novel. The Gospels abound with incidents in which Jesus' friends as well as his enemies misinterpreted his teaching (compare Mk 8:14-21). We can hardly validate our interpretation on the basis of what Jesus' listeners (mis)understood! Nor can we assume that when Jesus told his troubled disciples, "not everyone can accept this word," (Mt 19:11) that he either agreed with their interpretation or was saying that "no remarriage" is for disciples but not for unbelievers.

The fallacy of imposing our assumptions on Scripture, and thus creating the grid through which we interpret it, is clearly seen in the list on page 92: a list whose points are not found within any one passage of Scripture, but are drawn from various passages and assembled in a "proof text" manner.

In dealing with divorce and remarriage, it is particularly important that we interpret each relevant passage within its own context—and that we fight the tendency each of us has to interpret the passage according to our presuppositions. As I have noted, each of us is vulnerable. The very fact that so many different understandings of divorce-and-remarriage passages have emerged—each buttressed by careful exegesis and argument—reminds us that we must each hold our view humbly and accept our personal responsibility to study even more diligently to discern as best we can the will of God.

2. Does a second marriage while a first spouse is still living necessarily involve adultery? Heth's answer is an unqualified yes, and most of his chapter is devoted to showing why the "exception clause" in Matthew 19 is not an exception after all. But the critical passage is 1 Corinthians 7, and again the way we trace Paul's argument is crucial. In my contribution I have suggested that the *form* of Paul's argument has often been mistaken for its content. This error, and especially a failure to set that argument in the context of the questions disturbing the Corinthians, has led many to overlook the force of Paul's teaching. Simply put, a person whose spouse refuses to live with him or her is to first seek reconciliation and to remain unmarried. But that same person is "not bound" when it becomes apparent that there is no basis on which to expect reconciliation.

This does not mean that a divorced person should remarry. In fact, it seems to me that in many cases a life of celibacy is far more desirable. But, as Paul points out in the same chapter, this is a matter of "gift." As Jesus said, some do renounce marriage because of the kingdom of God, but "not everyone can accept this teaching."

And not everyone should!

Essentially, the reason for the divorce is not the issue, as so many evangelicals seem to feel. The issue is, when a person is *not married.* With Heth I believe the "not married" include those never married and those whose spouses have died. But unlike him, I believe the "not married" also include a vast number of persons who once were married, but whose marriages have been dissolved. For these persons, remarriage is undoubtedly a confession of having fallen short of God's ideal, and thus of sin. But for these persons remarriage can be in the will of God, and not a sin.

3

DIVORCE &
REMARRIAGE
FOR ADULTERY OR
DESERTION

Divorce & Remarriage for Adultery or Desertion

Thomas R. Edgar

*T*he opinion that the Bible allows divorce for adultery or desertion with the subsequent right to remarry is sometimes referred to as the standard Protestant view. Although this position has historically been associated with Protestants, in contrast to the Roman Catholic's sacramental view of marriage, it is not an official view. Neither can it be considered the traditional view among Protestants, as some imply, since among conservative Protestants the position which allows no divorce and no remarriage is more common. Nor can the position presented here be classified as either liberal or conservative. Many conservatives hold this position as well as other views, and some who fit the theological category of liberal hold to a strict "no divorce or remarriage" position. Rather, I would argue that the view presented here is the position most naturally derived from Scripture if we do not presuppose a sacramental view of marriage or its equivalent (marriage is indissoluble), and if we limit divorce and remarriage only to those instances specifically discussed in Scripture.

Those who state that there is never a valid reason for divorce and those who allow for some divorce but no remarriage are basically arguing that marriage can never be genuinely severed apart from the death of the spouse. Regarding marriage as indissoluble, these two views are fundamentally the same and follow the same arguments. The opinion that marriage is indissoluble may be held dogmatically, as in the Roman Catholic tradition, or may be derived from an alleged teaching of Scripture regarding the nature of marriage. No verse in Scripture explicitly teaches that marriage is indissoluble. However, those who are convinced of this tend to interpret every passage on divorce and remarriage with this assumption rather than following normal procedures for interpretation and the most natural meaning of the biblical passages involved.

We must not approach this subject with the assumption that it is inherently more spiritual to reject all divorce and remarriage. Some otherwise biblically oriented individuals, when confronted with arguments from Scripture which apparently allow some divorce and remarriage, frequently react as if, regardless of Scripture, it is inherently more upright or moral to be against divorce. However, only Scripture can give us the proper perspective on marriage and divorce.

God is the one who determines what is moral and immoral. Since God created the concept of marriage, he is the one who determines if and when it is proper to divorce and remarry. The view which allows for no divorce, even because of adultery, may seem to be more ethical. However, it could also be considered quite the opposite—as a more tolerant view of adultery—in that it treats adultery no differently than numerous other marriage problems.

We cannot *assume* that one of the views on divorce is inherently superior. We must turn to Scripture to see if God allows any exceptions to the general concept that "what God has joined together, let not man separate."

Common Misconceptions

There are two basic misconceptions often stated or assumed when discussing the issue of divorce and remarriage. One of these, often assumed at every phase of the discussion by those who deny all divorce and remarriage, is the concept that "the Bible clearly allows no divorce." The passages discussing divorce and remarriage are then approached with the idea that they cannot possibly be allowing any divorce or remarriage;[1] therefore, apparent exceptions must be explained in some other way. The nine passages usually referred to on the subject of divorce and remarriage are Genesis 2:24; Deuteronomy 24:1-4; Malachi 2:6-16; Matthew 5:31-32; Matthew 19:3-12; Mark 10:2-12; Luke 16:18; Romans 7:1-6; and 1 Corinthians 7:10-15.

The first, Genesis 2:24, says nothing explicit regarding divorce or remarriage. The second, Deuteronomy 24:1-4, obviously allows for some divorce and remarriage. God's statement, in the context of Malachi 2:14-16 that he hates divorce, refers to the divorcing of older, faithful wives in order to marry younger women. Thus, it cannot be automatically applied to all cases of divorce, neither can it overrule a God-granted exception.

The two passages in Matthew (5:31-32 and 19:3-12) seem to allow an exception where divorce and remarriage are permitted. Mark 10:2-12 describes the same statement by Jesus as that quoted in Matthew 19:9; therefore, the additional details in Matthew 19:3-12 must be understood in Mark 10:2-12. Mark's account does not deny any exception which is stated in Matthew. The seventh passage, Luke 16:18, merely refers to divorce as an example of one commandment of the Mosaic law. Romans 7:1-6 uses marriage as an illustration of how Christ's death releases the believer from the jurisdiction of the Mosaic law. No mention is made of divorce, and it would not be at all appropriate in such an illustration to bring up possible exceptions. First Corinthians 7:15 apparently teaches an exception allowing divorce.

In conclusion, four of the seven passages (excluding Gen 2:24 and Rom 7:1-6, which say nothing regarding divorce or remarriage) seem to allow for some kind of divorce and remarriage. However, not one of the other three passages definitely states that divorce and remarriage are never allowable. Since the majority of these passages imply that there are some instances where divorce and remarriage are allowed, we cannot properly assume that the Bible "clearly teaches" no divorce and remarriage. Apart from a detailed study indicating the contrary, it would be more accurate to assume that the Bible clearly allows for some divorce and remarriage.

Another invalid assumption that has influenced interpretation of the relevant passages is the idea that marriage is unbreakable or indissoluble. No biblical passage directly states such a concept. All of the arguments used to support such a view are indirect, such as the argument based on the alleged inherent nature of marriage as permanent. One popular argument focuses on the term *one flesh,* which occurs in the statement "the two became one flesh" (Gen 2:24). This expression is alleged to be equivalent to "blood relative," which requires a permanent unchangeable relationship just as that of blood relations. However, the term will not bear such an inference.

Its use in 1 Corinthians 6:6 to describe sexual relations with a prostitute can hardly be referring to an indissoluble relationship, especially one which disallows marriage to another. The term *one flesh* is not definitive and certainly has no necessary implication of indissolubility. To argue that "one flesh" means that a married couple— just as a blood relative—are in an unchangeable relationship, creates a logical dilemma. If "one flesh" means equivalent to "blood relative" in the full sense, then once married, the couple are blood relatives and in an incestuous relationship contrary to Scripture. It therefore follows that the term *one flesh* cannot possibly be equivalent to "blood relative" in the full sense of the term. This is, however, the very factor necessary to establish the claim of indissolubility since, if it does not mean equivalent to in the full sense, then it cannot be argued that equivalent results (that is, indissolubility) follow.

The term *one flesh* in Genesis 2:24 cannot imply indissolubility which precludes remarriage. Even if it were possible to prove that "one flesh" did mean blood relative and did imply an unchangeable relationship, the fact that persons are unchangeable blood relatives in no way restricts them from marriage to others; thus, the argument could not prohibit remarriage. Proponents of the "one flesh" argument select only those factors favorable to their presuppositions and ignore logical inconsistencies inherent in their position.

Their desperation is evident in their attempts to show that Deuteronomy 24:1-4 supports their position. This passage clearly teaches that a woman who is divorced and marries another man is so completely and permanently severed from her first husband that, if divorced from her second husband, she can marry anyone else but can never again marry her first husband. Contrary to any normal deduction, "one flesh" proponents urge this as proof that she is really still married to him; and this passage, which allows almost unlimited remarriage, is used as evidence against any remarriage.

Another argument of desperation is the claim that the aorist tense of the Greek word *joined together* in Mark 10:9 points to the permanence of the marriage bond.[2] This is based on an apparent misunderstanding of the aorist tense as implying "once for all" and is, in fact, an erroneous statement. As any Greek scholar can testify, the aorist tense implies nothing regarding permanence. It is, in contrast to the other Greek tenses, the tense which implies nothing regarding the action of the verb. The action is undefined, as even the name aorist ("undefined") implies, and is only stated as occurring in the past. The argument, therefore, is misleading. The term *one flesh* bears no implication of indissolubility, nor does the aorist tense indicate permanence. There is no evidence that marriage is indissoluble, but there are numerous indications to the contrary.

Whatever we may think of these arguments, no line of reasoning or any number of arguments regarding an alleged indissoluble nature of marriage can overrule direct statements of Scripture which allow for divorce and remarriage. God, who created marriage, can also declare if and when divorce and remarriage are valid. Therefore, since an alleged indissoluble nature of marriage cannot overrule God's direct statements, the proper focus is on the study of those passages which seem to allow for divorce and remarriage.

The main battleground concerns those New Testament passages which appear to specifically teach an exception regarding divorce and remarriage: Matthew 5:31-32; 19:3-12 and 1 Corinthians 7:10-15. The preeminent passage in this discussion is Matthew 19:3-12, since it contains the answer of the Lord Jesus Christ to the specific question of whether or not divorce is allowable. The allowed exception in Matthew 19:9 seems to be the same as that in the shorter passage, Matthew 5:31-32. Let us examine Matthew 19:9.

Matthew 19:9: Adultery Allows Divorce and Remarriage

Matthew 19:3-12 records a discussion between Jesus and the Pharisees. He answers the specific question with which we are concerned, "Is it acceptable for a man to divorce his wife for any reason?" (v. 3). Jesus refers to Genesis 2:24 and gives the general principle that a couple should not divorce (vv. 4–6). However, the Pharisees then refer to Deuteronomy 24:1–4 which seems to allow for divorce. Jesus answers that Moses allowed divorce due to human frailty, but this was not as it was "in the beginning" (before the Fall). He then gives his definitive statement on the subject in verse 9: "I say to you that whoever divorces his wife except for fornication and marries another commits adultery."

Matthew 19:9 Is Clear. Not only is this verse clear, but it is relatively simple, despite the disagreement over its interpretation. In fact, it could be said that it is the verse's clarity, rather than any complexity, which causes the problem for those interpreters whose presuppositions allow for no divorce or remarriage. Some of these interpreters give credence to any of several interpretive possibilities which nullify the force of the verse so that they can attempt to demonstrate that it cannot teach a genuine exception. The complexity of the arguments is due to the difficulty inherent in avoiding the plain teaching of the verse.

The English translation "Whoever divorces his wife except for fornication and marries another commits adultery" is accurate and gives a precise rendering of the original statement in the Greek text. The grammar and syntax of the verse are simple and not at all unusual. It is not helpful and does not give an accurate impression to imply that this verse is complex or strange due to the fact that the parts are in a different order than other verses.[3] This has no more significance than the fact that a certain house is unique since it is the only one in town with a porch on the left side and a circular drive in front. This does not mean that the house is strange or complex. Neither is there anything so strange or complex in Matthew 19:9 to justify an abnormal approach to interpretation. Apart from the invalid presupposition that it cannot allow for divorce and remarriage, it is extremely improbable that anyone would have difficulty understanding the meaning of this verse.

Remarriage Cannot Be Excluded. Many who allow divorce for the exception in Matthew 19:9 argue, at the same time, that no one is ever allowed to remarry. Even if someone is divorced for the exception, they believe that this verse does not allow for remarriage. In effect, they are claiming that the sentence refers both to *some* who divorce (all except those for fornication) and *all* who divorce and then remarry. This is a grammatically impossible interpretation. In the next section we will discuss the order of the words in Matthew 19:9 as it applies to the issue of remarriage. First, though, we must look at the grammar (syntax) of the verse.

The main verb in verse nine is "commits adultery." The subject of this verb, the one who commits adultery, is described by the relative clause "whoever divorces his wife except for fornication and marries another." The person who divorces his wife except for fornication is the same individual who marries another since both verbs are in one relative clause describing the one individual. Thus, the one who divorces his wife except for fornication is the same one who also marries another, and it is this same individual who commits adultery. It is grammatically impossible for this verse to refer to two different subjects.

Notice that this verse does not discuss an individual who merely divorces and does not remarry. It only concerns an individual who both divorces and remarries. The interpretation that this verse allows divorce but not remarriage is not merely improbable, it is grammatically impossible. The fact that this so-called patristic view was held by the church fathers is no proof of its validity since the church fathers are frequently unreliable, particularly in matters pertaining to marriage. Protestants have always held that Scripture, rather than the church fathers, is our supreme authority.

Wenham, in order to support the patristic interpretation, makes the grammatically and logically impossible claim that Matthew 19:9 (and 5:32) can be divided into two propositions: (A) to divorce except for *porneia* is adulterous and (B) to divorce and remarry is adulterous. Therefore, he concludes, all remarriage is adulterous and most divorce is in itself adulterous.[4] It should be immediately obvious that there is a problem with making divorce *alone* equal to committing adultery, if adultery is to be interpreted in any normal sense of the term or with any of the meanings normally associated with this verse. If adultery has some such weakened meaning in this verse, it must also have the same weakened sense in the case of remarriage. However, the real issue concerns the syntax of the verse.

Before discussing the grammar from a more technical perspective, we can use an equivalent example from English to show the impossibility of Wenham's statements and the untenability of the patristic view.

Consider an equivalent statement: "Whoever drives on this road except an ambulance driver on call and exceeds the speed limit is breaking the law." If this is interpreted as Wenham and others interpret Matthew 19:9, it would contain two propositions: (A) anyone who drives on this road except an ambulance driver on call is breaking the law and (B) to drive on this road and exceed the speed limit (including ambulance drivers on call) is breaking the law. It is clear that the original statement does *not* teach that merely driving on the road is illegal (compare with "merely divorcing is adultery"), nor that every one exceeding the speed limit including ambulance drivers on call is breaking the law (compare with "everyone remarrying, including the exception, commits adultery"). The original statement teaches neither concept; rather, both propositions are actually contrary to its real meaning.

The sentence has a *singular* subject "whoever." This person is the subject of the verb "to break the law." This *individual* is described as a man who drives on the road (excluding ambulance drivers) *and* exceeds the speed limit. The error in trying to interpret this as containing the two propositions A and B is that they refer to two different kinds of individuals. Proposition A has as its subject *some* of those who drive on the road (excluding ambulance drivers) and proposition B refers to *all* of those who drive on the road (including ambulance drivers) and exceed the speed limit. However, this is grammatically impossible. The sentence only refers to some drivers (excluding ambulance drivers) who also exceed the speed limit.

This error which says, in effect, that *all* who exceed the speed limit (including ambulance drivers) are breaking the law, is precisely equivalent to the so-called patristic view of Matthew 19:9, which attempts to prove that *all* who remarry (including those divorced for fornication) are guilty of adultery. It is also *contrary* to the meaning of the original statement. Neither of Wenham's propositions is in

Matthew 19:9.[5] In fact, both are actually contrary to Matthew 19:9.

Matthew 19:9 has only one singular subject, "whoever" ("he who," *hos*), of the singular main verb, "commits adultery" *(moichatai)*. This individual is described by the two singular verbs "divorces" and "marries." In other words, this individual is the subject of all three verbs ("divorces," "marries" and "commits adultery") and is the *only* subject of the sentence. A sentence diagram will demonstrate the syntax of Matthew 19:9.

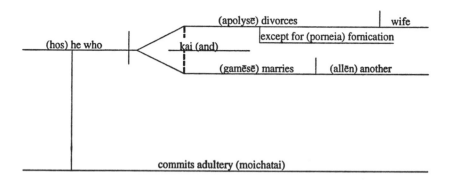

Jesus definitely states that the subject of the very "divorces" *(apolysē)* is someone who divorces for some reason other than fornication *(porneia)*. One who divorces for *porneia* is not mentioned. The subject of the verb *apolysē* is some divorceés, not all, and is also the subject of the other verbs in the sentence, "marries" *(gamēsē)* and "commits adultery" *(moichatai)*. The sentence thus says, and can only say, "Some (not all) divorcées who remarry commit adultery." To say otherwise is *contrary* to the verse. There cannot be two subjects at the same time, neither can the singular verb "divorces" have two different subjects *(some* and *all)* as the patristic view requires.

This verse definitely indicates that someone who divorces due to the exception and then marries another does not commit adultery. The exception is a real exception which allows for a genuine divorce so that the person may marry another. If a student asks whether it is permissible to leave the classroom during a lecture and the teacher replies that anyone who leaves without permission is wrong, the statement is meaningless if it does not mean that someone may leave with permission. In the same way, when Jesus answers the question of whether divorce is ever proper with the statement that if someone divorces except for fornication and remarries, he commits adultery, his answer is meaningless if it does not mean that in other cases it is acceptable. If we follow anything close to a normal approach to interpretation, then Jesus means that for anyone who divorces due to a spouse's fornication and marries another, the divorce is valid, and remarriage is permitted.

Heth and Wenham object to the idea that Matthew 19:9 allows remarriage. They argue that this would require the verb "divorces" to have two different senses in one verse. As evidence they argue that "divorces" has two meanings in the following statements. It means complete divorce with the right to remarry in the first sentence only and separation in the second:

1 Putting away for unchastity plus remarriage does not equal adultery.

2. Putting away for other reasons plus remarriage equals adultery.[6]

This objection fails on every count. Even with their assumptions, the word "divorces" does not have two senses in one verse. Their example is not *one* but *two* sentences. Of necessity, they invented the first sentence in order to have two differing concepts. Differing connotations in *two* different propositions cannot be evidence that they are different when they are present in *one* proposition. The problem is a hypothetical one due to the invention of a sentence which does not exist in the text. Only the second sentence exists; the other is implied. Thus, their objection fails.

Even if their reconstruction were assumed, the entire objection is based on a misconception of their own reconstruction. In their reconstructed sentences the issue which makes the divorce "complete" (remarriage is acceptable) or merely "separation" (remarriage is adultery) is not a different meaning for the verb "divorces," but whether or not the exception applies. Furthermore, they have confused the result of the verb action with the meaning of the verb. The exception affects the result, not the meaning, of "divorces." The meaning remains the same.

The problem may be illustrated by the sentence, "Bill shot and missed the target." The claim may be made that this sentence has two meanings for *to shoot*: "to shoot and miss" and "to shoot and hit." However, the sentence does not say anything about hitting the target, so the word could have only the other sense. But in reality, the verb *to shoot* does not change meaning because of the different result ("hit" or "miss"). It simply means "to release a projectile."

When two people take an examination, one may pass and one may fail. The meaning of *examination*, however, does not change. Thus the alleged problem in Matthew 19:9 does not exist. The entire premise is fallacious. Heth and Wenham's objection against a valid exception, based on the claim that it requires two meanings for the verb "divorces" will not stand. The patristic view, which they hold, however, does require two different subjects for each verb in this passage. But this simply is not a possible reading at all.

Word Order Allows Both Divorce and Remarriage. It is a common mistake to assume that if Jesus is teaching that fornication makes remarriage permissible, the exception clause should come after the statement "marries another" rather than after "divorces his wife." The error of such an opinion should be clear from observing either the Greek or the English. The exception clause is in the one position where it unambiguously teaches that a person who divorces due to a spouse's adultery may remarry. We must keep in mind that the English rendering is accurate and that the same person is the subject of all three verbs.

If the exception clause were placed after the verb *marries*, as some claim it should be if the verse were to allow remarriage, then it would read, "Whoever divorces his wife and marries another except for fornication commits adultery." This makes the exception the reason for the remarriage, rather than the divorce. This is absurd. With this view, anyone can divorce for any reason and not commit adultery so long as they marry another for the purpose of fornication. The only divorced person restricted from remarriage would be one who does not marry due to sexual lust.

To place the exception clause in other positions, such as before or after the entire sentence, merely produces other ambiguous statements. The exception does not qualify the basis for remarriage, but the basis for the divorce. Therefore, it must go with "divorces his wife," as it, in fact, does. When considering the statement, "Anyone who drives on this road except an ambulance driver and exceeds the speed limit is breaking the law," it cannot be argued that an ambulance driver is not allowed to exceed the speed limit unless the exception comes after "exceeds the speed limit." The subject of the first verb is also the subject of the second. In Matthew 19:9 the individual in question both divorces and remarries, but the action which fits the exception is the divorcing. If the divorce does not fit the exception and he remarries, he commits adultery. If the divorce does fit the exception and he remarries, he does not commit adultery. It is the validity of the divorce which determines whether or not the remarriage is adultery; therefore, the exception is properly the basis for the divorce and at the same time governs the validity of the entire action.

The Exception Is Adultery. The exception, fornication, is a translation of the Greek word *porneia.* The term *porneia* has the meaning "illicit sex" and can refer to illicit sex in general or, in a given context, to some specific immorality. The meaning in this context, therefore, is decisive for determining the nature of the exception. Matthew 19:9 is a discussion concerning the valid basis of divorce and states that some type of illicit sex on the part of the wife is the only proper basis for divorce. Therefore, the most natural way to interpret *porneia* is with the meaning "adultery."

A less likely, but plausible, opinion is that *porneia* does not have a specific reference here but refers to any type of illicit sex, including incest, homosexuality and sodomy. However, in a context concerning husbands and wives, particularly when using the term *porneia* for the wife's conduct and *moichaō* for the husband's, it is certain that the primary reference is to the sin of adultery. There is no valid reason to reject the meaning "adultery." To do so (and also to reject the possibility that this refers to illicit sex in general), meanwhile importing some other concept which is alien to the context, such as incest or betrothal unfaithfulness, demands conclusive evidence which has not been produced. The assertion of clichés, such as "an exception would contradict Jesus' teaching," is not evidence to reject the obvious meaning since this text is *also* Jesus' teaching.

If we dispense until later with the frequent objections to an exception, we can deal with the most common objection to regarding *porneia* as referring to adultery; namely, that *porneia* is not the specific word for adultery, and that *moichaō,* the specific verb meaning "to commit adultery," is used in this same verse. The objectors conclude that the use of two different terms in the same context indicates that a distinction is being made. *Porneia,* therefore, would refer to something other than adultery. But this argument will not stand up to careful examination.

It should be clear, even to someone familiar only with English, that the use of the general term *illicit sex,* in the statement "Whoever divorces his wife except for illicit sex" most naturally refers to adultery. Even in English a number of terms are used to refer to adultery, such as *unfaithfulness, immorality, having an affair, sleeping around* and other less refined descriptions. There is no real problem in using two different expressions meaning the same thing in the sentence, "Since his wife was involved in *immorality,* he *committed adultery.*" Neither is there anything unusual in using two different words in the Greek text to refer to this sin, particularly when one is a more general term which includes the other. A study of biblical Greek reveals several places where these two words occur in the same context and refer to the same sin. However, there is a much stronger reason to reject the argument against "adultery" as the natural meaning for *porneia* in this verse.

Jesus is speaking to a Jewish audience, living in the Hebrew culture, versed in and using the terminology of the Old Testament. A study of the Old Testament reveals that, although the specific words for adultery may be used for the wife, the most common words for a woman (including a wife) involved in illicit sex are the noun *porneia* ("fornication") or the verb *porneuō* ("to fornicate"). The general term *porneia* and particularly the underlying Hebrew word *zᵉnût* are primarily related to the woman. In contrast, a husband involved in adultery is not described by *porneia* but by the specific terms for adultery.

In other words, the use of the two different terms "fornication" *(porneia* for the woman) and "adultery" *(moichaō* for the man) is exactly in accordance with the expected usage. It is much less likely that the same term, rather than the two different terms, would be used, since it was contrary to the customary usage of the time. The objection based on the difference in words forces a modern-day English perspective on another culture. The proclivity of that culture to describe an adulterous woman by the term *porneia* (or verb *porneuō)* and the adulterous man by the specific terms *moichaō* or *moicheuō* is alone sufficient to explain the use of the two terms in Matthew 19:9.

In addition, the noun *porneia* occurs frequently in biblical Greek. However, the noun *moicheia,* "adultery," seldom occurs. Therefore, it is much less likely that, when the noun is required, as it is here, the wife's extramarital intercourse would be described by the seldom-used, specific noun *moicheia* than by *porneia.* Both the context and the normal usage of the terms involved show that the exception in Matthew 19:9 must be adultery. There is no justification for interpreting it otherwise.

The use of the two different words is therefore not a difficulty to be explained by proponents of the standard Protestant view; rather, an explanation is due from those who object to the use of two different words. Their argument is misleading and is apparently based either on an English translation or a failure to consider carefully the normal use of the Greek words involved. It is unreasonable to imply that the use of the term *porneia* in Matthew 19:9 indicates a meaning other than adultery.

More Than Merely Permissible. Some have admitted, occasionally grudgingly, that the exception in Matthew 19:9 is adultery, but they argue that divorce in such a case is merely permitted and still not proper. They intimate that the person who divorces due to the exception still has some spiritual or moral deficiency. However, not only is there no such negative implication in this passage, it implies the opposite. The question Jesus is answering concerns the acceptability of divorce. His answer, that to divorce and then remarry is wrong in all cases except for *porneia,* definitely implies that it is not wrong in this case. A comparison with Matthew 5:31-32 indicates no negative stigma of any kind.

Most agree that Matthew 19:9 and 5:32 are stating the same exception. Many have overlooked the parallel in the structure of Matthew 5:31-32 and 19:7-9. In both passages Jesus says, in effect, "Deuteronomy 24:1-4 states . . . , but I say . . ." His statement, in each case, is a contrast to Deuteronomy 24:1-4. In Matthew 19:9 his answer is in contrast to the apparent acceptability of divorce in Deuteronomy 24:1-4. His statement is definitive and so includes any exceptions. The effect of this contrast, however, is clearest in Matthew 5:31-32.

This passage is third in a series of statements where Jesus refers to an Old Testament concept by saying, "You have heard . . . , but I say . . ." In each passage Jesus states an Old Testament command and then gives the real spiritual meaning which God desires. For example, "You have heard that it was said do not kill . . . , but I say do not be angry." In each of the six cases, Jesus' statement contrasts with the concept they had heard and gives the spiritually desirable attitude on the issue. The same is true of Matthew 5:31-32: "It was said whoever divorces his wife let him give her a writ of divorce, but I say do not divorce except for *porneia*." Jesus' statement, which includes the exception (5:32), is the real, spiritually desirable attitude on the subject. This is parallel in structure to Matthew 19:7-9.

The exception clause stating that divorce for adultery and subsequent remarriage are proper is Jesus' definitive statement on this issue showing the desired spiritual attitude toward divorce and remarriage. Although Jesus does not require divorce in such a case, he indicates that it is perfectly proper and without stigma on the part of the innocent party. Matthew 19:9 clearly teaches that as a general rule divorce and remarriage are not proper; there is, however, an exception. Unfaithfulness or adultery is regarded as such a serious sin that it alone is acceptable as grounds for a genuine severance of a marriage, so that the innocent party may remarry. Adultery is not regarded as merely another in a series of imperfections which the spouse should overlook but as a heinous sin against the marriage relationship. The "no divorce" and "no remarriage" advocates seem to place more emphasis on the formal institution of marriage (a sacramental perspective) than on the sin of adultery. Jesus Christ, however, seems to regard fidelity in the marriage as far more important than the formal institution itself.

Belief in the Accuracy of Scripture Is Essential. My argument is based on the belief that the passages involved are accurate and without error. However, many of the presuppositions and objections of some of those who reject a valid exception in Matthew 19:9 are based on either an open rejection of the inerrancy of Scripture or on a precarious view of inerrancy. It is common among scholars to regard Mark 10:2-12, which does not include the exception, as Jesus' real statement on divorce and the exception clause as a later addition by Matthew. This is, of course, a direct repudiation of Matthew's accuracy since he definitely states that Jesus, on the occasion described, gave the exception.

Many conservatives, perhaps unaware, seem to hold a similar position. For example, those who insist that the exception is not "understood" in Mark 10:2-12[7] or that Mark 10:2-12 disallows any exception since it is determinative of Jesus' teaching on divorce have implicitly surrendered the inerrancy of Scripture. It must be kept in mind that both Matthew 19:3-12 and Mark 10:2-12 are recording the same historical incident and the same statements of Jesus. Neither is attempting to give his own view, nor the church's view on divorce; rather, both are reporting the very same conversation between Jesus and the Pharisees. Matthew explicitly states that, not only on a previous occasion (Mt 5:31-32), but in this very conversation, which is also described in Mark 10:2-12, Jesus specifically stated the exception. Unless Matthew 19:9 is inaccurate, in the conversation recorded in Mark 10:2-12 Jesus did state the exception. Therefore, it must be understood in Mark's account even though he does not record it. Mark, as often happens in other passages, merely omitted a detail which Matthew included.

Those who argue that Mark 10:2-12 gives Jesus' real view as allowing no exception and who reject the idea that the exception is "understood" in Mark are explicitly or implicitly denying the accuracy of Matthew. It is erroneous to consider Mark as determinative on this issue. Since the exception was actually stated as Matthew 19:9 records, although omitted by Mark 10:2-12, then Matthew 19:3-12, rather than Mark 10:2-12, is determinative for the existence, meaning and significance of the exception.

A frequent objection to the exception is the statement that Jesus clearly allowed no exception and that any view of divorce and remarriage, including the interpretation of Matthew 19:9, must agree with this fact.[8] This concept also requires an implicit rejection of the accuracy of Matthew. According to the Gospels, there are only three occasions on which Jesus mentioned this subject. One of these, Luke 16:18, is not really a discussion of divorce but simply a one-verse statement using divorce and remarriage as an illustration of the previous verse that the law was still in effect. This one-verse statement could hardly be expected to contain, nor would it be appropriate to be concerned with, an exception. On the two other occasions (Mt 5:31-32 and Mt 19:3-12/Mk 10:2-12) when Jesus spoke regarding divorce, he specifically gave the exception. To state that Jesus clearly does not allow an exception is not merely another perspective, it is definitely an erroneous perspective. That someone can make a statement so contrary to Scripture is due to basing one's perspective on only Mark 10:2-12 and implicitly rejecting Matthew 5:32 and Matthew 19:9.

The inspiration of Scripture also bears on another argument against a genuine exception in Matthew 19:9. Various arguments based on the alleged Jewish perspective of Matthew and the gentile nature of Mark are used as an explanation for the exception clause in Matthew. Several facts must be remembered. Both Matthew and Mark are recording an actual statement which Jesus made to the Pharisees prior to Calvary. They are not merely writing their own view on divorce as it applies to their addressees. The recipients of their respective Gospels, written years *after* Calvary, have no bearing on the meaning, significance or even the fact of Jesus' statement of the exception which was made prior to Calvary. To attempt to derive a position on Matthew 19:9 based on the recipients of Matthew or Mark is equivalent to reading Lincoln's Gettysburg Address in a modern high-school history book and then attempting to determine the actual content, meaning and significance of Lincoln's original speech by the fact that the historian reproduced it for modern teenagers.

Such erroneous approaches come from an unwitting acceptance of modern redaction-criticism which turns the Gospel authors into mere editors rather than accurate eyewitnesses. If persons argue that the exception in Matthew is only Jewish and Mark omits it because it does not apply to Gentiles, then they have lost sight of the fact that Jesus, in fact, said it to the Pharisees. To conclude that Mark excluded it in order to give the impression that Jesus did not say it would be to accuse Mark of giving a false impression. Jesus definitely stated the exception on two of the three occasions where he mentioned divorce and remarriage. It is incorrect to assume that Jesus taught no exception or that Mark's Gospel is against an exception.

An Exception Is Not a Contradiction. Often, contrary to a normal approach to interpretation or logic, some assume that a genuine exception in Matthew 19:9 (and 5:32) would be a contradiction of Mark. If Matthew is correct, Jesus gave the exception; therefore, it cannot be a contradiction of Mark, but *must* be understood as an omission of a detail by Mark. The assumption of a contradiction is based on an abnormal approach to the interpretation of the Gospels. Parallel Gospel accounts describing the same event are never interpreted elsewhere in such a manner by those who believe in the accuracy of the Scriptures. It is a common occurrence for two Gospel writers to describe the same event, but at the same time not to include precisely the same details. In no other place are the details which are included in one Gospel and omitted in the other considered to be contradictions. The fact that Matthew includes a detail which is omitted by Mark is not an unusual occurrence.

For example, in Mark 8:12 Jesus says, "There shall be no sign given to this generation." Yet, describing the same incident, Matthew 12:39 says, "There shall no sign be given to it, but the sign of the prophet Jonah." This difference is not considered contradictory, however. Nor is the fact that Mark omitted the detail concerning Jonah normally considered as evidence that Jesus could not have said, or did not say, it. The more detailed of the two statements is always considered to be the more accurate. To consider the less detailed account as determinative is abnormal interpretative procedure and questionable with respect to inerrancy. There *cannot* be a contradiction between two inerrant Gospel accounts.

Laney argues that the clearest account is to be preferred; therefore, Mark is preferred.[9] In this, however, he is actually reversing the normal procedure, since the clearer account in this case is Matthew since it is more detailed. Matthew 19:9 is not unclear; it is only unclear to someone who rejects its clear meaning. Certainly we cannot dismiss a detail not included in one Gospel by claiming the account that omits it is clearer than the account that includes it. This approach denies the possibility of any exception without any real consideration of Matthew 19:9 as it stands. In effect it denies the exception's existence.

This perspective which views an exception as a contradiction is contrary to logic. Such an approach would require that every time someone states a rule he must state all the possible exceptions; otherwise, any exceptions given on other occasions would be contradictions. One of the strangest assumptions is that an exception in Matthew 19:9 would contradict Matthew 19:6. Although Jesus states no exceptions in Matthew 19:6, to argue that an exception in verse nine would result in a contradiction is contrary to scriptural usage. Such an approach would mean that 1 Corinthians 7:11 contradicts verse 10. It would mean that if a policeman stated that no vehicles could exceed the speed limit and in the same conversation a listener asked if ambulances could do so, the policeman could not respond, yes!, without contradicting himself. With this perspective, no one could ever add exceptions as explanatory details in answer to a question (as Jesus does in Matthew 19:6-9) unless all of the exceptions were given immediately with the initial statement and on every occurrence. Such a perspective is not at all reasonable.

Attempts to Nullify the Exception. Many interpretations have attempted to nullify the force of the exception clause. These interpretations use what could best be termed as forced grammar and logic. They can be divided into two basic categories, those which deny that there is an exception in this verse, and those which explain *porneia* in a way which refers to an invalid marriage.

One attempt to deny the exception clause is the so-called preteritive view which interprets the exception as an exception to Jesus' entire statement rather than to the verb *divorce.* Matthew 19:9 would then mean, "I say to you that whoever divorces his wife (I am not speaking about *porneia*) and marries another commits adultery." This, however, would be an exception to the subject Jesus is discussing and have the grammatically impossible effect of making the exception refer to the verb "I say" when it is clearly an exception to the verb "divorces." Such a view is not even a serious possibility.

A similar view interprets Matthew 19:9 as "Whoever divorces his wife not even for fornication and marries another commits adultery." This is "linguistically impossible,"[10] particularly in the use of the negative. No examples of such a usage occur in the New Testament. Both of these views also founder on the fact that Matthew 5:32 gives the same exception as Matthew 19:9, yet cannot at all be interpreted in such a way.

Another view could be described as the "social pressure view."[11] Jesus' statement is interpreted to mean "whoever divorces his wife, unless the mores of Jewish society require it, and marries another commits adultery." In other words, "whoever divorces his wife, unless he is required to do so by the social mores of the community, and marries another commits adultery." This as well as the previous two views is a move of desperation. There is nothing in either the context or in Matthew 19:9 itself to intimate such an interpretation. It would require the addition of an alien concept as well as numerous words. Words should only be supplied when there is some necessity due to the syntax of the sentence or the context. There is no such necessity here. Thus, to supply an unnecessary clause, including an additional verb *(required)*, when the verse as it stands is clear, is entirely without warrant. Not only is this interpretation a grammatical improbability, it raises an additional question regarding how many other social mores may be considered as exceptions allowing divorce.

Invalid Marriage Interpretations. There are several approaches which attempt to interpret *porneia* in such a way that the exception does not refer to a valid marriage, and therefore, is not really an exception to a genuine marriage. Many of the arguments given to support each of these views are primarily arguments against an exception rather than arguments to support the respective view. Such standard "anti-exception" arguments as, "The Bible clearly allows no divorce," "Jesus allows for no divorce," and "Any exception would be a contradiction" have been shown to be inaccurate and actually contrary to the biblical perspective.

Another argument that needs to be discussed before considering individual views is the argument that the disciples' reaction to Jesus' statement is too strong for Jesus to have stated any exception. However, we do not know how strongly the disciples reacted since only their words that "it is better not to marry" are recorded. Their intensity or emotional pitch is not described. The disciples' answer may have been given in a very factual tone. Although the difference between those who allowed divorce for almost any reason (the opinion of Rabbi Hillel) and those who only allowed divorce due to adultery (the opinion of Shammai) was argued in Israel, the society as a whole was more lenient than Shammai. The followers of Jesus lived in this more lenient society. To hear their teacher state that the strictest view was to be followed could easily provoke a strong reaction.

In our present society many teach that no divorce is allowable or that divorce is allowable only for adultery (just as Shammai taught). Despite the fact that Christians have heard such views presented, many do react strongly to a statement that no one can divorce except for adultery since this still excludes a great number of divorces as biblically legitimate.

Another, although related, objection to any exception is the opinion that Jesus could not merely teach the view of Shammai, which only allowed divorce in the case of adultery. But Jesus Christ did not derive his position on divorce from Shammai. Jesus is teaching God's view on divorce; if Shammai agrees, he agrees with God's view. There is no inherent reason that Shammai could not be accurate in his interpretation of Deuteronomy 24:1-4 and other passages and thus be teaching the correct view on divorce. Are we to assume that no human can properly interpret God's Word and teach a correct view of Scripture? If not, then what is the problem if Jesus teaches the same view which Shammai taught? If the problem were stated more clearly, perhaps the objectors mean that to agree with the already known position of Shammai would not bring such a strong reaction. However, as we have seen, the reaction is not exceptional for the strict position which allows divorce for adultery only. We do not know how strong the reaction was, nor is a strong reaction to such a strict view surprising.

Invalid Mixed Marriages. The mixed-marriage view, as well as the next two positions, interprets *porneia* in a sense not at all implied in the passage. The basis for rejecting the obvious meaning for *porneia* and favoring the importation of a meaning foreign to the context is only reasonable on the presupposition that there can be no real exception which allows valid divorce and remarriage in a genuine marriage. Those who hold the mixed-marriage position interpret *porneia* as a reference to a mixed marriage between a believer and an unbeliever. They argue that there can be no exception, that *porneia* is not the specific word for adultery, that *porneia* can be used of a mixed marriage, and that mixed marriages were prohibited by the Old Testament and, therefore, could be grounds for divorce as in the instance where Ezra ordered the Israelites to leave their pagan wives. We have already seen that we cannot assume that the Bible allows no exception, since several passages imply an exception. We have also seen that the use of *porneia* does not, in any way, imply that Matthew 19:9 refers to something other than adultery. Although the Old Testament does prohibit mixed marriage in most cases, this does not mean that the marriages were invalid, nor do we know that Ezra's reaction is standard rather than unique. In any case, the mixed-marriage view which requires that a mixed marriage be invalid and indicates that, in such a case, it is proper to divorce, results in a definite contradiction with Paul's teaching in 1 Corinthians 7:10-15.

The apostle Paul states several things in this passage which contradict the mixed-marriage view. In 1 Corinthians 7:10-11 he refers to Jesus' statements regarding divorce and remarriage, apparently referring to Matthew 19:3-9, when he says, "I command, yet not I but the Lord" (v. 10). However, when Paul begins to speak regarding the subject of a mixed marriage, he states in verse 12 that the Lord did not speak on this issue. If, as Paul says, Jesus did not speak regarding mixed marriage, then Jesus could not be referring to a mixed marriage in Matthew 19:9. Another objection to the mixed-marriage view is that the apostle Paul definitely teaches in 1 Corinthians 7:12-14 that mixed marriages are to be maintained; that is, that the believer should *not* divorce the unbeliever. This would be in direct contradiction to Jesus' statement in Matthew 19:9 if the exception referred to divorce in the case of mixed marriages. Finally, the entire basis of Paul's argument that the believer should not divorce in the case of a mixed marriage is his argument in verse 14 that such a marriage is valid in God's sight (the unbeliever is "sanctified" in the sense that the marriage is acceptable). Therefore, rather than the marriage being invalid, it is valid.

The fact that Paul refers to mixed marriages, that he tells the believer not to divorce in such a case, that he teaches that the marriage is valid, and that he declares that the Lord did not speak to this issue are facts commonly recognized by interpreters. All of these facts, however, contradict the mixed-marriage view of the exception in

Matthew 19:9. Some may object that Paul speaks regarding Christians, but Jesus speaks of men in general. Thus, the situation is different. However, we should note that in 1 Corinthians 7:10-11 Paul refers to Jesus' statements and uses this as basic to his whole argument regarding Christian marriages and mixed marriages. Therefore, Paul must regard the statements of Jesus in Matthew 19:3-12 (Mk 10:2-12) as applicable also to Christians.

Betrothal Unfaithfulness. Another attempt to nullify the exception in Matthew 19:9 is the claim that it refers to unfaithfulness discovered before the marriage is actually consummated. Some discussions seem to confuse the betrothal period with any premarital status. If "premarital unchastity" is substituted for "betrothal unfaithfulness," the implications and applications broaden considerably. The following arguments will also apply to any "premarital unchastity" view. Insisting that Matthew 19:9 applies to divorce before the marriage is consummated avoids the sundering of a genuine marriage. Otherwise, those holding this view would be in the illogical position of allowing severance of a consummated marriage for either premarital or betrothal unfaithfulness, while refusing it for unfaithfulness after marriage. This would place a higher value on faithfulness prior to marriage than on faithfulness once married.

The obvious problem with this view is that the Pharisees' initial question, their subsequent question, Jesus' initial answer and the Old Testament passages quoted (Gen 2:24; Deut 24:1-4) refer only to married people. How can the idea of betrothal, therefore, fit? In order to show some basis for importing the concept of betrothal into this passage, the proponents of this view argue that Jewish betrothal is the same, or as binding, as marriage.[12]

This premise, that Jewish betrothal is the same as marriage, is easily shown to be incorrect. Does it not seem odd that someone can argue that marriage is indissoluble while betrothal is not, and at the same time argue that they are equally binding? In order to import betrothal into the marriage context, one is in the unenviable position of arguing that Jewish betrothal and marriage are the same, in order to eventually prove that the exception does not apply to marriage but to something not as binding, that is, to betrothal. If betrothal were as binding as marriage, the exception would also apply to marriage. It seems clear that proponents of the betrothal view cannot really mean, what they in fact say, that Jewish betrothal and marriage were the same, since in that case their view self-destructs.

Jewish betrothal and marriage, however, were not the same. Such a concept would have been unthinkable to anyone in Israel at the time. If betrothal were the same as marriage then why would the couple still need to be married? Why would they still live separately? Why would the husband not support the wife? Although it may not be apparent to the proponents of this position, it would certainly be apparent to the engaged couple that betrothal and marriage were not the same. One basic argument for this view is that both involved a formal agreement and both required a divorce. Another argument is that the couple are called "husband" and "wife" during the betrothal period.[13] Neither of these arguments demonstrates the alleged point. The fact that we may need a license to drive and a license to fish, even though both require a license, does not mean that driving and fishing are the same.

The divorce, both in Jewish marriage and betrothal, was merely a formal notification of severance required in each case and in no way indicates they were the same. With respect to the argument based on the terms *husband* and *wife,* some have apparently overlooked the fact that we are actually dealing with Greek and Hebrew. There is no specific word for "husband" or "wife" in either language. In both languages the words under discussion mean "man" and "woman" and any more specific meaning is derived from the context. They may be used to mean "man," "woman," "fiancé," "betrothed," "husband" or "wife." The biblical text does not use the terms *husband* or *wife* for an engaged couple, neither should an English translation use *husband* and *wife* to refer to an engaged couple.

Even if the betrothal view were correct, the resulting meaning of Jesus' statement is often ignored. Jesus' statement would then be, "Whoever breaks his betrothal except for unfaithfulness and marries another commits adultery." This would mean that it is wrong to break a betrothal except for *porneia.* For those who also hold that even in the case of the exception remarriage is not permitted, it is even worse, since the verse would then mean that once betrothed, marriage to another is always wrong, even in the case of the exception.

This becomes an indissoluble betrothal. The person is condemned to permanent singleness before having been married once. Some may try to avoid these obvious problems by claiming, "but we are only referring to a Jewish concept of betrothal." This, however, is not true to the passage which says that Matthew 19:9 is Jesus' (God's) concept of marriage and betrothal, if betrothal is in view.

Not only does the betrothal view result in logical inconsistencies and in an almost impossible meaning for Matthew 19:9, it is also grammatically impossible. It requires that the word *porneia* refer to unfaithfulness during the betrothal period and that *gynaika,* the word translated "wife," means *only* "betrothed" or "fiancée." The proponents of this view have made the distinction between the betrothed before marriage and the wife after marriage. The word *porneia* can only refer to the illicit sex or unfaithfulness itself. If, as this view requires, it does refer to premarital unfaithfulness, then it can only imply the time the unfaithfulness occurs. *Porneia* can in no way imply when the divorce occurs or the category of the person divorced. The meaning of *porneia* cannot indicate whether the *divorce* occurs before or after the marriage is consummated.

In Matthew 19:9, this implication can only be in the meaning of *gynaika,* "woman." If *gynaika* refers to a betrothed, the divorce is before marriage. If it refers to one who is already married or to both a wife and a betrothed, then the divorce for premarital unfaithfulness can occur with respect to a wife, as well as to a betrothed. Perhaps a series of sentences covering the three situations will demonstrate this more clearly. In each sentence the meaning of *porneia,* "fornication," will be the same, betrothal (premarital) unfaithfulness. The meaning of "woman," *gynaika,* will be changed to demonstrate the problem. The basic sentence is "Whoever divorces his *gynaika* except for betrothal unfaithfulness and marries another commits adultery."

1. Referring to both: "Whoever divorces his wife or fiancée except for betrothal unfaithfulness, and marries another, commits adultery.

2. Referring only to a wife: "Whoever divorces his wife except for betrothal unfaithfulness and marries another commits adultery."

3. Referring only to a betrothed: "Whoever divorces his betrothed

except for betrothal unfaithfulness and marries another commits
adultery."

The third sentence alone, which refers only to a betrothed, fits the
betrothal view. The first two sentences, since they also include reference to those actually married, mean that a wife can be divorced
for unfaithfulness, after marriage as well as before. The word *gynaika,*
"woman" must keep the same meaning whatever it refers to. It cannot change back and forth in meaning to suit the needs of a view
which does not fit. The exception allowing divorce for unfaithfulness
during betrothal *must* apply to divorce of the *gynaika,* whoever she
is. Therefore, if the *gynaika,* who is put away for *porneia* means "wife,"
then a woman in a consummated marriage may be divorced at any
time for unfaithfulness which happened during the engagement.

The only way this verse can be restricted to a fiancée is for the
verse to refer *only* to a fiancée and not at all to a wife. It is a grammatical impossibility for this word, in the same sentence, to change
meanings back and forth, at one time meaning "wife" and at another
time meaning "betrothed," in order to suit the whims of the interpreter. To understand it as only referring to a betrothed woman, however,
is all but impossible in a passage which discusses marriage. It is even
less likely in the other verse which discusses the exception (Mt 5:32)
and in the closing statements of Mark 10:2–12.

If *porneia* refers to betrothal unfaithfulness or premarital unchastity and Matthew 19:9 in any way includes a reference to a wife, then
a wife can be divorced at any time for such *porneia.* This would not
only open the door for numerous divorces, but, as previously stated,
it would also mean that divorce for unfaithfulness during marriage
(adultery) would be disallowed, while divorce for unchastity or unfaithfulness before marriage would be allowed. The betrothal view is
impossible in this passage, a fact for which we should all be thankful
unless we desire indissoluble engagements. It is amazing that the
disciples did not respond, "It is better not to be engaged," rather than,
"It is better not to marry."

Those who hold that 1 Corinthians 7:36 refers to an engaged couple or fiancée have a problem if they also hold the betrothal view of
Matthew 19:9. This would require that, on the one hand, Paul would
say, "Do not follow through and get married," but, on the other hand,

Jesus would say, "The betrothal cannot be broken." One thing seems definite. The "betrothal view" of the exception in Matthew 19:9 is not at all realistic.

Invalid Incestuous Marriage. A view which seems to be popular among modern interpreters is that the exception in Matthew 19:9 refers to incestuous marriages prohibited in Leviticus chapter 18. Despite its popularity, this is, however, the least probable of all views. In addition to the fact that there is not the slightest hint of such a meaning in this passage and that it is highly unlikely that anyone hearing Jesus would understand it this way, the view has inherent difficulties. The incestuous-marriage view, as the other invalid marriage views, has as its foundation the premise that Matthew 19:9 must refer to some invalid marriage since there cannot be an exception to a valid marriage.

Marriage is alleged to be indissoluble because the couple become "one flesh"; that is, just like blood relatives. Therefore, they are in a permanent relationship which can never be dissolved. It seems to be a contradiction in logic to argue that a couple who are "one flesh" to begin with and then consummate a new marriage provides the only instance in which the one-flesh rule of permanence (indissolubility) does not apply. Some will answer this apparent inconsistency by saying that the marriage is not valid. But, we ask, "Why not?" The couple followed exactly the same procedure which makes others "one flesh." If becoming "one flesh" is that which makes a marriage indissoluble, why would the consummated marriage of a couple who are already "one flesh" not be at least as indissoluble as the marriage of other couples? If someone objects that the marriage is sinful or that God does not recognize it so that it is not really "one flesh," we must remind him that a sexual relationship with a prostitute is also sinful, and God does not recognize it as a valid marriage. However, according to 1 Corinthians 6:6, it is still a one-flesh relationship.

This paradox demonstrates that either the argument that becoming "one flesh" makes a marriage indissoluble or that the incestuous-marriage interpretation which regards a one-flesh relationship as the only valid reason for divorce, is incorrect or both. The one-flesh argument for indissolubility has previously been shown to be fallacious. Even 1 Corinthians 6:6 reveals that becoming "one flesh" with a prostitute can hardly imply that the relationship is indissoluble. Apart from the one-flesh argument for indissolubility, alleged evidence that Matthew 19:9 must apply only to an invalid marriage is scarce. Without this assumption, the incestuous-marriage view has no basis for existence. It also creates the logical paradox of allowing as the only grounds for divorce the same factor which allegedly created the indissolubility.

Would Jesus really imply that a breaking of an incestuous relationship was merely permissible rather than required? The tone of the passage implies that because the wife is guilty of *porneia,* the husband who divorces her is blameless, but in an incestuous marriage both would be guilty. Although Jesus is only referring to the correctness of the divorce and remarriage itself, is it likely that he would refer to wrongful divorce as adultery and yet, in contrast, merely state that an incestuous couple who divorce are not in adultery? We should notice that Jesus refers to a specific passage, Genesis 2:24, when discussing the subject of marriage. The hearer's question regarding the exceptions allowed under the Law refers to a specific passage, Deuteronomy 24:1–4. However, if the exception is the case of incestuous marriage, it is odd that there is no reference to the Old Testament passage which describes the alleged exception.

The incestuous-marriage view regards *porneia* (the exception) in Matthew 19:9 as a reference to marriage of blood relations. If so, this is contrary to the prohibited relationships in Leviticus 18:6–18 and is assumed not to be a valid marriage. Therefore, the exception is not really an exception, since it does not actually concern divorce but an annulment. Although this is often meant to include Jewish incestuous marriage, or any incestuous marriage, some refer this verse specifically to gentile incestuous marriages. They feel that the Levitical rules against incest would be so well known by Jews that they would not need to be stated by Jesus, however, some gentile converts may have been involved in incestuous marriages.[14]

Heth and Wenham give another perspective by describing the view as relating to a problem for Jewish-Christians regarding gentile converts involved in incestuous marriages. Matthew solved this problem by adding the exception.[15] The stipulation that the incest involved Gentiles is an attempt to avoid the obvious problem that Jesus would have little reason to mention something to his Jewish audience which was well known as a violation of the Mosaic Law and abhorrent to them.

Both of the views that the exception refers to gentile converts involved in incestuous marriages depend on an implicit denial of the inerrancy of Scripture. They depend on the assumption that Matthew *added* the exception clause to meet the problem confronting the church regarding gentile converts in incestuous marriage. Jesus, according to this position, did not give the exception even though Matthew explicitly attributes the statement to Jesus. In fact, even if proponents of such a view do allow that Jesus stated the exception, he could not have been speaking regarding a Gentile-Christian problem to the Pharisees before the church came into existence and years before there were any gentile converts to Christianity.

This opinion, that those involved in incestuous marriage were Gentiles, produces yet another illogical scenario. Most of those who hold this position also hold the position that Matthew is Jewish in perspective and Mark is basically addressed to Gentiles. Many make it even more specific by arguing not only that this perspective is the reason Matthew includes the exception and Mark omits it, but that Mark does not include the exception specifically because it is not applicable to Gentiles. It certainly seems illogical to hold these opinions regarding the difference between Matthew's and Mark's Gospels and at the same time regard the incestuous marriages as those of Gentiles.

Is it logical to argue that the exception concerns Gentiles and to argue, at the same time, that Mark omits it because he writes to Gentiles and that Matthew includes it because he writes to Jews? It is even more of a logical paradox to hold that the exception is not in Mark because it does not apply to Gentiles and also to hold to the "gentile convert in incestuous marriage" concept. This produces the situation that Matthew, writing to Jews, includes an exception specifically allowing Gentiles in incestuous marriages to divorce, but Mark writing to Gentiles does not include the exception because he does not allow it to Gentiles.

Even if we hold that the incestuous marriages are Jewish, and at the same time hold that the exception is in Matthew due to his Jewish perspective and omitted in Mark because he writes to Gentiles, the problem is not completely alleviated. The Gentiles were as susceptible to incestuous marriages as were the Jews, so for what reason would Mark exclude the exception due to the fact that he addresses Gentiles? Jesus' original statement was made to Jews in Israel, but if it concerned incestuous marriages, would not Gentiles likewise be concerned with what he said? To argue that it applies to Jews merely because it was against their law and unacceptable, ignores the fact that the Romans also had laws against incest and that it was not acceptable. Is incestuous marriage a sin in the case of the Jews merely because it violates the Mosaic Law, a sin so serious that it alone can sunder a marriage, but apart from the Mosaic Law so insignificant that it is not an exception for Gentiles?

Let us look at the basic arguments used to prove that *porneia* in Matthew 19:9 refers to incestuous marriage.[16] It is argued that "incest" or "incestuous marriage" is a possible meaning for *porneia*, that 1 Corinthians 5:1 uses *porneia* to refer to incest, that the same word is used in Acts 15:20 and 29 in the decrees of the Jerusalem Council which were sent to Gentiles and that *porneia* in these decrees refers specifically to Leviticus 18:6–18 which concerns incestuous marriages. The final step is that this is, therefore, a possible interpretation of *porneia* in Matthew 19:9.

Additional support is claimed from the allegation that an extrabiblical example using *porneia* to refer to incestuous marriage has been found. The argument that "incestuous marriage" fits the Jewish nature of Matthew and its exclusion fits the gentile perspective of Mark is standard but, as we have seen, illogical. Another argument is that "incestuous marriage" fits the historical situation, since Jesus is in the territory of Herod Antipas who married his brother's wife. Before we analyze these arguments, it is necessary to point out that this position must interpret *porneia* not as merely meaning incest, but as specifically meaning incestuous *marriage*.

If *porneia* refers to incest, then instead of an invalid marriage, incest on the part of the wife is the exception and becomes an acceptable basis for divorce in a valid marriage. This would not only disprove the concept of indissoluble marriage, but once the concept of indissoluble marriage is abandoned it would be highly illogical to select such an isolated meaning for *porneia* when other common meanings such as "adultery" would fit. It would also be illogical to allow divorce in a real marriage for incest and yet reject adultery as a grounds. The "incestuous marriage" position depends on the fact that *porneia* refers to an invalid marriage. However, there is insufficient evidence to establish that *porneia* was ever used to refer to an incestuous *marriage*, or that any of the hearers would have understood it to carry that meaning in Matthew 19:9.

The main argument for this interpretation depends on an improbable linking of several passages in order to establish an alleged connection with Leviticus 18:6–18. This indirect linkup is necessary, since the term *porneia* does not occur in Leviticus 18:6–18, nor does this passage specifically mention incestuous marriages, nor is there adequate evidence to show that *porneia* ever had such a meaning. The need to establish such a meaning and the scarcity of any evidence for it are revealed in Fitzmyer's attempt to find an example. Although some have made the claim that he has found clear proof in an example from extrabiblical literature,[17] a study of the evidence reveals that his interpretation is highly questionable. There is no definite evidence for such a meaning for *porneia*.

The first link in the alleged connection between Matthew 19:9 and Leviticus 18:6–18 is based on the fact that *porneia* refers to incest in 1 Corinthians 5:1. However, it does not refer to incestuous *marriage*, and although Paul writes to the church in which the incest occurred, he realizes that the word *porneia* would not necessarily be understood as referring to this sin. He realizes that without a specific explanation of the *porneia* involved, no one would recognize his meaning. Therefore, Paul specifically describes *porneia* as incest.

The next step in the argument is to move to the same word *porneia* in Acts 15:20 and 29 and then attempt to connect this passage with Leviticus 18:6–18, asserting that the latter passage refers to incestuous marriage. This series of connections is, however, one in which each link in the chain fails to connect with the following link. In 1 Corinthians 5:1 *porneia* needed to be defined in order to be recognized as meaning "incest." This implies that incest is not commonly understood by the use of this word, including its use in Acts 15:20 and 29. Further, this parallel in meaning between 1 Corinthians 5:1

and Acts 15:20 and 29 is highly improbable.

Porneia in 1 Corinthians 5:1 refers to something "not even among the Gentiles," but it also seems clear that Acts 15:20 and 29 refer to something common to and even acceptable among the Gentiles. This passage can hardly refer to the same thing as 1 Corinthians 5:1. Its connection with Leviticus 18:6-18 is likewise improbable. The decree written to the Gentiles in Acts 15:20 and 29 mentions four items from which the Gentiles are requested to abstain: idol sacrifices, blood, things strangled and *porneia*. There is no indication in the context of Acts 15:20 and 29 or in the decree itself which makes a definite connection with Leviticus 18:6-18 or with any other specific passage in the Old Testament. The only implication in the context is that these four items occur in the writings of Moses.

It would not be at all obvious to anyone reading the decree, particularly the gentile recipients, that this refers to incestuous marriage. It is, in fact, not obvious to most modern readers. The argument for the connection is based on the four items mentioned and the order in which they are stated. Laney, for example, argues that the four items occur in Leviticus in the following order: "idol sacrifices" (Lev 17:8-9), "blood" (Lev 17:10-12), "things strangled" (Lev 17:13-14) and *"porneia"* (Lev 18:6-18).[18] It is asserted that only in this passage are these four specific items found and found in this order; thus, this passage must be the one to which Acts 15:20 and 29 refer. However, when we study the passage in light of this argument there are certain discrepancies.

Leviticus 17:8-9 does not specifically mention idol sacrifices, nor are the words used in Acts 15:20 and 29 found in this passage. Although Leviticus 17:10-12 does mention eating blood, the term *strangle* or *things strangled* does not occur in Leviticus 17:13-14 or anywhere in the immediate context. Leviticus 17:13-14 continues the discussion of blood, as is particularly clear from verse 14, but it is only assumed that this includes prohibition of things strangled. If the prohibition of things strangled is understood in the prohibition against blood, then the number of separate items is three, not four; the order of three items is less significant. However, since "idol sacrifices" is also not mentioned in Leviticus 17:8-14, we are left with one item in this passage ("blood" or "things strangled") and one in Leviticus 18:6-

18 *(porneia)*. The corresponding order of these two items is of little significance. It is of no significance when we realize that the relative order of these two remaining items differs between Acts 15:20 and Acts 15:29.

The argument based on order will bear no weight as evidence for a connection with Leviticus 18:6–18. The argument that these four items occur only in Leviticus 17:8—18:18 is likewise of little import when we notice that only two separate items, blood (by implication "things strangled") and illicit sex, are discussed in both passages, for these occur elsewhere in Moses' writings. When we further understand that the term *porneia* does not occur in the Leviticus passage, we should realize that of the four Greek words used in Acts 15:20 and 29 to describe the prohibitions, only one occurs in Leviticus 17:8—18:18, namely, "blood." The alleged correspondence does not exist. Since a prohibition against blood occurs elsewhere, there is no reason to relate this specifically to Leviticus 18:6–18. Some may argue that, although the word *porneia* does not actually occur in this passage, the passage discusses illicit sexual relationships which are in the category of *porneia*. However, this is stretching the point.

There is another flaw in attempts to relate Acts 15:20 and 29 specifically to the incestual sins of Leviticus 18:6–18. The prohibited incest occurs within a larger section (Lev 18:6–23) which prohibits several illicit sexual relationships which could be described as *porneia*,[19] including adultery and homosexuality. Therefore, even if Acts 15:20 and 29 do refer to Leviticus, the argument from terminology and order cannot support the selection of only the incest prohibitions out of an entire section of prohibitions against various forms of illicit sex. They all occur in the same section and in the same relative order. The fact that the term *porneia* can describe incest does not specify that only the incestual sins are in view. *Porneia* can also describe the other sins. There is no reason to select the incest prohibitions and overlook the other illicit-sex prohibitions.

Laney tries to support such a selection by arguing that the decree in Acts 15:20 and 29 referred to items acceptable to Gentiles but offensive to Jews. He argues that the incest prohibitions in Leviticus 18:6–18 are ceremonial and not moral issues; therefore, they are acceptable to Gentiles. He also uses 1 Corinthians 5:1 to argue that this was an apparently "live issue" and acceptable to Gentiles.[20] First Corinthians 5:1, which states that the *porneia* in question "is not even among the Gentiles," is an unlikely witness to prove that this is an acceptable or "live issue" among the Gentiles, since it states just the opposite. There is sufficient evidence that incestuous marriage was not completely acceptable among the Gentiles.

We also ask, is it really true that the prohibited incestual relationships of Leviticus 18:6-18 were not moral issues, but only ceremonial? If they were only ceremonial due to the Mosaic Law, why did the Romans also have laws against incest? Is it at all likely that the incestual relationships were not moral but only ceremonial and of so little moral significance that the Jerusalem church would consider them "gray areas," as Laney says, and not definitely wrong for Gentiles? Are we to believe that Jesus Christ states that such "ceremonial" relationships invalidate a consummated marriage and are the sole grounds for breaking an otherwise indissoluble relationship which cannot be severed by a definitely unacceptable and severe sin such as adultery? This is improbable.

Not only does the term *porneia* fail to occur in Leviticus 18:6-18, and not only are the above arguments sufficient to show that no real connection can be made between Acts 15:20 and 29 and Leviticus 18:6-18, but the incest portions of Leviticus 18:6-18 do not refer to incestuous *marriage* but to incest. There is still no established link to connect *porneia* with the meaning "incestuous marriage," nor is there a link with Matthew 19:9.

The only verse in Leviticus 18:6-18 which discusses marriage (v. 18) is often used as evidence that the passage refers to marriage. The terminology in the passage shows that except for this verse the subject is not marriage but illicit sexual intercourse. Moreover, this single verse does not even refer to incest but to a particular form of polygamy (marriage to both a woman and her sister). Such a marriage is prohibited, not due to incest, but due to the very practical issue of jealousy between sisters. The section prohibiting incest begins in Leviticus 18:6, which states that no one is to have sexual intercourse with a "blood relative of his." The prohibitions concerning blood relatives end in Leviticus 18:17, and it is clear by a comparison with verse 18 that a different issue is involved. It should also be clear that to marry two sisters who are blood relatives to each other is not the same as marrying one's own blood relatives.

This change of aspect after verse 17 includes the prohibition against having sisters as wives, adultery, homosexuality and sodomy. The only prohibited marriage is the one which involved marriage to sisters, which is hardly the exception occurring in Matthew 19:9. Neither is there any implication that such a marriage, if it occurred, would be invalid. There is no specific connection of Leviticus 18:6-18 with Acts 15:20 and 29 and no basis for understanding *porneia* as a reference to incestuous marriage.

Every link in the chain which allegedly connects Matthew 19:9 with Leviticus 18:6-18 has been shown to be defective, and there is no link of any kind to connect 1 Corinthians 5:1 and Acts 15:20 and 29 with Matthew 19:9. It is extremely unlikely that *porneia* in Matthew 19:9 refers to incest and even less probable that it refers to incestuous *marriage.* There is nothing to imply such a meaning. Some indication would be necessary in a context where all concerned would normally understand the meaning as "adultery" and could hardly be expected to recognize such a remote meaning as "incestuous marriage." There is no adequate evidence to support the meaning "incestuous marriage" for the exception in Matthew 19:9.

An illustration will demonstrate the incongruity of interpreting *porneia* as a reference to incestuous marriage rather than adultery or some other common use of the term. If a night guard for a factory in Ohio should ask his supervisor whether he should allow anyone to enter, the supervisor could well reply, "Do not let anyone in this building." If the guard responds that in the past, certain people were allowed in, does it seem likely that the answer would be, "I tell you, do not let anyone in except the president of the United States." Would there be any need to mention such an exception? Is this a likely response when the guard was seriously attempting to obtain the answer to a situation which might well confront him? Such an answer would be considered somewhat sarcastic. Yet we are asked to believe that in answer to a question concerning a situation likely to confront many of the hearers, a question for which there were some differing but commonly accepted answers, Jesus would ignore the commonly debated answers and give an answer with an exception so remote yet so obvious that no one would think it necessary to mention. The situation in the incestuous-marriage view is even more incongruous.

Jesus used a common term which in the context would have a commonly understood meaning, but, according to the incestuous-marriage view, would actually mean something for which the term was never or rarely used. If the above illustration is to parallel such a view, the supervisor would respond with the seemingly congruous answer, "I tell you, do not let anyone enter except an appropriate official." However, by "appropriate official" he does not mean what one would normally understand, but only the president of the United States. Would the guard or anyone else have even the most remote reason to think this referred not to officials of the factory, but only to one unlikely possibility not at all obvious in the term? Yet this is what we are asked to believe is a reasonable interpretation of Matthew 19:9.

To argue that this meaning could be expected, since Jesus was in the territory of Herod Antipas who married his brother's wife, is unacceptable. This incident concerned a royal family which not only did as it pleased, but also often engaged in intermarriage. This does not imply that incestuous marriage was a factor among the general populace, or even allowed. It also ignores the fact that even in Herod's case it was not accepted as proper. Herod, himself, probably did not consider it as completely acceptable in a moral sense. If the historical context is to provide a basis for selecting a specific meaning for *porneia*, certainly the prevalent sin of adultery would be the more obvious choice than this isolated instance concerning Herod. To use Herod's marriage as evidence that *porneia* in Matthew 19:9 means "incestuous marriage" bears as much force as an argument that the guard in the illustration should have understood that "appropriate official" meant "president," since the historical context shows that the president has visited factories.

The incongruity of importing the concept of incestuous marriage into this context is even more apparent if we keep in mind that, according to this view, this is not regarded as a genuine marriage. In answer to a normal question regarding normal marriage, for Jesus to omit any reference to the specifics normally encountered in such a discussion and refer to an instance which is not really a marriage—and is not likely to happen and is disallowed by the society as a whole—is improbable.

Divorce and Remarriage for Adultery. The most reasonable interpretation of *porneia* in Matthew 19:9 (and 5:32) is "adultery." The only other reasonable interpretation is to understand *porneia* in the general sense of "illicit sex." Other interpretations are based on illogical and faulty concepts. Some argue that since *porneia* is a general term for illicit sex, it is just as restrictive to interpret it with the specific meaning "adultery" as it is to interpret it in some other specific way such as betrothal unfaithfulness or incestuous marriage.[21] Apart from the extensive problems with either of these latter two interpretations, this argument is inaccurate. The basic issue does not concern "restrictive interpretations," but appropriateness in the context. The word *ball* has several meanings, any of which are "restrictive" to one concept. If we are attending a baseball game and apart from some indication of another meaning, someone asks "where is the ball?" it is not restrictive in any inappropriate sense to interpret this as referring to a baseball. It is, however, unreasonably inappropriate and unnecessarily restrictive to interpret it, in such a context, as referring to a dance. The natural meaning of *porneia* in Matthew 19:9 is adultery. Therefore, we conclude that Jesus Christ himself teaches that adultery is the one completely valid basis for divorce which also allows for remarriage.

Divorce and Remarriage for Desertion

The preceding discussion has shown that valid divorce and remarriage are possible. There is at least one other situation where Scripture seems to indicate that divorce and remarriage may be allowed. Since Jesus stated that there is only one valid ground for divorce and remarriage, how can there be another? Jesus' statement in Matthew 19:9 refers to the one situation where it is proper to initiate the severance of the marriage. The other situation, described in 1 Corinthians 7:15, is one where the spouse initiates the separation, although the one abandoned may carry out the legal technicalities for divorce.

There is no question in the context of 1 Corinthians 7:15 regarding the issue. The unbelieving spouse leaves the believer. The difference of opinion is not over this fact, but whether or not the believer is then free to remarry. The specific issue concerns the meaning of the statement, "The believer is not bound." Does it mean, as some say, merely not bound to stay with the unbeliever, or does it mean not bound in the sense of being freed from the marriage tie so that remarriage is possible?

Many of the arguments used against an exception here are the same as those used against an exception in Matthew 19:9. The same answers apply here and need not be repeated. A specific objection to an exception in 1 Corinthians 7:15 is that 1 Corinthians 7:10-11 allows no exception at all. Therefore, any exception would be a contradiction to these verses. This is the same basic argument that claimed that any exception in Matthew 19:9 would contradict Matthew 19:6 (since it states no exception) and also Mark 10:2-12. The same answers apply. The argument was erroneous in the case of Matthew 19:9, and it is erroneous here.

Paul definitely states that the position on divorce and remarriage in 1 Corinthians 7:10-11 was given by the Lord. Since the Lord spoke specifically on the subject of divorce and remarriage on the occasion described in Matthew 19:3-12 (Mk 10:2-12), and to some extent in Matthew 5:32, Matthew 19:9 (and 5:32) must be the instance to which Paul refers. It is unreasonable to refer Paul's statement to the occasion described in Luke 16:18 (a one-verse comment used merely as an illustration of the point in the previous verse). Jesus' statement recorded in Matthew 19:9, to which Paul refers in 1 Corinthians 7:10-11, definitely included the exception, so that the exception *must* be understood in 1 Corinthians 7:10-11, just as it must be understood in Mark. Not only is there no logical reason to expect exceptions to be given every time a subject is mentioned, there is an obvious reason why it would not be specifically stated in 1 Corinthians 7:10-11. Paul is not giving the information in 1 Corinthians 7:10-11 to provide a complete discussion on divorce and remarriage. He is answering the question whether or not it is acceptable for a believer to stay married to an unbeliever; he says that which is appropriate to his argument. He states that the general principle in marriage is for those married to stay married; the believer should stay married to the unbeliever. There is no need to mention exceptions which would allow for divorce, since the issue is not whether there are any exceptions, as in Matthew 19:3, but the acceptability of mixed marriages.

Paul's reference to Jesus' statements and his application of these to the situation in Corinth reveals that he considered Jesus' statements on divorce and remarriage as foundational for his discussion and as applicable to Christians. Thus, the exception must be understood in 1 Corinthians 7:10–11. The statement "If she divorces, let her remain unmarried, or be reconciled to her husband" necessarily applies to one who divorced for reasons other than the exception. Otherwise, as is clear from Matthew 19:9, they are allowed to remarry. In effect, 1 Corinthians 7:10–11 could be summarized as follows: "Divorce and remarriage are excluded but for the exception of Matthew 19:9; however, if a wife divorces her spouse for other reasons she should stay unmarried or be reconciled to her husband." Since the exception is understood in this passage, it is also understood in the case of a mixed marriage. In a mixed marriage either spouse may divorce the other for adultery. A believer is not required to stay with an adulterous, unbelieving spouse.

The crux of the issue is the meaning of 1 Corinthians 7:15. The arguments against interpreting this verse as referring to a divorce and allowing remarriage are few. It is argued that the verse only refers to allowing the partner to leave and says nothing about remarriage. If such an approach were followed elsewhere, many doctrines, including the doctrine of the Trinity, would be lost. The situation Paul refers to either allows remarriage or it does not. This is what needs to be determined.

Another objection to interpreting "not bound" as a reference to being released from the marriage tie is that a different verb *(deō)* is consistently used of the marriage tie rather than the verb *enslaved,* used in 1 Corinthians 7:15. However, this verb means approximately the same thing and may even be stronger than the verb *deō.* In any case, there is no reason to assume that only one verb can be used of the marriage tie. There is, of course, the possibility that to use the verb *deō,* which commonly occurs in the tense used here with a meaning equivalent to "to be married," could cause confusion, since it is a standard term for the marriage tie. It could conceivably be interpreted to give the erroneous idea "Let him go, the brother or sister is not married in such cases." Contrary to Paul's point that mixed marriages are valid, such an understanding could appear as a contradiction. This is at least a plausible reason that Paul uses a different verb, but whatever the reason, he is not bound to use only the one verb *deō*. The meaning of "not bound" must be determined from the context.

Matthew 5:32; 19:9; and 1 Corinthians 7:10-13 concern the party who initiates a divorce. They reveal that the general rule is to maintain the marriage. It is wrong to divorce one's spouse and marry another unless it is because of adultery. If the wife divorces for some other reason, she should stay unmarried or be reconciled to her husband. This same perspective applies even if she is married to an unbeliever. However, 1 Corinthians 7:15 concerns a different situation; that is, when the other party leaves. Therefore, the previous rules (vv. 10-11) do not necessarily apply. The issue in 1 Corinthians 7:15 then is whether or not the verse refers to acceptable divorce.

The verb translated "depart" in 1 Corinthians 7:15 is commonly used for "divorce." In a context such as this "divorce" would be the expected meaning. The action in 1 Corinthians 7:15 is in contrast with that in 7:12-13. There, if the unbeliever is willing to stay, the believer is not to divorce the unbeliever. The word translated "divorce" *(aphiēmi)* definitely means "divorce" in these verses. The natural contrast to the statement, "If the unbeliever is willing to stay do not divorce," is the concept, "If the unbeliever is not willing to stay you may divorce him."

The difference in the two words "divorce" *(aphiēmi)* and "depart" *(chōrizō)*, although both mean "divorce," indicates where the initiative for separation lies. In verses 12-13 the believer is not to send away ("divorce") the other, but in verse 15 the unbeliever *leaves* ("divorces") the believer. The meaning of the verbs and the contrast between verses 12-13 and verse 15 imply that divorce is in view in verse 15. It is also highly unlikely that the unbeliever would leave the believer without intending a divorce and remarriage. It is further questionable that "not bound," in 1 Corinthians 7:15 means only "not bound to stay with," since if the unbeliever leaves, the believer can hardly have any choice in the matter and, therefore, even if bound, could not stay with the departing unbeliever.

Since Paul presents it as acceptable for the believer to allow this to happen and since a biblically valid divorce allows for remarriage, it is most probable that Paul allows not only divorce but subsequent remarriage in the case of desertion by an unbeliever. Although it is not definitely stated that desertion by a believer likewise allows for divorce and remarriage for the deserted spouse, according to 1 Corinthians 7:10-14 there is no substantial difference between the validity of a mixed marriage and the marriage of two believers. The mixed marriage is acceptable to God and completely valid. Therefore, although not specifically stated, desertion even by a believer may be grounds for divorce and remarriage.

Some argue that the deserted believer is not permitted to remarry, because the entire context of 1 Corinthians 7:17-24 urges the believer to remain as he or she is and not to change his or her status.[22] This opinion ignores the details of the context. The *preference* for remaining as is refers also to those never married and to widows and widowers. If this aspect of the context prohibits remarriage, it prohibits *all* marriage. The passage actually teaches the preference of staying single, but if you desire to marry it is *not sin.* Although this statement may not specifically allow remarriage of divorced persons, on the other hand, the context does not specifically deny it unless it denies all marriage. Paul implies in 1 Corinthians 7:10-12 that he has something to say that was not specifically covered by the Lord. Since Jesus' statement in Matthew 19:9 is true for all, including believers and unbelievers, Paul must be doing more than repeating the same teaching for application to a mixed marriage. If he merely repeats in verse 15 what he said in verses 10-11, that divorce and remarriage are prohibited (except for adultery) and that separated people should remain unmarried, then he has stated nothing that the Lord did not already say. If verse 15 is mere repetition, why then would Paul state that the Lord did not speak regarding this matter?

Conclusion

The Bible specifically states that God intended for marriage to be maintained. Just as specifically, Jesus states that there is only one valid reason for which a person may properly divorce the other and subsequently marry someone else—adultery on the part of the spouse. This is clear and specific. There is no valid basis on which to reject this teaching. First Corinthians 7:15, since it does not specifically mention remarriage, is not as clear. However, the most probable meaning is that if the spouse initiates the separation, the deserted spouse may divorce and remarry. This position does not overlook the factor of sin, however.

The sin and responsibility in the first situation lie with the spouse who commits the adultery. In the second case the sin and responsibility lie with the spouse who deserts. Marriage is a concept created by God for us. We should not sever that which God has joined. The guilt and sin lie not with the innocent party but with the person basically responsible for the failure, the adulterer or the deserter. Many approach the subject of divorce and remarriage as a policeman would who is not primarily interested in stopping robberies, but more interested that the criminals not enjoy the benefits of their crime. They seem less interested in avoiding marriage failures and more interested in keeping the divorced from remarriage. Remarriage, however, is a secondary issue in that it only arises as a result of the basic problem, which is divorce. God seems more interested in maintaining marriages than in keeping people unmarried. However, for adultery and apparently for desertion, he allows divorce and subsequent remarriage.

We might well ask, regarding the various attempts to avoid any real exception (particularly in Mt 19:9), why such an unusual method of interpreting parallel passages in the gospels is used? Why all these illogical paradoxes? Why this attempt to interpret contrary to the context? Why illogical suppositions that an exception must be stated constantly or be a contradiction? Why this consistent interpretation contrary to the apparent meaning of passages? Why interpret contrary to normal rules of language or syntax? Why are all of these unusual approaches converging on one passage and on one issue? It is not due to the intellectual deficiencies of the interpreters, since many well-known scholars are involved. It is due to a presupposition contrary to the passages as a whole, the assumption that the passages cannot teach any exceptions. The view presented here is, as stated at the beginning, the one most naturally derived from Scripture. It allows Scripture to speak rather than subduing the melodious and harmonious voice of Scripture to the insistent clanging of a dogmatic presupposition.

Case Study

Pete was in his third year of ministry and his wife Patty was expecting their first child. What the congregation did not know about Pete was that he was schizophrenic and that contrary to the appearances of being a loving husband, he was cruel and abused his wife. Patty had lied to outsiders about the bruises and the broken arm she had suffered while she was working to put him through seminary. Patty has been very fearful for the safety of her baby because Pete has threatened to kill her baby. In desperation, Patty finally told her pastor what was going on. He took Pete to the hospital where he was admitted for psychiatric testing. Pete was diagnosed as schizophrenic with no hope of rehabiltation. He did not respond to therapy. After a year, Patty filed for divorce. Three years later, Patty has met another man whom she would like to marry.

Answer

Regarding the case in question, several factors must be considered. It is difficult to understand the seemingly casual acceptance of the psychiatric diagnosis by the church. Pete was able to conceal his problem through three or four years of seminary, three years after that and presumably during the period he courted Patty prior to marriage. Obviously, he did not assault his seminary professors, fellow students, church members, employers, policemen or strangers on the street. Therefore, there is no question that he is in control of his actions whenever he desires. He resorts to violence only when he thinks there will be no repercussions.

The primary responsibility of the church, since Pete can control his actions, is to bring church discipline to bear on him. This includes, at the minimum, removing him from the ministry and insuring that he neither re-enters the ministry nor marries someone else. Pete is the instigator of this marriage problem, not Patty. For the church to be concerned over the validity of Patty's possible remarriage, but to have taken no disciplinary action against Pete, is little more than hypocrisy. If the church has taken no action against Pete and in addition, contrary to Scripture, accepted the idea that he is beyond rehabilitation, then why is it only concerned about Patty's remarriage?

Pete's present marital status also enters into consideration of Patty's possible remarriage. Since it is three years after the divorce, has he remarried or become involved in *porneia* with some other woman? If so, he has committed adultery in relation to his original marriage to Patty, and the exception of Matthew 19:9 applies. She is free to remarry.

Assuming the situation as in the scenario, I find it strange that the church did not counsel Patty to separate and allow time for Pete to change, rather than to proceed with divorce. It seems clear that, in general, the Bible is against divorce. The fact that remarriage after divorce (except for *porneia)* is adultery (Mt 19:9) is because the divorce is not valid. However, the additional step of remarriage is necessary before it becomes adultery. First Corinthians 7:10-11 seems to make some allowance for extenuating circumstances when it states that the wife should not divorce, but if she does, then she is to remain unmarried. This is not to say that divorce is encouraged or desirable. The church leaders need to thoroughly explain the biblical statements to Patty, but in the final analysis, the responsibility for the divorce and the consideration of extenuating circumstances must rest on the person initiating the divorce. The church cannot require Patty to live in a situation which endangers her life and the baby. They should, at the least, allow for separation.

Since the divorce has already occurred and since Patty is in no way at fault for the situation, the divorce should be allowed without any stigma against Patty. The real crux of the issue is Patty's potential marriage to another man. There is no biblical statement which allows for remarriage in this situation. It would be erroneous to indicate to Patty that she is free to marry another. She should remain unmarried. If this seems unnecessarily harsh, it may be necessary to point out that when society as a whole has discouraged divorce, many spouses, including non-Christians, have maintained their marriage in situations as tenuous as Patty's original marriage. They have not even divorced. It should not be impossible for a Christian, by God's grace, to remain single. The extenuating circumstances of Patty's situation do not make it any more difficult for her to remain unmarried than it is for other divorcées without such extenuating circumstances, or who were even the guilty party. Yet, the church expects these to remain unmarried. Patty should remain unmarried, since it is not definite that she has biblical grounds for remarriage.

If she does remarry, her situation should be handled and she should be treated, however, in light of the fact that she is a victim of the extenuating circumstances beyond her control. She was not responsible for the difficulty of her situation. Therefore, I would not, as a pastor, feel that the church should take any official action against Patty.

Notes

[1] William A. Heth and Gordon J. Wenham, *Jesus and Divorce* (London: Hodder and Stoughton, 1984), pp. 112, 140, 141, 144, 176; J. Carl Laney, *The Divorce Myth* (Minneapolis: Bethany House Pub., 1981), pp. 59, 67, 78.

[2] Laney, *The Divorce Myth*, p. 56.

[3] Heth and Wenham, *Jesus and Divorce*, p. 114.

[4] G. J. Wenham, "The Syntax of Matthew 19:9," *JSNT* 28 (1986):17–23. His propositions *cannot* be formulated from the original sentences. His attempts to find exegetical support for his approach from other verses are improbable.

[5] This same thinking is apparent in Heth and Wenham, *Jesus and Divorce*, p. 120.

[6] Ibid., p. 134.

[7] Ibid., p. 121.

[8] Laney, *The Divorce Myth*, p. 67.

[9] Ibid., p. 52.

[10] Friedrich Hauck and Siegfried Schulz, "πόρνη," *TDNT*, 6:592.

[11] Heth and Wenham, *Jesus and Divorce*, pp. 125–26.

[12] Ibid., pp. 169–70; Laney, *The Divorce Myth*, p. 69.

[13] Heth and Wenham, *Jesus and Divorce*, pp. 169–70.

[14] G. J. Wenham, "Matthew and Divorce: An Old Crux Revisited," *JSNT* 22 (1984):100.

[15] Heth and Wenham, *Jesus and Divorce*, p. 154.

[16] Ibid., pp. 154–60; Laney, *The Divorce Myth*, pp. 71–78.

[17] Heth and Wenham, *Jesus and Divorce*, p. 159; Laney, *The Divorce Myth*, p. 74. See also Joseph A. Fitzmyer, "The Matthean Divorce Texts and Some New Palestinian Evidence," *To Advance the Gospel* (New York: Crossroad Pub. Co., 1981), pp. 79–109.

[18] Laney, *The Divorce Myth*, p. 73.

[19]William F. Luck, *Divorce and Remarriage* (San Francisco: Harper and Row, Pub., 1987), p. 99.

[20]Laney, *The Divorce Myth,* p. 74.

[21]Heth and Wenham, *Jesus and Divorce,* p. 135.

[22]Gordon J. Fee, *The First Epistle to the Corinthians,* New International Commentary on the New Testament (Grand Rapids: Eerdmans Pub. Co., 1987), pp. 302–03; also, Heth and Wenham, *Jesus and Divorce,* p. 143.

Response

J. Carl Laney

Whereas I find myself in agreement with virtually every point made by Bill Heth, I strongly disagree with nearly every point made my Thomas Edgar. Yet, he does make several comments in the conclusion of his document with which I heartily agree. Edgar writes, "The Bible specifically states that God intended for marriage to be maintained" (p. 191). He also states, "We should not sever that which God has joined" (p. 191). It is surprising that Edgar can make such strong statements regarding God's design for marriage and then take the entirety of his article to argue the legitimacy of divorce and remarriage.

Although I have not met Thomas Edgar, I am aware that we both graduated from Dallas Seminary. I am confident that we share much in common theologically. On the issue of divorce and remarriage however, we are poles apart. I have read his document carefully and intend to respond as a Christian and as a gentleman to his presentation.

I am disappointed that Edgar's document is primarily a rebuttal of the books and articles published by Bill Heth, Gordon Wenham and myself instead of providing the reader with a positive presentation of his own position. Such a point-by-point refutation has already been published in the more exhaustive book, *Divorce and Remarriage.*[1] The presentation of Edgar's own viewpoint is limited to the first six pages of introductory remarks and the last eight pages of his manuscript. There he argues that divorce and remarriage is permitted for adultery and desertion. As it is, the positive presentation is little more than a statement of the traditional Protestant viewpoint. I believe that his approach is uneven and certainly not the concept envisioned in planning this project.

I am also disappointed in Edgar's approach in dealing with those of different viewpoints. For example, Edgar states that many of the objections to a valid exception in Matthew 19:9 are "based on either an open rejection of the inerrancy of Scripture or on a precarious view of inerrancy" (p. 165). He remarks that those who insist that an exception is not "understood" in Mark 10:2-12 have "implicitly surrendered the inerrancy of Scripture" (p. 166) and "are explicitly or implicitly denying the accuracy of Matthew" (p. 166). His comment that "such erroneous approaches come from an unwitting acceptance of modern redaction-criticism which turns the Gospel authors into mere editors rather than accurate eyewitnesses" (p. 167), is reactionary and unfair. These kind of remarks discourage students of Scripture from exploring the options for fear of being labeled a heretic. Such labeling, all too typical among evangelicals, hinders church unity and discourages the pursuit of truth.

In responding to Edgar's presentation, I will first speak to general issues representative of the position he holds. Then I will relate to some specific comments made in the paper. As one who once held the viewpoint espoused by Thomas Edgar, I have a reasonably good understanding of the position. It was the viewpoint I was taught in seminary and taught others during my early years of teaching. Over time, however, I became troubled by the apparent inconsistencies in the Protestant evangelical position. After considerable study on the subject I came to my present view that Scripture disallows divorce and remarriage.

A major difficulty with Edgar's viewpoint is the absence of an exception in Mark 10:1-12 and Luke 16:18. According to Edgar, Mark "merely omitted a detail which Matthew included" (p. 166). I would have to say that Mark's omission of an exception to the permanence of marriage is more than a detail! Eusebius records that Mark carefully recorded the teaching of Peter for the church at Rome after Peter's death.[2] The church at Rome was apparently not taught by Peter that there was an exception to the permanence of marriage. Peter's preaching contained no exception. Neither did Mark's Gospel. Neither were the gentile readers of the Gospel of Luke informed as to an exception. This is not a minor historical detail. This omission would have a significant impact on the lives and marriages of Mark's readers.

Careful study of the New Testament takes into consideration introductory matters such as author, date and audience. It cannot be ignored that the readers of Matthew are Jewish and the readers of Mark are Roman. Why the omission of the exception when Mark's Gospel actually provides the more complete account? In my study I have come to conclude that it has to do with his readers and purpose. The omission was not inadvertent but intentional. Neither Mark nor Luke saw the exception as applicable to their Roman or Greek readers.

Another major concern I have with Edgar's view is that it seems to leave little place for the biblical practice of forgiveness. Certainly adultery is a devastating and disrupting sin. But is it beyond forgiveness? Is divorce the way to deal with an unfaithful spouse? What did Jesus say about forgiveness in Matthew 18:21-35? Disciples are called upon to forgive others without limit, as they themselves have been forgiven by Christ. The book of Hosea presents God's alternative to divorce in the case of adultery. Hosea was commanded, "Go again, love a woman who is loved by her husband, yet an adulteress, even as the LORD loves the sons of Israel, though they turn to other gods and love raisin cakes" (3:1 NASB).

And where in Edgar's viewpoint is the place for promise keeping? It seems that the Bible places a high priority on promise keeping. God spoke to Moses, "If a man makes a vow to the LORD, or takes an oath to bind himself with a binding obligation, he shall not violate his word; he shall do according to all that proceeds out of his mouth" (Num 30:1, see also Eccles 5:4-5 NASB). Psalm 15 describes the godly man as one who "swears to his own hurt, and does not change" (15:4 NASB) The story of Joshua and his covenant with the Gibeonites suggests that God would have his people keep their promises even when entered into wrongfully (Josh 9:3-27). When the covenant with the Gibeonites was broken by Saul, God brought judgment by way of famine (2 Sam 21:1-6). According to the Bible, God is a promise-keeping God who delights in those who make and keep their marriage vows.

Significantly absent from Edgar's discussion is a biblically based definition of marriage. It is difficult to adequately discuss deviation from God's plan unless God's plan for marriage is clearly spelled out. Nowhere does Edgar present his understanding of marriage. Is marriage merely a human agreement? A divine institution? A covenant commitment? What "ends" when divorce takes place? I submit that one's view of marriage will effect one's view of divorce. What is Edgar's view? Is his view biblically based?

The major objection I have to Edgar's presentation is the lack of any canonical continuity. His treatment of the Old Testament passages is quite sketchy. In the New Testament, he focuses on Matthew 19:9, excluding discussion on such passages as Luke 16:18 and Roman 7:1-6, mere "illustrations" according to Edgar. I would expect that a biblical presentation on divorce and remarriage would include all the texts relating to the issue. Edgar has chosen to exclude from his consideration two texts which strongly affirm that divorce and remarriage is adultery.

Instead of presenting a thorough biblical study of the subject, Edgar continually appeals to logic and states that the arguments of the opposing viewpoint are illogical (compare, pp. 173, 179, 180, 186, 192). I would hasten to point out that many biblical doctrines—such as election and free will—do not fit our categories of logic. How is the doctrine of the Trinity—three equal persons in one godhead—logical? Frankly, I would rather be biblical than logical if a choice is demanded.

I find that Edgar is repeatedly guilty of gross overstatement. Concerning the issue of *porneia*, Edgar writes that "it is certain that the primary reference is to the sin of adultery" (p. 162). Is it "certain" to F. F. Bruce, Joseph Fitzmyer, Charles Ryrie? Apparently not. Elsewhere he states, "The exception clause is in the one position where it unambiguously teaches that a person who divorces due to a spouse's adultery may remarry." Apparently it was not so unambiguous to the church fathers since they did not permit remarriage for divorced persons.

Edgar's quotation of Matthew 5:31–32 on p. 164 is neither an accurate quote or a paraphrase. Putting the statement in quotation marks misleads the reader who is unfamiliar with the specific text.

Edgar wrongly equates indissolubility with a "sacramental view of marriage" (p. 151). A sacramental view of marriage regards marriage as a sacrament that bestows grace. I would maintain indissolubility on the basis of biblical evidence, but would certainly deny that marriage is a sacrament. Interestingly, it was the sacramental view of Erasmus that led to the Protestant view espoused by so many evangelicals today. Protestants have abandoned the sacrament of marriage, but not the implications drawn by Erasmus.

Edgar refers on several occasions to the "desperation" of those who regard marriage as permanent. I certainly do not feel any desperation in my teaching or writing on this issue. I ask my students not to merely accept my view, but to use my research to further their own understanding of what God has revealed in his Word. I have nothing to gain or lose whether marriage be permanent or not. All I ask my students to consider is the biblical evidence. God's truth does not need our desperate defense.

On page 155 Edgar accuses me of misunderstanding the nature of the Greek aorist tense in my comment on Mark 10:9. Although the aorist generally is timeless and does not mean "once for all," the culminative aorist does view an event from the viewpoint of its existing results. Jesus taught that since God has yoked (aorist tense) the husband and wife, they should not be separated. Both the tense and context imply permanence.

Edgar goes to great length to refute my view that *porneia* refers to incestuous marriage (pp. 176-186). Whether right or wrong, the view does coincide well with the history, culture, geographical situation and Jewish background. These factors are as much a part of our Protestant hermeneutic as Greek word studies.

Edgar's own view—that *porneia* refers to adultery appears (pp. 186-187) sketchy and inadequately defended. In his discussion of 1 Corinthians 7:15 Edgar is honest enough to admit that the allowance for remarriage by the deserted spouse "is not definitely stated" (p. 190). His argument for the remarriage of a deserted spouse is based on what Edgar thinks is "most probable" (p. 191).

Edgar may persuade many through his forceful and dogmatic presentation. I trust that my brief remarks will encourage readers to keep studying the issue and remain open to another viewpoint.

Notes
[1]William F. Luck, *Divorce and Remarriage* (San Francisco: Harper & Row, 1987).
[2]Eusebius *Historia Ecclesiastica* 3:39.

Response

William Heth

*T*homas Edgar's presentation of the view that the Scriptures allow divorce *and* remarriage in the two instances of adultery and desertion takes up one of the two main pillars that John Murray built his view upon nearly forty years ago. But Edgar suggests some new and interesting ways of looking at those who disagree with him over how to harmonize this famous exception with the teaching in Mark, Luke, Paul and the early church.

I tend to agree with Edgar that a wife's adultery is probably the most natural way to understand the reference to *porneia* in the context of the exception clauses. He makes some good arguments against two of the more obscure ways of understanding the exception clauses, but beyond that our differences are many.

Edgar's approach to the scriptural teaching on divorce and remarriage presents a marked contrast to the positive, practical and pastoral presentation of Laney. From the outset Edgar is on the attack. He does not like the suggestion that his view is considered the traditional or popular view among (evangelical) Protestants. He is opposed to having his position labeled as liberal or conservative. Then he claims in the opening paragraph that his view "is the position most naturally derived from Scripture." I certainly agree that no view should be labeled as loose or strict, conservative or liberal, and that no approach "is inherently more spiritual" or "superior" to another. What is important is how each position handles all of the biblical data it appeals to for support. But this is precisely where it becomes difficult to assess Edgar's surprisingly absolute claims.

The only text he treats in detail is Matthew 19:9, and even there his discussion is primarily confined to his insistence on *the* one and only one way of reading it. We receive some lessons in logic and are given way too many examples of how *not* to read Matthew 19:9. But the larger and more important biblical/theological picture is all but omitted as a control factor in Edgar's framework.

To be specific, I find it extremely significant that Jesus bases his divorce and remarriage sayings in Matthew 19:9 and Mark 10:11-12 on the combination of two verses from Genesis 1:27 and 2:24. But Edgar claims that this verse and the covenantal and kinship concepts that it shares with other passages in the Old Testament teach us "nothing explicit regarding divorce or remarriage" (p. 153). He states that the biblical kinship view of marriage creates a logical dilemma, but I find this to be consistent if it is read on its own terms. The dilemma is created by Edgar, not the Scriptures, for they never imply the problem he raises.

Thus we are left to guess just how Edgar interprets the terms *leave* and *cleave* and *become one flesh*. Does he really mean to imply that the kinship aspect of marriage is nowhere to be found in the Old Testament and that it is irrelevant to the question of remarriage after divorce? Did not Jesus in particular focus on the one-flesh aspect of the marriage union when he said: "Consequently they are no more two, but *one flesh"* (Mt 19:6, NASB, italics mine). Something is amiss when, on the one hand, Edgar can say that Genesis 2:24 has nothing explicit to teach us regarding divorce or remarriage, and, on the other hand, Murray can say in the preface to his classical defense of the view Edgar himself adopts, "At the very outset this [Gen 2:23-24] enunciates the nature and basis of marriage and clearly implies that divorce or the dissolution of the marriage bond could not be contemplated otherwise than as a radical breach of the divine institution."

There is certainly no need to work through Edgar's chapter point-by-point and respond in like fashion to the case he makes for his view. I feel it would be most helpful if I first note Edgar's working definitions, then consider his hermeneutical presuppositions and finally make some comments about his treatment of Matthew 19:9. In doing so I will do my best not to misrepresent him.

The first set of working definitions that we should consider are found in Edgar's opening paragraph.

1. Anyone who forbids remarriage after divorce presupposes this point. It cannot be found in Scripture.

2. Anyone who forbids remarriage after divorce holds a sacramental view of marriage or its equivalent (marriage is indissoluble).

3. The view that allows divorce and remarriage for desertion and adultery is the one most naturally derived from Scripture (p. 151).

I find it difficult to see the logic here. Do I hold a "sacramental view of marriage or its equivalent" because I do not allow remarriage after divorce? Yes, according to Edgar; and yet I am not a sacramentalist. Have I derived my no-remarriage view from an exegetical study of the biblical data? No, according to Edgar, because anyone who comes up with a no-remarriage view presupposed this from the outset. How can I get out of this straitjacket?

Apparently when Wenham and I abandoned an understanding of the divorce texts comparable to Edgar's, we did so not by a careful study of Scripture but by way of presupposition—in particular, a presupposition that implicitly adopts a sacramental view of marriage. As far as I know the Roman Catholic view of marriage as a sacrament has nothing to do with Wenham's, my own, or others' understanding of marriage as a kinship relationship. Nor does it have much to do with those who defend a no-remarriage position based on their understanding of covenant relationships (that is, vows made before God). Edgar seems to have misrepresented the no-remarriage position right from the start. Having built a straw man, he then proceeds to tear it apart, only to return at the very end to restate the assumption he began with: Whoever concludes that Jesus did not permit his disciples to remarry after any divorce subdues the voice of Scripture "to the insistent clanging of a dogmatic presupposition" (p. 192).

Edgar's operating framework is carried a step further in his second paragraph. There he wants his readers to understand the following:

1. Those who argue that there is no valid reason for divorce are one and the same as those who allow some divorces but no remarriage; the marriage relationship is dissolved only by the death of a spouse.

2. This opinion may be held dogmatically (for example, Roman Catholics) or it may be derived from an alleged teaching in Scripture regarding the nature of marriage (for example, Heth, Wenham and Laney).

3. No verse in Scripture teaches that marriage is indissoluble. Therefore, anyone who argues for a no divorce or no-remarriage position presupposes indissolubility and violates "normal procedures for interpretation and the most natural meaning of the biblical passages involved" (p. 152; compare p. 153).

Within this framework it seems that anyone who disagrees with Edgar's views is damned from the start. We presuppose what we want to prove, and we violate normal hermeneutical procedures. I wish Edgar would give more credit to those who disagree with him.

I believe that the Achilles' heel of Edgar's understanding of the New Testament teaching on divorce and remarriage is his insistence on the very same point that Murray argued some forty years ago: the exception clause qualifies both the divorce action and the remarriage action in the double conditional protasis of Matthew 19:9 (that is, the *if* portion of the situation that Jesus envisages). Thus remarriage after divorce in the case of the genuine exception does not constitute adultery. Edgar *insists* that this is the clear and simple meaning that emerges even from an English translation of this verse. He claims that there is nothing unusual about the Greek grammar and syntax of the verse. The exception clause simply *demands* the interpretation that he argues for throughout this chapter. (For a critique that will make Edgar look just as "dogmatic" as he claims that Wenham and I are, see *Jesus and Divorce* pp. 90-93, 113-20.)

In all fairness, Edgar should have admitted that his understanding of the function of the exception clause is one possibility among others. It is not as obvious as he insists. The analogies and illustrations that he cites in favor of his own view of Matthew 19:9 can easily be duplicated by those who take a no-remarriage view (compare *Jesus and Divorce*, pp. 234-35, n. 20). It all depends on what one wants to argue. Edgar uses the following analogy as a foil to argue for the absurdity of Wenham's view (pp. 158), "Whoever drives on this road except an ambulance driver on call and exceeds the speed limit is breaking the law." This is not even comparable to what Wenham is arguing and presents only part of Wenham's argument. Wenham understands that the lustful look and divorce, except for immorality, are presented *in the context of Matthew 5:27-32* as violations of the spirit of the seventh commandment. To even begin to come close to Wenham's propositions, Edgar should first have noted that some kind of road sign stood at the beginning of this particular street stating that in all but one case *driving* on this road is a violation of the law. The conceptual parallels between Edgar's example and Wenham's understanding of Matthew 5:32 (in the context of vv. 27-32) and 19:9 are so different and so imprecise as to be totally unhelpful.

Everyone who knows the role that Greek grammar plays in exegesis realizes that grammar and syntax involve possibilities. Grammar, though absolutely necessary, is seldom solely determinative for choosing one reading of a passage over another. Thus for Edgar to insist that his reading is the only possible one is to go far beyond the possibilities allowed by grammar and syntax. That both his and Wenham's (and my own) understanding of the syntax of Matthew 19:9 are *only possibilities* was demonstrated clearly in Jacques Dupont's superb exegetical work, *Mariage et divorce dan l'évangile* (1959). Edgar shows no evidence of having read this landmark treatment of the divorce texts, and, in particular, the syntax of Matthew 19:9.

To set the record straight, the only reason Wenham and I included a discussion of the syntax and word order of Matthew 19:9 in our book was to show that Murray's (and now Edgar's) *insistence* that the exception clause qualifies both the divorce and the remarriage actions is *not* demanded by either the grammar or the structure of the verse. Those who read the presentation of my view in this volume will see that the syntax argument is not high on my priority list—it is not determinitive for or against my view. Edgar's view, however, stands or falls at this point. It only needs to be shown that his reading of Matthew 19:9 is one among other possibilities.

Edgar claims over and over again that his reading of Matthew 19:9 is the most natural and plain reading of this "clear" text. He never says that the construction in Matthew 19:9 is unparalleled in the Gospels. So if this conditional relative clause—with a double conditional protasis containing an exception that is formally linked only to the act of divorcing—is a unique construction in the Gospels, how can Edgar possibly appeal to the plain, normal (even apparent in English) meaning of this sentence? There are no other precise parallels with which to compare it! As far as I am aware, Murray was the first person in the history of the church to appeal to the syntax of Matthew 19:9 to justify divorce and remarriage for adultery. The early Greek-speaking fathers never debated this issue, and though certainly not determinitive, this is an interesting point to note. Thus from an exegetical standpoint the syntax argument is at best a neutral vote.

Other factors are decisive for me: 1) the preceding and especially the following context of Matthew 19:9; 2) the absence of the exception in Mark and Luke (Note how Edgar plays down the significance of the one verse in Luke on this subject!) and Paul; 3) one's understanding of the nature of marriage in the creation accounts; and 4) the fact that where Paul does mention specifically the possibility of remarriage he also mentions the death of one of the spouses (compare Rom 7:2–3; 1 Cor 7:39).

Once it is realized that Edgar's reading of Matthew 19:9 is only possible, but certainly not demanded, then Wenham and I cannot be accused of holding "a peculiar view of the inerrancy of Scripture," or "implicitly surrender[ing] the inerrancy of Scripture" (p. 165) and unwittingly accepting redaction-critical principles (p. 167). These are sorry accusations.

If, from page 165 on, the reader inserts *"my particular interpretation of"* before almost every one of Edgar's references to Matthew 19:9, he or she will catch the force of what I am saying. For if Edgar's interpretation of Matthew 19:9 is only possible but not demanded, then he cannot say that it is best to read Mark and Luke and Paul in the light of it. (Even if his interpretation of Matthew is accepted I am bothered by his very selective harmonistic approach.) On the contrary, the explicit absence of the exception *as Edgar interprets it* in the rest of the New Testament persuades me to shy away from Edgar's particular reading of Matthew 19:9.

In closing, I would like to note two points. First, it is clear from Edgar's discussion of the betrothal view that he has not understood the view as it is defended by Abel Isaakson, *Marriage and Ministry in the New Temple* (1965). Thus he again builds a straw man and knocks it down. Second, I count it an honor to have my views on 1 Corinthians 7:15 placed alongside the conclusions of Gordon D. Fee in Edgar's last note. That is the greatest compliment Edgar could have paid me.

Response

Larry Richards

*T*homas Edgar has made a significant contribution to our discus-sion. His careful analysis and persistent faithfulness to text show the weaknesses in the views of our first two contributors. The assump-tion that marriage is indissoluble, which underlies their exegesis, real-ly cannot be sustained.

I believe that Edgar has shown us from Scripture that a marriage can be "genuinely severed apart from the death of the spouse." I believe he has also shown that only by tormenting the text, and an implicit retreat from the full inspiration and authority of Scripture, can the "no divorce" and "divorce, but no remarriage" positions be maintained. I agree with his conclusion that remarriage is valid in the case of adultery or desertion. But I want to add a few words of warning.

First, "valid" does not imply desirable or best. A person can divorce an unfaithful spouse. But Hosea reminds us we may be called to imitate God's persistent, redeeming love for unfaithful Israel in our marriages. Adultery, as terrible and destructive as it is, may be a symptom of marital dysfunction rather than its cause. At times a loving, forgiving Christian spouse, and a wise counselor, can bring healing and redemption to marriage partners—and to their marriages as well.

It may be correct for us to advise the injured party that he or she "can" divorce. But it is not for us to advise that he or she should. Instead we need to work toward the healing first of the persons involved, and then of the marriage.

Second, it is a fiction to suppose that the "innocent" party in a divorce occasioned by adultery or desertion can remarry, but the "guilty" part cannot. Paul's treatment of divorce in 1 Corinthians 7 is eminently practical. The Corinthian believers were desperate to know how to obey both Paul's injunction not to be unequally yoked with unbelievers, and Christ's teaching on the marital ideal. Paul first told them not to initiate divorce, even from an unsaved spouse. But if they did divorce, they were to remain unmarried and seek reconciliation. Then he went on to release those whose unsaved spouses would not live with them from guilt and from bondage. If a husband or wife deserted the relationship, the believing partner was "not bound" and, by clear implication, free to remarry.

As Edgar points out, since marriage is an institution for all humanity and not just for believers, this principle can be extended to the marriage between two Christians as well as between a Christian and an unbeliever. If any husband or wife deserts the relationship, the marriage is in fact ended. This is the reality of the situation. And, if there is no marriage bond, the ex-spouses as unmarried persons are free to marry again.

This view does not make light of the sin that corrupted the marriage relationship. It does not make light of remarriage, which any who have failed once must approach most cautiously and prayerfully.

It also avoids the contradiction of holding that an innocent party is unmarried, and free to marry again, but a guilty party is somehow still "married," thus can never marry again.

This view also avoids the spiritual contradiction of affirming grace and forgiveness for one sinner, while insisting that in this instance at least there is neither grace nor forgiveness for the person we consider a greater sinner!

But enough of this. It's my turn next, and in the final contribution to this vital debate you'll better understand the reasons for the position I have been led to take.

4

DIVORCE & REMARRIAGE UNDER A VARIETY OF CIRCUMSTANCES

Divorce & Remarriage under a Variety of Circumstances

Larry Richards

I *have yet to meet a Christian who, when he or she stood before* pastor and family and church to say "I do," planned on divorce. I have yet to meet anyone who enjoyed divorce. For each person involved there is pain: worry about the children, uncertainty, sudden loneliness, financial hardship, the lingering and agonizing death of hoped-for love and belonging.

For most Christians there is also a sense of guilt, the awful realization that somehow they have failed, falling dreadfully short of God's ideal of a permanent, lifelong relationship. Even the "innocent party" feels guilt. What did he or she do wrong? What might he have done differently? What happened to destroy a relationship she entered with such joyous expectation?

It is true that in our society divorce is all too common. It is also tragically true that the Christian community has proven as susceptible as the general culture. Most churches have men and women attending who have been divorced and, in many cases, have remarried. I have no statistics on the Christian community, but the most recent study I've seen suggests that about 51% of Americans who marry for the first time will divorce. Many of these divorces will be unnecessary. If both parties were willing to receive counseling, to work at the relationship, most marriages that end in divorce could probably be saved.

With divorce epidemic in our society and infecting our churches, I can understand why so many Christian leaders feel its necessary to take a stand. The mandate for "no divorce" rings from many pulpits. And "no divorce" is counseled by many pastors who, though they hurt for abused wives and for husbands who have been deserted, feel they have no right to encourage something that is contrary to God's will. Those who reluctantly take this position find biblical texts that support—or compel—their stand.

"I hate divorce," the Lord says through Malachi (Mal 2:16). And Matthew 19:4-6 seems to nail down the "no divorce" position. Jesus taught: "at the beginning, the Creator 'made them male and female,' and said, 'For this reason a man will leave his father and mother and be united to his wife, and the two will become one flesh.' So they are no longer two, but one. Therefore what God has joined together, let man not separate." In view of such clear biblical statements, how can any Christian consider divorce, or any minister of the Word of God hold that divorce and remarriage is a possibility for believers?

Approaching Divorce and Remarriage
There are two dangers to guard against if we are to come to a correct conclusion on the sensitive and vital issue of divorce and remarriage.

First, we must guard against being so swayed by sympathy for hurting people that we ignore or reject Scripture. As Oswald Chambers once wrote, "It is possible to have such sympathy with our fellow man as to be guilty of red-handed rebellion against God." Now I confess to a great sympathy for many struggling with the option of divorce. One of our neighbors, whom I'll call Brenda, has an abusive husband. For some ten years he has belittled and sworn at her, constantly ridiculing her. What troubles Brenda now is that her husband treats their two girls the same way. How can she stay with him and see her daughters emotionally damaged for life by his verbal abuse? Is it right for her to stay in a relationship where not only she but her girls are victimized?

In another nearby home the problem is sexual abuse. Here the wife fiercely denies that her husband has been abusing their six-year-old. If she finally does admit the truth to herself, what can she do? Like most child abusers, the man seems unlikely to accept responsibility for his actions or even to admit to them. The little girl in that home is in serious danger. And damage has already been done. What will happen if that couple stays together until the daughter reaches her teens?

It is easy to be moved by compassion for persons in such relationships. Most today would probably advise the two women to dissolve those marriages. Why not flee a relationship which has become so destructive that God's intent for marriage—to be a nurturing, upbuilding relationship—can never be realized?

The Christian, however, has to hesitate here. If divorce isn't God's will, ever, then we can't advise it. If divorce isn't God's will, ever, we have to take the radical position that a sovereign Lord is able to turn evil into good. God must intend to work good in the lives of the innocents involved. We cannot be swayed by sympathy, but are bound by our allegiance to the Word of God.

This brings us to the second danger—misunderstanding God's will. We must guard against using proof texts or developing a legalism that turns biblical principles into inflexible rules. We must guard against drawing conclusions from Scripture without regard to the whole counsel of God and without consideration of various understandings of passages, putting aside our preconceptions. We must guard against a logic that says, "If A, then B," without stopping to consider that God often turns our logic into foolishness by infusions of a grace so overwhelming that we can barely comprehend its implications.

Take, for instance, the passage I quoted earlier, which seems to demand a "no divorce" position. Through Malachi, God announced, "I hate divorce." Logic seems to demand that if God hates divorce, then we must not permit divorce. But is the conclusion warranted?

If it is, how then could God permit Moses to make provision for divorce in the Old Testament (Deut 24:1-4)? And, if remarriage is never an option, how can those same verses from Deuteronomy speak of the divorced wife becoming "the wife of another man"? If A ("I hate divorce") means B ("No divorce can be permitted"), how could God, through Ezra, actually demand that members of the post-exilic generation put away their foreign wives (Ezra 10:11)?

Looking more closely at Malachi, we note that something happening in our society today was also happening then: Men were deserting the "wives of their youth." This phrase, repeated twice in Malachi 2:13-16, makes it clear that these were older couples and suggests that, then as now, older men were deserting their first wives to marry younger, more sexually attractive women.

Partnerships forged by years of shared struggle and joy were being broken up by men who "failed to guard themselves in their spirits." This phrase, also repeated twice, reminds us that as men grow older they, like Solomon, become more susceptible to sexual temptation. So it is clear from the context of Malachi that when God said "I hate divorce," he was speaking of divorces motivated by lust, divorces that involved abandonment of women who had been faithful, loving partners through years of married life. You and I also hate this kind of divorce. We recognize its source in selfishness and sin. We see the anguish it causes a partner who has lavished years of loving care on a person who now pushes her aside. No godly person treats another in this way. And nothing can justify such a divorce.

But notice that it is not valid to conclude from Malachi 2:16 that God hates every divorce. As we study the wider context of the Old Testament, and even the narrower context of the passage, God's "I hate divorce" in Malachi simply does not imply "no divorce."

"If A, then B" may be logical, but the logic is faulty. God hates every divorce that involves the selfish rejection of a faithful partner. Yet this same God, through Moses, made divorce an option. This same God actually demanded in Ezra's day that some Israelites divorce their wives!

If we are to deal faithfully with Scripture, we must be willing to do more than pull out proof texts that seem to support our position. We must interpret while paying strict attention to the context and argument of the passages where our texts are found.

It seems to me that there is only one way to avoid the two dangers I have identified above. On the one hand, we must avoid arguing from human experience. It would be easy to list case after tragic case and to so play on emotions that any sensitive reader would cry out, "No! Let him or her go!"

It would be almost as easy to list case after case of selfish and unnecessary divorce and to trace their tragic consequences. But we Christians do not find moral guidance in human experience. We find moral guidance in Scripture, and we then apply Scripture to help us evaluate experience. Thus any valid discussion of divorce and remarriage must begin with a study of the Word of God, not with appeals to have compassion on hurting people.

Yet when we turn to Scripture, we must be careful. We must first of all note that different views on divorce are held by persons who honor God's Word equally. This suggests that the Bible's teaching on this issue is not as cut and dried as some insist. The very existence of different opinions warns us that we must probe deeply and avoid any tendency to accept what may at first seem "obvious."

We must approach the question of divorce and remarriage on three levels: (1) we must study relevant texts with careful attention to their context; (2) we must test our interpretation against patterns seen in the whole Word; and (3) we must check the harmony of our conclusions against Scripture's most basic context, that of the grace of our God.

It is this threefold approach I want to take in what follows. But, for the sake of brevity, we will only be able to study one of the more critical passages, perhaps the most significant one of all, Matthew 19:3-9. For a more thorough examination of every relevant passage see my book, *Remarriage: A Healing Gift from God* (Word, 1981).

The Teaching of Matthew 19:3-11

Some Pharisees came to him to test him. They asked, "Is it lawful for a man to divorce his wife for any and every reason?"

"Haven't you read," he replied, "that at the beginning the Creator 'made them male and female,' and said, 'For this reason a man will leave his father and mother and be united to his wife, and the two will become one flesh'? So they are no longer two, but one. Therefore what God has joined together, let man not separate."

"Why then," they asked, "did Moses command that a man give his wife a certificate of divorce and send her away?"

Jesus replied, "Moses permitted you to divorce your wives because your hearts were hard. But it was not this way from the beginning. I tell you that anyone who divorces his wife, except for marital unfaithfulness, and marries another woman, commits adultery."

The disciples said to him, "If this is the situation between a husband and wife, it is better not to marry."

Jesus replied, "Not everyone can accept this word, but only those to whom it has been given." (NIV)

The context. The context within which we must interpret these verses begins with Matthew 18 and runs through Matthew 20. Jesus' disciples asked a question about greatness in God's kingdom (Mt 18:1), and all that follows develops Jesus' theology of greatness.

As Matthew 18 unfolds, Jesus draws attention to a child's responsiveness to his Word (18:2-5), then goes on to say that God's "little ones" must live together without causing one another to sin (18:6-9). Jesus uses three illustrations, each of which focuses on interpersonal relationships and the power of forgiveness.

He says we are to view each other as sheep who tend to go astray. We must search for wanderers and, when one is found, restore him or her with joy (18:10-14). He says we are to remember that like children in any family we will sin against and hurt each other. When this happens, we must give priority to restoration and be willing to forgive even "seventy times seven" (18:15-22). He says that if forgiveness seems hard, we are to remember that, like the servant in his illustration, we have freely been forgiven an unpaid debt by our King (18:23-35). These three stories establish Jesus' teaching: greatness in God's kingdom is found in maintaining loving, nurturing relationships with God's other children.

Jesus then goes on to sketch three useless routes people sometimes take in a search for spiritual greatness. The Pharisees, who raise a legal question about divorce, represent the way of Law (19:1-15). A rich young man, who takes pride in his humanitarianism, represents those who seek greatness by doing good works (19:16-30). Workers in a vineyard represent those who seek greatness by working harder than others in God's service (20:1-16). In each case Jesus shows why the route chosen is useless as a way to spiritual achievement.

With the flaw in each of these approaches to greatness exposed, Jesus announces his coming death (20:17-19) and calls his disciples to a servanthood like his own (20:20-28). A last incident illustrates this vividly. Jesus, setting out toward Jerusalem and the cross, is appealed to by two blind men. He stops and asks, "What do you want me to do for you?" (20:34). In the willingness of Jesus to set aside his own deeply felt needs to minister to others, we realize what greatness is—and what it costs to serve others.

We need, then, to understand Christ's dialog with the Pharisees in this broader context. Jesus' intent is to dispose of their legalism as a ground of spiritual pride. To do so, Jesus uses the Pharisees' question about divorce. In the conversation that follows, he exposes the shallowness of every Pharisee-like approach to faith.

Given this context, several of the statements found in Matthew 19:3-8 take on great significance.

"Is it lawful?" This was the issue that consumed the attention of the Pharisees. This group of dedicated Jewish men was committed to keep each and every statute of the Mosaic code. By strict obedience they were sure they would attain a spiritual stature greater than the ordinary Jew.

The background of the "Is it lawful?" query emerges from the rest of the question. They asked, can a man divorce his wife "for any and every cause?" Two positions on divorce were held by the rabbis of Jesus' day. One school of rabbinic thought held that the only valid ground for divorce was some kind of sexual uncleanness in the wife. The other rabbinic school was far more liberal, holding that anything "displeasing" in the wife was sufficient grounds for a divorce. The Pharisees, being strict legalists, would use any waffling on this issue against Jesus if they could.

There are two things to note here. The first is that the Pharisees asked the wrong question. Rather than inquiring about what grounds legitimize divorce, they should have asked: How can a troubled marriage be saved? How can hurting husbands and wives be healed and mutual commitment restored? If they had asked these questions, Jesus could have pointed them to what he had just taught—healing and restoration are possible if we accept one another's "sheep-hood" and go looking for one another when we stray. Healing and restoration come as we bring our hurts to one another and respond to confession with forgiveness. Healing and restoration come as, remembering how much we have been forgiven by God, we find through his love the grace to forgive others just as freely.

If Christians today would choose to live with their spouses in the way Jesus outlined in Matthew 18, the question of "Is it lawful?" would not need to be asked. And, perhaps, if we who minister the Word of God did a better job preaching, teaching and counseling how to live with others in God's way, we might not have the plague of divorces that have struck our churches.

At any rate, the Pharisees were concerned only with the Law. They didn't ask the right question. Strikingly, Jesus did not answer the question they did ask. He did not deal with divorce as a matter of law at all.

"In the beginning the Creator." What Jesus did was to return to God's creation to identify God's ideal for the marriage relationship. Long before law was introduced, God shared a one-flesh vision of marriage. God intended marriage as a gift to bond two people together in a wondrous unity that enables each to enrich the life of the other as they meet life's trials and share life's joys together.

Note that Jesus did not go back to creation in order to lay the foundation for a new, stricter law. He returned to creation to point out that the law, which the Pharisees viewed as the ultimate expression of God's will for humankind, was not the ultimate expression they thought. The ultimate expression of God's will in any matter is the divine ideal, not laws that give the ideal a more-or-less perfect formulation.

At this point the Pharisees, sensing that Jesus was somehow cutting the ground from beneath their feet, objected. "Why then did Moses command that a man give his wife a certificate of divorce and put her away?" This question led directly to two more significant statements by Christ.

"Because your hearts were hard." The creation ideal to which Jesus appealed was established before the Fall. Some time after Adam and Eve consummated history's first marriage, the serpent deceived Eve and she ate Eden's forbidden fruit. Adam, knowing all too well that what he was about to do violated God's command, took the fruit from his wife's hand.

Since that moment history has flowed in a tragic course. Human hearts have been hardened—toward God and toward others. Anger, bitterness, selfishness and pride have found expression in injustice, crime and war. Hardness of heart has also found expression in the twisting of that most intimate of relationships—marriage, which God intended as a matchless gift—into what has become, for some, a horror.

What do Jesus' words "Moses permitted you to divorce because your hearts were hard" imply? Simply that God, in grace, has taken the warping of humankind into account. He gave his permission in Moses' Law for human beings to take a course of action which actually goes against his own ideal. The Law's provision for divorce is proof that the Law in which the Pharisees put such trust is in fact a lowered standard, a *lowered standard* that demonstrates God's willingness to accommodate himself to fallen humanity's weaknesses.

Jesus' statement, and the very existence in the Law of provision for divorce, should make us hesitate. If God treated human frailty so graciously in the age of the Law and permitted not only divorce but also subsequent remarriage, how can we, in this age of grace, treat divorce and remarriage so legalistically?

If God, sensitive to the fact that human hardness of heart would turn some marriages into destructive caricatures, announced through Moses that marriages could be ended, how can we deny divorce to those few whose suffering cries out that their marriages, too, should end? If Jesus recognized hardness of heart as the rationale for permitting divorce in Old Testament times, how can we insist that there is *no* rationale for divorce today, even when one spouse persistently sins against his or her partner?

Nevertheless, the ideal remains. Christians should endorse the ideal, and every one of us should strive in our marriages to reach it. With God's help, we can. But Jesus' statement of the ideal must not be distorted by Christians. It must not be mistaken as the promulgation of a new and higher law. Not when the very context of Jesus' words takes explicit notice of our frailty and of the hardness that sin brings to every human heart.

"Let man not separate." To understand this saying, we need again to remember the context. The Pharisees came to Jesus and raised an issue much debated by the rabbis. The rabbis dedicated their lives to the study of the Scripture and its traditional interpretation within Judaism. Their goal was admirable. They eagerly desired to understand the Word of God with the end that every Jew might obey God fully, thus keeping the covenant their forebears had made with the Lord. In this process, the rabbis gradually assumed the role of judges. Questions of law were taken to them and, sitting as ecclesiastical courts, they announced decisions that were considered binding in Israel. In Jesus' words, "the teachers of the law and the Pharisees sit in Moses' seat" (Mt 23:2).

The Pharisees who raised the divorce issue had probably reached their own conclusion already. No doubt, they were more than ready to sit as an ecclesiastical court of domestic affairs and pronounce who could and who could not divorce. We know that many Pharisees sat on the Sanhedrin, the supreme religious and legal court of Judaism. And we know that the decisions of this body on matters of the law were binding.

The question "Is it lawful?" then, was raised by the Pharisees as an issue to be resolved by an ecclesiastical court. When a person appealed to it, the court would sit, once agreement had been reached, and pronounce "You can" or "You can't." At the very least, the court would determine the broad conditions under which divorce was valid and under which divorce was not "lawful." It is against this background that Jesus said firmly, "What God has joined together, let man not separate."

While this saying is frequently taken as a command to the married, no couple considering divorce stood before Jesus when these words were uttered. This is an important point, for it is a basic rule of hermeneutics that we note to whom a particular saying is addressed. For instance, the promise of offspring made to Abraham cannot be claimed by every childless couple. Similarly, Jesus' call to the rich young ruler to "sell all you have" need not be taken as a general command binding on all Christians. In Matthew 19, the men who stood before Jesus were leaders who assumed that divorce was a matter for an ecclesiastical court. And it was to these men that Jesus spoke. To paraphrase, what Jesus said to this audience was, "You are not competent to serve as judges on the issue of divorce. You have no right to say 'this marriage can' or 'this marriage cannot' be put asunder."

Support for this interpretation is found in the very Old Testament passage that provides for divorce. There Moses pictures a situation in which a man divorces his wife. He is, Moses said, to write her a certificate of divorce, give it to her and send her from his house (Deut 24:1). The fascinating thing here is that the divorce action is taken by the couple with no appeal to an outside tribunal in spite of the fact that a system of courts did exist in Old Testament times.

During the wilderness years, Moses organized the people in groups of tens, fifties, hundreds and thousands. Officials over each of these groups handled disputes and, if an issue was too difficult to be resolved on any of these levels, it might be brought to Moses himself (Ex 18). Later, local elders functioned as judicial bodies. They were responsible to judge the facts of cases brought before them and then follow the law in applying any penalties required (Deut 19:15-20). Deuteronomy 18:18-20 indicates that "judges and officials" ruled over tribes as well. And cases too difficult to be dealt with on a local level might be brought to the priests who served at God's tabernacle (Deut 19:17).

Thus at the time Deuteronomy 24:1-3 was written, a system of ecclesiastical courts existed that decided cases brought before them in accord with the divine law. Yet, when a couple was determining whether or not to divorce, they were not told to bring the issue to one of these courts. In fact, the court systems were ignored, and the issue was decided by the couple involved and by that couple alone. If they chose to divorce, the husband simply wrote out a bill of divorce and gave it to his wife, and she left. And both were then free to marry others.

Jesus' command "let man not separate" has great significance for modern debates on divorce, like the one conducted in this book.

Jesus' words warn us that pastors and other Christian leaders have no more right to stand in judgment over the dissolution of a marriage than did the Pharisees. His words tells us that theologians have no right to decree, "People in this situation can divorce and remarry, but people in that situation cannot." Jesus' words to the Pharisees confront us if we, like those jealous men of long ago, take it upon ourselves to convene our ecclesiastical courts to make pronouncements on an issue which must in the last analysis be a personal decision— a personal decision that Christians will consider only as a last resort, and then prayerfully and purely, with a heartfelt desire to know and to do God's will for them.

Jesus' words "let man not separate" fixes the responsibility for divorce on husbands and wives alone. It makes each couple responsible to answer the question "Has hardness of heart so distorted our relationship that God calls us to abandon it?"

In practice, by the time such a question is even asked, many marriages will be over—in fact if not legally. One or both parties will have chosen not to live with his or her partner as Jesus taught—with compassion for human waywardness, with sensitivity to hurts and with a commitment to forgive repeatedly.

When is a marriage over? When is damage beyond repair? When is it appropriate to take the legal step of divorce? It is just these questions that only the husband and wife involved can answer. It is just these questions that no ecclesiastical court, of Jesus' day or of ours, is competent to decide.

"The kingdom of heaven belongs to such as these" (19:14). Before we deal with the question of marital unfaithfulness and adultery, we should sum up the impact of this dialog concerning the view the Pharisees had—namely, that strict obedience to law provides a pathway to spiritual superiority. The summary is as follows:

The Pharisees asked the question concerning divorce "Is it lawful?" Jesus did not answer this question but went back to creation to state the divine ideal for marriage. When the Pharisees asked why God permitted divorce if this was not in harmony with his ideal, Jesus answered that the law's divorce provision was included because of their hardness of heart. That is, God, knowing sin would corrupt and distort some marriages unbearably, graciously permitted divorce as a way out. Jesus even went on to say that ecclesiastical courts are not competent to rule on the permissibility of a particular divorce!

What has this done to the Pharisees' approach to religion? First, it demonstrated that the Law is *not* God's highest standard. The Deuteronomy divorce regulation shows that the law is a relatively *low* standard—proof of God's willingness to deal graciously with humanity rather than hold lost people unconditionally responsible to live up to his ideal. Thus, as law is a flawed standard, law can hardly lead us to spiritual greatness. Second, Jesus' refusal to permit the Pharisees to bring divorce before an ecclesiastical court shows that law is not competent to speak to every issue in life.

In this way, with brief, decisive strokes, Jesus completely cut the ground from under the Pharisees. Their zeal for the Law and their belief that by keeping the Law more rigorously they would advance spiritually must be wrong. Dedication to the law offers no real hope of spiritual success.

What then can?

Here Jesus returns to his earlier theme of "little children." Matthew 19:13-15 says that little children were brought to Jesus. His disciples rebuked them, but Christ said, "Let the little children come to me, and do not hinder them, for the kingdom of heaven belongs to such as these."

What is significant about these little children? The Greek word found here *(paidia)* is typically used of children up to age seven. Even the most rigorous of the Pharisees thought a boy was ready to take on the obligations of the Law only after he reached the age of twelve or thirteen. "Little children" of seven or less related to God in a much more direct and personal way.

When Jesus said that the kingdom of heaven belongs to *paidia*, he summed up the impact of his interchange with the Pharisees. God's kingdom is made up of people who relate to the Lord directly, intimately, responsively—*not* through the agency of the law. What has law to do with greatness? Nothing. What does a legalistic approach to the issues of life have to do with our relationship with God. Again, nothing. The Pharisees had built their hopes, their very lives, on a crumbling foundation. God's kingdom is made up of little children, whose sole desire is to love and to respond directly to their Lord.

If we were to draw tentative conclusions at this point, I believe they would be these: (1) God does permit divorce and remarriage; (2) the rationale for divorce is human hardness of heart, which so distorts a marriage that its covenant character is violated beyond repair; and (3) the decision to divorce is not a matter for ecclesiastical courts, but must be made by the persons involved in the marriage themselves.

At this point let's stop to see whether these conclusions fit the three criteria for interpretation which I mentioned earlier. First, does the interpretation fit the context of the text? Yes, it takes full account of the role of the discussion of divorce in Jesus' larger treatment of greatness in his kingdom.

Second, does the interpretation match patterns seen in the rest of Scripture? Yes, it carefully notes the relationship of the creation ideal to both the Fall and to the introduction of law. It also is in full harmony with the divorce teaching of the Old Testament, not only in the fact of its permissibility, but also in the personal, rather than judicial, way in which divorce was handled then.

Third, does the interpretation fit the broadest context of all, what we know of God as a God of grace? Yes, for once again God is revealed as a God of compassion, who knows our frame and who remembers that we are but dust (Ps 103:3–14).

I can't help expressing here the pain I feel when I see pastors and other Christians leaders retreat to legalism to deal with the heart-rending issue of divorce and remarriage. We are so quick to make up our lists of rules and to issue our decrees about when divorce is lawful or not. All the while, we miss the fact that Jesus Christ has denied us the right to sit in judgment on this issue.

We miss the teaching that divorce and remarriage is not a matter to be dealt with by laws. We misconstrue Matthew 19's exposition of grace and are blind to Jesus' statement that God understands when hardness of heart drives even the most saintly of his people to divorce. What a tragedy to find ourselves unwittingly taking sides with the Pharisees against our Lord! What a travesty to impose on Christians a burden that even Old Testament Law takes pains to relieve!

"Any one who divorces his wife, except for marital unfaithfulness, and marries, another woman commits adultery." This statement of Jesus, added to his explanation of hardness of heart, seems at first

to cast doubt on our whole understanding of Christ's conversation with the Pharisees. It is also the text used by some to resolve divorce and remarriage questions by assuming that Christ introduces here a so-called exception clause.

Divorce is not permitted, we say, unless there is adultery. In that case, divorce is permissible and remarriage is an option for the innocent party. But three considerations cause problems with this interpretation.

First, it fails to fit the context of Jesus' talk with the Pharisees. Taking this statement as an exception clause would require Jesus to actually adopt the Pharisees' legalistic position and promulgate his own higher interpretation of the Law. Yet the flow of the argument clearly shows that Jesus views law as an inadequate and flawed means of relating to God.

Second, this interpretation views adultery as the exception that makes divorce and remarriage permissible for the innocent party. Yet Jesus does not identify adultery here as the exception. He spoke of what the New International Version calls "marital unfaithfulness," a translation of the Greek word *porneia. Porneia* does *not* mean "adultery"; the Greek word for "adultery" is *moicheia.* Moreover, to understand adultery as the exception does not fit with the testimony of the rest of Scripture. On the one hand, the Law's penalty for adultery is death by stoning, not divorce (Lev 20:10). On the other hand, the way to treat a wayward spouse, as illustrated by God's treatment of adulterous Israel and Hosea's treatment of his adulterous wife, Gomer, is to seek reconciliation and renewal (see Hos 1, 11). Adultery may be grounds for forgiveness, but it is not grounds for divorce!

Finally, the "exception clause" approach to divorce and remarriage fails to address the nature of the "marital unfaithfulness" cited by Christ. The New International Version translation here is unfortunate, but illustrates the confusion of scholars over the exact meaning of *porneia.* Whatever it may mean, however, *porneia* is not *moicheia.* While, ordinarily, appeal to the exception clause holds that divorce is valid if one party in a marriage commits adultery, this is clearly not what Jesus was saying. The following chart makes this clear.[1]

	Adultery	Prostitution (Fornication)
OT	nā'aP	zānâh
NT	moicheia	porneia
Differences	usually refers to men relations with a married person not spouse not a professional prostitute death penalty appropriate	usually refers to women relations outside of marriage often a professional prostitute death penalty not appropriate
Similarities	both are forbidden by God both are used figuratively to represent spiritual and moral unfaithfulness in God's people both merit and will receive divine punishment	

The questions we have to ask, then, are these: What did Jesus mean when he said that remarriage after any divorce except for *porneia* involves the commission of adultery? And what did he *not* mean?

To explore these questions adequately we might check the meaning of *porneia*. And we might look for clues in parallel passages, especially Matthew 5:31-32 where the same language is used and the same exception is noted—and most importantly the same issue, that of law, is being addressed.

What is porneia? An article in the *The New International Dictionary of New Testament Theology*[2] sums up possible meanings of this term.

3. In later Jewish Rab. language, *z^enût (porneia)* is to be understood as including not only prostitution and any kind of extra-marital sexual intercourse ... but also all marriages between relatives forbidden by Rab. law. ... Incest ... and all kinds of unnatural sexual intercourse were viewed as fornication *(porneia)*. One who surrenders to it shows ultimately that he has broken with God. ... Thus Jub. can even call *porneia* an unforgivable mortal sin (33:13,18). In order to avoid fornication, early marriage was recommended. ...

1. There was also prostitution in Israel at the time of Jesus. Whereas, however, according to Jewish law, prostitutes and tax

collectors were excluded from the people of God and thus from salvation, Jesus proclaimed to them God's forgiveness on the basis of their faith, and thus the way of salvation (Matt. 21:31f.; Heb. 11:31; cf. Jas. 2:25). Their faith is held up as an example for the self-confident priests and elders of the people. This in no way softens Jesus' rejection of prostitution (Mk. 7:21 par.). But it does mean that, along with other sins, it is no longer excluded from forgiveness. It is not absolutely clear whether *porneia* in the "exceptive clause" (Matt. 5:32; 19:9) is to be understood simply as extra-marital sexual intercourse in the sense of *moicheia* or as prostitution. . . . Some exegetes argue that the reason for divorce could only be that during the marriage the woman's earlier activity as a prostitute became known. Most exegetes, however, suppose that *porneia* is to be understood synonymously with *moicheia* as adultery. Whether in Matt., by contrast with Mk. 3:4; 10:2-12 and Lk. 16:18, we have a secondary, mitigating qualification of the prohibition of adultery, and whether the Matt. version goes back to Jesus himself are disputed.

Actually, attempts to define *porneia* do not seem to help us clarify Jesus' meaning. Is he speaking of some previous sexual sin of the divorced partner that in effect invalidates the marriage so no stigma of adultery remains? Or is this simply an illustration of hardheartedness in a marital partner? Or does Jesus imply a special class of divorce and remarriage cases? Our appeal to first-century Greek usage and Jewish custom leaves us with no certain answer.

What did Jesus teach in Matthew 5:31-32? A look at this passage that parallels Matthew 19:9 does help us—immensely. It helps us for the simple reason that here we have a different context for Christ's statement, a context that sheds tremendous light on what Jesus meant. The relevant verses read as follows:

It has been said, "Anyone who divorces his wife must give her a certificate of divorce." But I tell you that anyone who divorces his wife, except for marital unfaithfulness *[porneia]*, causes her to become an adulteress, and anyone who marries the divorced woman commits adultery.

How does the context for these verses help us understand their teaching and thus the parallel teaching of Jesus in Matthew 19?

The relevant context begins with verse 5:17 and continues to verse 48. In Matthew 5:17 Jesus announces that his words should not be mistaken as an attack on the law. "I have not come," Christ said, "to abolish [the Law or the Prophets] but to fulfill them." How Jesus would "fulfill" the Law has been widely misunderstood by Christians. His hearers, however, knew full well that it was the ambition of every Jewish rabbi to "fulfill" the Law—a technical use of "fulfill" by which the rabbis meant "to express the Law's true intent and meaning." Jesus, then, is about to reveal the true intent and meaning of the Law.

After saying this, Jesus warned his listeners that his explanation of law would uncover a righteousness required to enter the kingdom of heaven that "surpasses that of the Pharisees and the teachers of the law" (5:20).

What follows is a series of six teachings: on murder (5:21-26), on adultery (5:27-30), on divorce (5:31-32), on oaths (5:33-37), on retribution (5:38-42) and on relating to one's enemies (5:43-48). Each teaching follows the same pattern. Jesus begins, "You have heard that it was said." He follows this with a quote from the law. He then says, "But I tell you."

These six teachings have another characteristic in common. Jesus shifts our attention from a behavior described in the law to a heart attitude. The first two cases illustrate. Jesus says, "You have heard that it was said to the people long ago, 'Do not murder, and anyone who murders will be subject to judgment.' But I tell you that anyone who is angry with his brother will be subject to judgment" (5:21-22). God's concern is not only for the act of murder but also for the anger which motivates the act.

Again, "You have heard that it was said, 'Do not commit adultery.' But I tell you that anyone who looks at a woman lustfully has already committed adultery with her in his heart" (5:27). God's concern is not only with the act of adultery but also with the lust that motivates the act!

We begin to see now what Christ is doing. He is teaching that the law, which can deal only with behaviors, was never an adequate exposition of righteousness. Law merely pointed Israel toward righteousness.

The Pharisees, who were so zealous to keep the law, achieved at best an inferior "behavior-righteousness," which was not enough for them to enter the kingdom of God. God demands a surpassing "heart-righteousness." The righteousness that God requires will not just conform to the Law's prohibitions against murder and adultery, but will keep a person free from the anger and lust that motivate these sins. It is within this context that Christ next speaks of divorce. What does this context tell us about what Jesus means in this text?

First, he means that the Law, which says "give her a certificate of divorce," does *not* express God's highest standard or ideal. The Pharisees thought that it was righteous to divorce one's spouse as long as the legalities were observed. Jesus makes it clear that, while it is permissible to divorce, it is not *righteous.* Divorce falls short of God's will for us and reveals human failure. In view of God's ultimate standard for us, divorce, while permissible, is still sin. And remarriage, while permissible, involves an act which measured against the ideal must be acknowledged as adultery.

If we return now to Matthew 19, we can better understand what Jesus was saying and why he made this statement to the Pharisees. These zealots were so concerned with legalisms that they actually treated divorce trivially! "Oh," their attitude seems to imply, "if the law says we can divorce, there's nothing wrong with it." Jesus disagrees! Divorce and remarriage are not trivial. Although they are permitted, they are wrong.

Jesus' explanation that God permitted divorce because of hard-heartedness must never be construed to suggest that divorce is not wrong. Divorce is not to be undertaken lightly—as an act with no real meaning. Jesus bluntly says to those who would blithely accept divorce that "anyone who divorces his wife, except for marital unfaithfulness, and marries another woman, commits adultery."

God's standards are far higher that those expressed in laws that regulate behavior. God calls us to realize that *any* falling short of his glory is, and must be acknowledged as, sin. Yes, there is here a mysterious exception that removes this stigma from some divorces and remarriages. But since we cannot be sure what *porneia* involves, it is best to affirm that any divorce involves sin. And that any remarriage involves an act of adultery.

It is far better to bow humbly before God—and if divorce does come, to confess our failure—than to pretend as the Pharisees did that "our" divorce is right because some human court has announced rules that make what we have done legitimate.

I said when we began this look at Matthew 5:31-32 that we needed to discover what Jesus' statement about remarriage involving adultery meant. I also suggested that we need to discover what it does *not* mean. What it does mean, I believe, is that we are called to acknowledge the failure of a marriage as sin. We are not to justify ourselves or pretend that something terrible has not happened. We are not to assume that divorce and remarriage are trivial things, for they are not.

But it may be even more important to specify what Matthew 5:31-32 and Matthew 19:9 do not mean. Let me list several things and explain each.

	Matthew 5	Matthew 19	Mark 10
Occasion	Christ "fulfills" the law in response to charge that he is law's enemy	Pharisees ask about "lawfulness" of divorce for "any cause"	Pharisees ask about "lawfulness" of divorce
Christ's argument	Law is an inadequate expression of God's ideal for humanity	Law is a lower rather than higher standard	Law is a lower rather than higher standard
Ideal	Not stated	Creation's intended "oneness"	Creation's intended "oneness"
Judgment of divorce	Wrong	Wrong, but permitted because of "hardness of heart"	Wrong, but permitted because of "hardness of heart"
Expected outcome of divorce	Remarriage	Remarriage	Remarriage
Adultery involved	For both parties when either remarries	For the "one divorcing" upon remarriage	For the "one divorcing" upon remarriage
Exception	Divorce for πορνεια (porneia)	Divorce for πορνεια (porneia)	None stated

Matthew 19:9 and 5:31-32 do not mean that Christ has forbidden divorce and remarriage. Remember that in Matthew 5 Christ's teaching on divorce immediately follows after his teaching on murder and adultery, and it follows the pattern they establish. In this pattern Christ states a law which deals with an *action,* then moves beyond behavior to deal with *motive.* In the case of murder, Jesus condemns the anger which motivates it. In the case of adultery, Jesus condemns the lust from which it springs. While the law can deal with acts of sin, no legislation can address a person's hidden motives and desires.

In teaching this, Jesus was not calling for new laws that would impose the penalty for murder on a person who shouted out angrily at a brother. Christ was not suggesting a law that would impose the penalty for adultery on a person whose eyes lit up with lust at the sight of a beautiful woman. Jesus' teaching was obviously not a call for new social legislation. It was a demand that each listener face that he or she had violated the spirit of the Law, if not the letter of the Law! If the true implications of Mosaic Law are rightly understood, then no one can claim to be righteous.

Who would be so foolish as to call for laws that apply the penalty for murder to anger or the penalty for adultery to lust? Neither is Christ attempting to impose a new law against divorce and remarriage. It would be inconsistent at best to contend such when the two parallel teachings do no such thing!

Let me put it bluntly. Anyone who takes these statements out of context and teaches that they are Jesus' rules for marriage and divorce has distorted, and done violence to, the Word of God.

Matthew 19:9 and 5:31-32 do not mean that remarriage is an adulterous state. The issue of remarriage is confused by a misunderstanding of the nature of the "adultery" involved. Some have taught that to remarry is to enter an adulterous relationship. By this interpretation, to live with a second husband or second wife is to live in a state of sin. This is a very unlikely interpretation. In the Old Testament, adultery was not only condemned, it was to be dealt with by stoning the adulterous pair. Yet, according to Old Testament law, remarriage was a valid social institution. If an adulterous *state* were involved, God surely would have dealt with the sin more severely. He would at the very least have commanded the separation of couples who had entered into second marriages.

But there is no hint of such teaching in the Old Testament. There is no hint of such teaching in the New Testament either. Jesus is clear about the ideal, and he is clear about the sin. Yet in no place does God prescribe separation for those who have remarried. Even when a second marriage does involve adultery, we must conclude that the adultery relates not to the marriage as a whole but only to the act by which the second marriage was initiated. The physical consummation of the new union may technically and in reality be an adulterous act. In such a case it must be acknowledged as sin and dealt with as sin. It must be brought to the Lord in confession, with the expectation that the Lord will keep his promise and forgive. But at the same time, the second union *is* initiated. A new and valid marriage relationship has been established. And within that relationship sexual relations once again take on the holy and undefiled character of any valid marriage.

Matthew 19:9 and 5:31-32 do not mean that divorce and remarriage are unforgivable. Jesus confronted those who heard his Sermon on the Mount with evidence that each listener had sinned and fallen short of the glory of God, if not by actively disobeying the letter of the Law, then surely by a failure to achieve the high standard implied by its spirit. Jesus confronted them, not that they might despair, but that they might confess and find forgiveness.

Christ's teaching on divorce and remarriage should have the same impact. Should divorce or remarriage come, a person must sense the reality of his or her failure. But then he or she should celebrate the wonder of God's forgiveness. He or she should let the Scripture's grand proclamation of God's love for us in Christ wash away the guilt and free him or her for a new start.

How great and how good God is! He does remember our frame, that we are dust. And he does have compassion on us.

It seems to me that much of the church has set about deliberately to withhold awareness of God's compassion and forgiveness from those who divorce and remarry. It is almost as if the church is determined to punish divorce as Scripture's true "unforgivable" sin.

Too many pastors and teachers insist that there is no forgiveness for the divorced, no fresh start. In many Christian communities, if your marriage fails, you are marked forever and dismissed to a lifetime of loneliness—unless, of course, by some legalistic twist or turn you can be pronounced the "innocent party."

In many Christian communions a punishing attitude is made explicit in church polity—no divorced person can teach Sunday school or sing in choir. No divorced person can serve on a committee. And, horror of horrors, no divorced person can be remarried in church.

A divorced or remarried person can attend and put money in the offering plate. They can listen to our preaching and send their children to Sunday school. But no divorced or remarried person can participate fully in the life of the church. For such a person has sinned.

How strange! We would invite a converted murderer to give testimony from our pulpits. Yet we will not permit a person who has been divorced and has remarried to praise God in our choir.

What is most sad, however, is that such institutional denial of divine forgiveness prevents many hurting brothers and sisters from experiencing the wondrous grace and forgiveness of our God. Our judgmental attitude communicates a condemnation that is not of God, for God understands our frailty; he does forgive, even the sin of divorce.

It pains me deeply to say this, and I say it humbly with an overwhelming awareness of my own faults and flaws. But, dear brother and sister—you who set up rules for who can and who cannot divorce and remarry, you who refuse those who divorce or remarry in violation of your criteria the opportunity to serve in your church, you who refuse to marry in your church those who wish to begin a new life together by committing themselves to one another before God—you unjustly sin against Christ's little ones and do violence to the spirit of the Gospel. I appeal to you to come again to the Word of God. Trace the argument of each passage from which you draw your texts. And with an open mind, ask the Holy Spirit to be your guide.

When I was in seminary, I studied the question of divorce and remarriage. I expected to be a pastor and saw the question of divorce as one on which I had to have well-grounded convictions from the first. When I studied this issue then, I came to far different conclusions than I hold now. Actually, I resisted re-studying divorce and remarriage. Only repeated requests from a dear friend, whose Bible study group then included a number of young women just going through divorce, led me to return reluctantly to the Scriptures. When I did, I carefully examined every relevant biblical passage. And I was amazed by what I found. Hesitantly, but driven by what I then believed Scripture teaches, I changed from a person who took a relatively hard line on divorce and remarriage to what most would now consider a rather liberal position.

Much of my understanding was shaped by Matthew 19. But to be valid, any position must be in harmony with the whole of Scripture. How does my view of Christ's teachings square with Paul's teaching in 1 Corinthians 7?

It is clear in reading this chapter over that the Corinthians were as much confused about marriage issues as we are today. To understand what Paul is saying, we need to reconstruct as much as we can of the situation there.

Three issues surface immediately. First, is marriage itself wrong? Second, should marriage to pagan spouses be dissolved? And third, what principles govern the case of a Christian whose [pagan] spouse deserts him or her?

The answer to the first question is found in 1 Corinthians 7:1-9. Paul thinks the unmarried state is better. But he realizes that celibacy is a matter of gift. God has instituted marriage to meet the sexual needs of human beings, as well as for procreation and companionship. Therefore, those with strong sexual drives should marry (7:1-2, 7-10), and married couples should not opt for sexless "spiritual" marriages (7:3-5).

The answer to the second question, as to whether Christians should divorce their pagan spouses, is related back to the direct teaching of Jesus (7:10-11). It is the Lord himself who commands us "not [to] separate" from our spouses. So, if a Christian wife has an unsaved husband, this is no reason for instituting a divorce. Indeed, a wife in Corinth who has separated from her husband is told to "remain unmarried or else be reconciled to her husband" (7:8-9). In the same way "a husband must not divorce his wife" (7:10).

The third question has to do with Christians whose pagan spouses have initiated the divorce or have abandoned them (7:12-16). These anxious individuals must have suffered: how could they obey God's command to maintain a marriage with an unwilling spouse? Were they doomed to a single life or to endless waiting in hope that the one who abandoned them would be converted and return? Paul's answer must have been a source of great comfort: "If the unbeliever leaves, let him do so. A believing man or woman is not bound in such circumstances" (7:15). The abandoned individual is freed from the marriage bond.

We can draw a number of important principles concerning divorce and remarriage from Paul's discussion of the issues that troubled the Corinthian church. First, a single, permanent marriage relationship is unquestionably God's will for his people (7:10). There can be no debate over this question. Marriage is intended to be a lifetime commitment, in which couples share not only their bodies but all of life, and especially their spiritual life.

Second, in Corinth as today, that ideal may be beyond the grasp for some couples. Paul deals specifically with the case of a mixed marriage, in which [we assume] one partner converted after marriage and the other has not. What is important here is that, in dealing with this situation, Paul exhibits a spirit of grace often absent in modern attitudes toward divorce. He says that the abandoned spouse is "not bound" by the marriage vow, implying that he or she is now "unmarried" and thus free to remarry. Past failure to achieve the ideal does not disqualify the divorced person from another try!

Even so, the passage is troubling. To clarify we need to look at the meaning of several key Greek words. And we need to look carefully at the flat, and apparently exceptionless command, "A wife must not separate from her husband."

The Greek Words

Agamois. This compound word is constructed from the Greek word for "marry" and the negative prefix, *a.* In verse 8, Paul tells the unmarried he thinks it is better if they remain in this state, but "if they cannot control themselves," he suggests they should marry. Etymologically there is no way to tell whether "unmarried" includes the divorced, or only widows and those who have never married. However, in this very passage, in 7:11, Paul uses this very Greek word of a woman who is separated from her husband! It appears then that in Paul's thinking, a divorced person as well as widows and those who have not previously married is included among the unmarried Paul speaks to, advising marriage if this is their gift from God (see v. 7).

Chōristhēnai, aphienai. These words mean, respectively, "separate oneself, be separated" and "send away, cancel." In New Testament times both words were commonly used of divorce, the first specifically of the breaking of a marriage contract, and the second also in a legal sense. It is important to understand here that when Paul speaks about "separating" from one's spouse he is not using the word in the modern sense of a legal separation which is distinct from a divorce. In using either of these words, Paul intends his readers to understand an actual divorce.

Dedoulōtai. In 7:15 Paul says that the Christian whose unbelieving spouse has deserted him or her is "not bound." In its particular form the verb might be rendered "is not in a continuing state of bondage." While the import of this term here has been much argued, it is clear from the context that what Paul means is that the marriage bond no longer continues. The abandoned believer can consider himself or herself unmarried and thus is free to remarry.

While the lexical meaning of the key words Paul uses in 1 Corinthians 7 is not decisive in itself, the way in which the words are used in Paul's argument makes it clear that the unmarried are free to marry, and that at least some of the divorced are included among the unmarried!

The Exceptionless Statement. The most serious objection to a more liberal attitude toward remarriage rests on Paul's use of apparently exceptionless language in 1 Corinthians 7. "To the married I give this command (not I, but the Lord): A wife must not separate from her husband" (7:10). This flat statement would seem to rule out even the possibility of divorce for Christians, making the issue of remarriage moot. If "you can't divorce," it is clear that you can't remarry!

The only trouble is, despite the exceptionless form of the statement, Paul himself immediately goes on to discuss, not the ideal which he has just expressed, but the reality of divorce in Corinth. So he says in the next verse, "But if she does [divorce], she must remain unmarried or else be reconciled to her husband" (7:11). Again we have a statement in exceptionless form. But again, almost immediately, we have Paul himself discussing an exception! What about the Christian who has been abandoned by his unbelieving spouse? Must he or she also "remain unmarried or else be reconciled"? No, Paul says. In this case the Christian is "not bound," because "how do you know, wife, whether you will save your husband?" (7:16). Paul's reasoning seems to be that while conversion of the departed spouse is possible, there is no basis on which to expect it. And it would be unreasonable to ask the abandoned spouse to wait for his or her mate's possible conversion and return. Paul thus concludes that the abandoned Christian is now unmarried and, if unmarried, we must assume free to remarry.

Despite the exceptionless form of some of Paul's saying in 1 Corinthians 7, his statements about remaining unmarried or else being reconciled, and even his command not to divorce, are not exceptionless at all! It surely is the epitome of legalistic interpretation for modern Christians to demand "no remarriage" for divorced believers based on verses which Paul himself does not apply in that way.

But what does this treatment of 1 Corinthians 7 do to our high view of Scripture? Are we not to take God's words literally? Of course we are. But the literal meaning here is defined by the context, not by our presuppositions. Paul treats these statements, despite their exceptionless form, as guiding principles rather than rigid laws. And if we are to treat Scripture with respect, we must take the same course! If we do, what does this passage seem to teach?

First Corinthians 7 teaches us that a permanent marriage is God's ideal. Paul's emphasis on celibacy was not intended to suggest Christians should divorce their spouses or opt for sexless, "spiritual" marriages. Even if one's spouse is an unbeliever, the Christian is not to initiate a divorce. But if the marriage breaks down because of the other person's choice, the Christian is free of his or her responsibility for the relationship and may remarry.

Applying this to our own day, we too are to affirm the marital ideal. We are not to use divorce as an easy out but rather, as Matthew 18 teaches, follow Christ's own prescription to develop a truly loving and nurturing relationship. His principles are to guide us in our efforts to prevent divorce.

If divorce comes in spite of our efforts, we are still to remain open to and even seek reconciliation. We surely must at that point also consider the option of remaining unmarried and, if this is our gift, choose this option. However, when there is no reasonable expectation of reconciliation, we may be considered released from the marriage bond and free to remarry.

This last principle would seem to apply clearly in situations like the following: (1) the divorced spouse remarries; (2) the divorced spouse enters a homosexual relationship; (3) the divorced spouse takes a live-in lover; (4) the divorced spouse leaves the community and cuts off contact; (5) The divorced spouse remains hostile and abusive.

Guided both by the principles Paul uses and the grace he displayed in the case of Corinthians abandoned by their unsaved spouses, we can confidently conclude that God sanctions remarriage for the divorced; a remarriage not contingent on the particular cause of the divorce, or on the believer being the supposed "innocent" party.

Principles Guiding Divorce and Remarriage

1. God's goal in marriage is a lifelong union, within which two people love one another and enrich one another's lives. Successful lifelong marriage is possible for any two people willing to follow Jesus' guidelines for developing a supportive personal relationship (see Mt 18).

2. Because human beings are marred by sin, it will not always be possible for a marriage to achieve this ideal. In some cases, hardheartedness may so distort the marriage relationship that a divorce is the best one can do.

3. Hard-heartedness may be displayed in a variety of ways, including mental and physical abuse, sexual abuse, repeated adulteries, and emotional and spiritual abandonment of the relationship, even when two persons live in the same home. In such ways, the marriage covenant may be abandoned by one or both parties, whether or not a legal divorce takes place.

4. It is the sole responsibility of husband and/or wife to determine whether or not the marriage is really over and it is time to divorce. No ecclesiastical court has ever been granted the biblical right to determine who can and who cannot divorce. It is, however, the responsibility of spiritual leaders to give guidance and to enable those willing to keep on trying to live with their spouses in Jesus' way.

5. Persons who divorce for any reason do have the right to remarry. However, spiritual leaders are responsible to lead such persons to accept responsibility for the failure of the first marriage, to confess the sin involved to God, and to enter another marriage only upon the clear and definite leading of the Lord.

6. Persons who have divorced and are remarried have the right to be fully involved in the life of the local church, without prejudice. Their spiritual gifts are to be recognized and affirmed, and they are to be encouraged to find the place of service for which their gifts equip them.

Guided by these convictions, how might leaders in the church deal with divorced persons and persons considering divorce or remarriage?

Persons considering divorce. Spiritual leaders have no right to stand in judgment over particular cases. Our obligation is to do all we can to heal those with marriage problems. Ideally this will involve the healing of the marriage.

We want to work with both husband and wife, although usually only one partner will seek our help. In many cases we'll encourage professional counseling. But we will also teach Jesus' way of living with others as God's "little ones." We will encourage forgiveness, even in cases of adultery by one partner. And we'll hold out the hope that God, who works miracles in the hearts of his people, may work a miracle in the marriage.

At the same time, we will be honest about the divorce option. We will explain that God permits divorce where hardness of heart in one or both parties has destroyed the covenant character of the relationship. We will explain that divorce does involve sin, as falling short of any divine ideal involves sin. And we will tell each person who comes to us that he, and he alone, is responsible to decide before God whether his marriage is hopeless or not. We will help each person who comes to us to accept the burden of that responsibility. But we will urge her to pray long and urgently for guidance before deciding to divorce, and we will pray with and for her.

Persons who have divorced. We will be especially sensitive to the pain experienced by persons who have divorced. We will understand the grief of loss and the guilt of failure. We will be aware of the burden faced by young men or women trying to bring up children alone. We will sense the deep need of brothers and sisters who have failed in life's most significant relationship for belonging and acceptance and worth.

As ministers of God's good news, we will affirm the forgiveness that the divorced can claim. We will show by our own warmth and caring that Jesus values them, despite the worthlessness they now frequently feel.

In our churches we will try to provide social groupings where the divorced can feel they belong. We may sponsor seminars to help them deal with unexpected feelings and tasks for which they are not equipped. If we are uncertain how to minister to the needs of the divorced, we will take the initiative and purchase a helpful book, such as the 1987 Zondervan release *Effective Divorce Ministry* by Sue Richards and Stan Haggameyer.

We will encourage the divorced to serve in our Sunday schools and other church agencies, demonstrating that they do belong and are needed in our fellowship. During those first, most painful months and years after the divorce, we will remain especially sensitive and encourage others in our congregation to reach out in friendship and caring.

At no time will we be judgmental, even though you or I might not have made the choice a brother or sister made. As Paul reminds us, "Christ died and returned to life so that he might be the Lord of both the dead and the living" (Rom 14:9). We will let Jesus be Lord in the divorced person's life and will stop playing God.

Persons considering remarriage. Here too we will let Jesus be Lord. We will recognize that a person whose first marriage has ended has a right to remarry. But we will, as spiritual leaders, intervene to provide a certain guidance. There are questions that a person planning remarriage needs to face. Has he identified his role in the breakdown of the earlier marriage? Has she acknowledged the sin and sought God's forgiveness? Has he considered whether God might be calling him to a single, celibate life? Has she prayed and sought God's guidance in this particular relationship?

Frequently those who have divorced rush too soon into a new relationship. Generally speaking, at least two years will pass after a divorce before a person has experienced enough healing to be able to handle the stress of a new marriage.

Another common problem is that a divorced person will often be attracted to an individual who displays the flaws of his or her ex-spouse. We need to be aware of potential problems like these and help those who hope to remarry seek a mate wisely and with a firm determination to marry again only in God's will.

When decision to remarry is made, it is time for us to stand with our brother or sister. We need to make our church available for the wedding and encourage the local body of Christ to celebrate with the couple. We need to affirm once more God's amazing readiness to forgive us when we fall and then enable us to stand.

In these ways, with compassion and with love, in confrontation and by offering emotional support, we will witness to our church and to the world of the surpassing grace of our God, who has chosen in Christ not to treat us as our sins deserve or to repay us according to our iniquities.

Case History

Tom has been married twice previously. He is a respected business-man, articulate and very successful. He is a warm, caring, people person. People gravitate toward his charisma. Children are naturally drawn to him. Wanda has been married once before. Their relation-ship has developed, and they have decided to get married. Tom has been divorced from his last wife for three years, and Wanda has been divorced for fifteen years. They both have received counseling in preparation for marriage. Would you marry them?

They are married and one year later Tom files for divorce. Tom moves to a neighborhood where he is not known, enters into a new fellowship of believers and finds another woman to marry. This would be his fourth marriage. Would you marry Tom again? How is his recurring marriages not a mockery of the bond we must "let no man put asunder"?

Would it make any difference in your view if Wanda refused to have sexual relations with Tom and she would not seek counseling?

Answer

There are actually two cases here: the first, Tom's marriage to Wanda, and the second is his fourth marriage after divorcing her. Let's take them one at a time.

Whenever any person wants to remarry, it is important to help him or her deal with the causes of the earlier marital breakdown. In doing this the pastor or counselor is not to take the role of an ecclesiastical court to decide if the parties can marry, but the role of a spiritual advisor to help the individuals mature spiritually. In the case of multiple remarriages, talking with previous spouses is important. It is conceivable that in the course of such counseling serious personality flaws may be discovered. In such cases, both of the engaged parties should be confronted. Tom may need professional help to deal with personality problems. Wanda must certainly be helped to realistically evaluate her prospects of a successful marriage with Tom. When divorced persons plan to remarry, more intense pastoral care and counseling are called for.

In the case of a couple like Tom and Wanda, the marriage should be monitored. The best way to do this is to have a mature Christian couple meet regularly with Tom and Wanda during the first two years of their marriage. They can offer support and teaching on building the marriage relationship, as well as alert the pastor if more serious problems develop.

All too often a pastor will approach the Toms and Wandas in our churches as if his or her responsibility is to determine whether or not to perform the marriage. Like the priests who asked Judas "what is that to us?" when Judas confessed betraying innocent blood, Christian ministers can be more concerned with their own technical purity than with opportunities to minister—even though they know Tom and Wanda will just find someone else who will marry them and will certainly not turn to the pastor for help if marital problems develop.

But what about the second part of this case history? What if a year later Tom files for divorce? Should a pastor marry Tom if he finds a fourth willing woman? To be honest, this kind of case history approach irritates me. It reminds me so much of the Pharisees of Matthew 19. "Let's define the legalities!" the Pharisees cried, never realizing that God's concern is not with the kind of complicated situations they delighted to debate, but with the human beings involved.

The fact is that if Tom and Wanda's marriage breaks down in one of our churches today, the chances are much of the fault lies in the weakness of initial counseling, in our modern hesitation to confront and our typical failure to provide continuing support for any couple launching into married life.

Would it make a difference if Wanda had refused sex? Of course, it would make a difference. It would make a difference to Tom and to Wanda too, for a vital element in Christian marriage would be lost. But the time to deal with Wanda's refusal is not after a divorce, but during the marriage!

Would it make a difference if the two would not seek counseling before going ahead with the divorce? Of course it would—to Tom and Wanda. They would be failures again, falling short when wise, loving and supportive help from others might have turned their marriage around. But does it make a difference, legalistically, as to how we would assign fault, or who we would excuse, or whether or not a minister should officiate at another wedding for Tom? If we were Pharisees, it would. But if we are ministers of the grace of God, according to the spirit and letter of the Word of God, then the real difference it should make would only be in the way we counsel and support. And here Tom's and Wanda's past should make a big difference indeed!

Would I marry Tom and Wanda the first time? Yes, but not without careful, confrontative counseling. And not without setting in place some kind of monitoring of their relationship. Would I marry Tom a fourth time? Yes, if his intended insisted on going ahead with the marriage after being confronted with everything I knew or could find out about the breakdown of his three previous marriages. And if I could receive a commitment from them for regular, professional counseling during the first two years of their marriage.

God did not charge me, or any other pastor, with the task of deciding who can or cannot marry. He did not tell us to set up ecclesiastical courts. But God did charge each of his servants: "feed my lambs," providing the support and guidance and help that his people need. Those seeking remarriage do not need judges. They need ministry. They do not need Pharisees. They need the loving touch of a Jesus who, on his way to the cross, stopped at the cry of two blind men, and said, "What do you want me to do for you?" (Mt 20:32).

Notes

[1]Taken from *Expository Dictionary of Bible Words* by Lawrence O. Richards, p. 22. Copyright © 1985 by The Zondervan Corporation. Used by permission.

[2]H. Reisser, "πορνεύω," *The New International Dictionary of New Testament*, 3 vols., ed. Colin Brown (Grand Rapids, Mich.: Zondervan, 1975), 1:499–500.

Response

J. Carl Laney

*I*have enjoyed reading *Larry Richards's position regarding divorce*
and remarriage. I appreciate the fact that he devoted himself to a
positive statement of his viewpoint and has made a good case for
what he believes. And I find that I am in agreement with him on many
points.

I agree with Richards's comment on 1 Corinthians 7:10, "A single,
permanent marriage relationship is unquestionably God's will for his
people" (p. 239). "Divorce falls short of God's will for us and reveals
human failure" (p. 233). I affirm as well that "any divorce involves sin.
And that any remarriage involves an act of adultery" (p. 233). Yet, I
also agree with Richards that remarriage following divorce does not
constitute an "adulterous state" (p. 236). I deal with the problem of
the present tense "commits adultery" (Mk 10:11) in my book *The*

Divorce Myth (pp. 120–121). Finally, I agree with Richards that divorce and remarriage are not "unforgivable" (pp. 236–37). God's grace is sufficient to forgive and cleanse. This does not mean, however, that divorce and remarriage will not result in wounds and scars which may have long-lasting effects on the life and ministry of a believer.

I found Richards's presentation quite stimulating and creative. His approach is quite unique and thus provides opportunity for fresh thinking and interaction on the subject. The negative aspect is that he does not seem to be in touch with the work that other expositors and scholars have done on this subject. This is reflected in the lack of endnotes (just two, in contrast with Heth's 107). Creative thinking has its place, but the conclusions must be checked with the exegetical work of equally knowledgeable authorities.

Another feature I appreciate in Richards's work is his concern to treat the various Scripture texts in their biblical context. He makes repeated appeal to the "context" of the passage (pp. 218, 219, 220, 229). Unfortunately, he has often introduced a foreign context into the discussion of biblical passages. He introduces the consideration of "sheep who tend to go astray" into his comments on Matthew 18:2–5. "Sheep" do not appear until 18:12, and there it is God who searches for the sheep, not the disciples. Jumping contexts leads Richards to conclude that Jesus' purpose in his dialog with the Pharisees was to "dispose of their legalism as a ground of spiritual pride" (p. 221). No doubt that the Pharisees were guilty of spiritual pride and legalism. But Jesus makes no mention of this issue in his response.

A more serious violation of context appears in Richards's discussion of 1 Corinthians 7. He believes the context (1 Cor 7:15, "not bound") informs the meaning of Paul's statement, "But if she does [divorce], she must remain unmarried or else be reconciled to her husband" (1 Cor 7:11). Richards argues that the "exceptionless" form of Paul's saying in 1 Corinthians 7:11 is modified by the context. One could as reasonably argue that the context of 1 Corinthians 7:11 informs the interpretation of "not bound" in 1 Corinthians 7:15. What

Richards has failed to note is that the context changes in 1 Corinthians 7:12. While context is one key to interpretation, one must be careful to avoid importing the wrong context into the study of a passage.

I found Richards's pastoral concern for those in hurting relationships very encouraging (pp. 216–19). Often these issues are debated with seeming little concern for those facing divorce or struggling as divorced people. The problem is that personal involvement with divorced and hurting people may result in an inadvertent personal bias toward a particular viewpoint on divorce and remarriage. Richards relates that he changed his own view as a result of involvement in some ministry to the divorced (p. 238). In spite of his statements to the contrary, (p. 216–17), I wonder if Richards's personal experience affected his shift from the more traditional viewpoint.

One of my concerns with Richards's work is his low view of the Old Testament Law. He declares (p. 227) that "the Law is *not* God's highest standard" and is in fact a "flawed standard." Later he equates the Law with legalism. This leads Richards to a rejection of any basic guideline in the Old Testament Law concerning divorce and remarriage. I fear that he tends toward antinomianism at this point. Paul called the Law "holy" and the commandment "holy, righteous and good" (Rom 7:12). The Law was God's gift to a redeemed people designed to guide them in the path of "life and prosperity" (Deut 30:15).

Consistent with Richards's low view of the Law is his lack of serious interaction with Old Testament texts on the subject of divorce and remarriage. He begins his discussion on the scriptural teaching with Matthew (p. 219). A canonical approach in which every text, both Old and New Testament, is considered provides a broader basis for the development of biblical doctrines.

I am also concerned by Richards's low view of the single life. Without the possibility of remarriage, he regards divorced people as "doomed to a single life" (p. 239). This is certainly not Paul's view of the single life (compare 1 Cor. 7:7, 32–35). Paul refers to the single life as "better" (1 Cor 7:38) and "happier" (1 Cor 7:40). I believe that many divorced people remarry because they have never been taught what the Bible says about the single life. Jesus found meaning and fulfillment in life as a single person. Richards speaks of God's grace as the basis for remarriage after divorce. Couldn't God's grace also serve as the basis for remaining single?

Richards is in error when he states that "God actually demanded in Ezra's day that some Israelites divorce their wives" (p. 218). Ezra 10 records that the Israelites "put away" their wives (the normal word for divorce is not used), but this came as the suggestion of Shecaniah, not the command of the Lord (see the comments in my essay).

I object strongly to Richards's statement that God "gave permission in Moses' Law for human beings to take a course of action which actually goes against his own ideal" (p. 223). God never "announced through Moses that marriages could be ended" (p. 223). These statements reflect Richards's failure to understand the grammatical structure of Deuteronomy 24:1-4. There God *describes* what he does not necessarily *prescribe*. Although divorce and remarriage is described in Deuteronomy 24:1-3, only in 24:4 does a specific command of God appear. Moses never said, "write her a certificate of divorce," (p. 225). This comment is based on the King James translation which incorrectly makes a command out of a descriptive statement. The only command given in Deuteronomy 24:1-4 is that a man may not remarry his former wife if there has been an intervening marriage. Divorce was "permitted" in Mosaic Law only in the sense that it was not prohibited by divine command.

Richards inserts the concept of an "ecclesiastical court" into the contest of Matthew 19 and concludes that Jesus was teaching, "You are not competent to serve as judges on the issue of divorce. You have no right to say 'this marriage can' or 'this marriage cannot' be put asunder" (p. 225). On this basis Richards concludes that divorce, for whatever reason, is a "personal decision" which no one has the right to judge or prohibit. Only the husband and wife can decide when the damage is beyond repair and the marriage is over (p. 226). This does away with any sense of accountability to pastors or church elders (contrary to Mt 18:15–18, Heb 13:17, 1 Pet 5:5) and may lead to the antinomian ethic which prevailed in the time of the judges when "everyone did what was right in his own eyes" (Judg 21:25).

Richards writes of a marriage whose "covenant character is violated beyond repair" (p. 228). Is there such a thing? Where does God's grace come into the picture? I wish I had space to report examples of modern-day Hoseas whose marriages were devastated by alienation and adultery. Yet God in his grace has brought about restoration! After couples have said, "this marriage is over," God has shown the power of his renewing and redeeming love. We must not lose hope. Shattered marriages *can* be restored by God's grace.

Although Richards does not specifically address the issue of church leadership, he suggests that Christians should not refuse those who divorce or remarry opportunity to serve in the church. While I would agree that divorce and remarriage should not disqualify one from all service in a church, the office of elder and deacon have a specific marital requirement, "husband of one wife" (1 Tim 3:2, 12, Tit 1:6). While divorce and remarriage is a forgivable sin, it would be disqualifying in terms of church office.

Richards refers to the "gift" of remaining unmarried as a requirement for remaining single after divorce (p. 238-39). We often think of celibacy as a gift which one has or doesn't have. It is better to think of the "gift" of celibacy as a divine enablement which God provides for those who face life without a spouse. I had that enablement before my marriage, and believe I would receive it again should my wife precede me in death. The point is, God will enable divorced (or widowed) people to cope with single living. There is no special "gift" which is required.

Response

William Heth

*T*he chapter by Larry Richards, more than any of the others, helps those who have never experienced marital failure think more seriously about the actual distress, pain, guilt and agony that accompanies the breakdown of life's most intimate relationship. In the other chapters in this book we are confronted with what God thinks about divorce and remarriage. We are given either detailed exegetical discussions of individual passages throughout the Bible or analogies and exercises in logic that are supposed to redirect our thinking on what Matthew 19:9 really means. But in Richards's chapter we are confronted with a sensitive concern for the human side of divorce. We are called to acknowledge any marriage failure as sin. And we must never withhold the promise of Christ's love, forgiveness and mercy from people with deep emotional scars.

I must confess, as Richards does in his introduction, that it is difficult not to be taken in by the details of specific divorce cases, especially when one of the marriage partners endures great suffering and has clearly been treated unjustly. How much more so when marital breakdown occurs within one's immediate family. When I hear someone arguing for a particular view of divorce and remarriage, I cannot help but consider that someone in their family or some very dear friend of theirs may be divorced or remarried. There are very strong emotional and psychological needs to view that friend or family member's situation in a particular light. I have pondered on more than one occasion whether or not I would be willing to stick to my exegetical and theological convictions if one of my three sons or my daughter were divorced? What if Julie, now three, marries a young man and within two years of the wedding her husband leaves her and marries another woman? And what if she was my only child and my only hope of experiencing the life of a grandparent? And what about her own desires to marry, to experience the birth of one or more children and to have the kind of family life that she grew up with?

I also agree with Richards that it is not always morally wrong to separate or get a legal divorce. I am thinking of situations in which getting out from under the same roof as one's mate is motivated by a concern for doing what is right and just in the eyes of God. Does anyone really believe that Jesus would prohibit a wife from doing whatever is necessary to get her children out of a home in which their father is sexually abusing them? And if in this extreme situation the father fails to provide for his children—and it seems obvious that this is what will happen—may we not hesitantly suggest that the wife exercise a kind of "tough love" and take whatever legal action is necessary to force the father to be the kind of father he ought to be—at least in the area of child support? Unfortunately we still seem to live in a "man's world." Recent cases suggest that legal decisions in favor of the wife in similar situations will be difficult to obtain. But this is where the church comes in. The body of Christ must be a community that cares about justice and compassion and does whatever it needs to do to "make things right."

I am pleased Richards takes this opportunity to mention that the "I hate divorce" of Malachi 2:16 occurs in the context of older men divorcing their Jewish wives for pagan women. This is Ezra 9 and 10 revisited. Richards draws our attention to the same problem in contemporary society. Then as now, older men were divorcing their first wives to marry more sexually attractive younger women. Richards's sensitivity to the terrible pain that such pleasure-motivated divorces create reminds me of the very moving description that occurs in the practical application section on this passage in Lange's series:

> The phrases, "wife of thy youth," and "companion" are thrown in to show the aggravated nature of this offense. "She whom you thus wronged was the companion of those earlier and brighter days, when in the bloom of her young beauty she left her father's house, and shared your early struggles, and rejoiced in your later success; who walked arm-in-arm with you along the pilgrimage of life, cheering you in its trials by her gentle ministry; and now, when the bloom of her youth is faded, and the friends of her youth have gone, when father and mother whom she left for you are in the grave, then you cruelly cast her off as a worn-out, worthless thing, and insult her holiest affections by putting another in her place."[1]

To read Malachi 2:16 with this in mind should not lead us to argue, however, that God actually sanctions divorce *with a view to remarriage* in certain "approved" situations. I think Richards and I agree that any divorce is a violation of God's original plan for marriage. But I do not believe that divorce automatically implies the right to remarry. Even though the Hebrew text of this section of the Book of Malachi is difficult to sort out, I am inclined to agree with Laney when he says that verse 15 "appears to refer to the original institution of marriage when God made one partner for Adam (Gen 2:24)." It is interesting to find that the NIV translation of this verse appears to follow the JB and NEB suggested emendation of one of the Hebrew words in this verse. It involves the change of only one vowel point. (These are "punctuation" points not present in the original Hebrew text.) The word *remainder/remnant* is changed into *flesh.* This is the same Hebrew word for flesh that Leviticus 18:6 combines with the Genesis 2:24 word for *flesh* to describe those who are "near of kin," that is, close relatives. This is further confirmation of my own understanding of the biblical kinship view of marriage. The suggestion by Paul House, my colleague and professor of Old Testament at Taylor University, may well be correct: Jesus also has in mind this passage from Malachi when he concludes from Genesis 2:24: "Consequently they are no more two, but *one flesh.* What therefore God has joined together, let no man separate" (Mt 19:6 NASB).

In addition to the Malachi passage, Richards alludes to two other passages from the Old Testament which, along with Malachi, seem to be seminal in his thinking on the subject of divorce and remarriage. Both Laney and I felt the need to address these two passages in some detail in our contributions to this book. The way Richards alludes to all three of these Old Testament texts and what he concludes from them I think justifies our concern:

> Through Malachi, God announced, "I hate divorce." Logic seems to demand that if God hates divorce, then we must not permit divorce. But is the conclusion warranted? If it is, how then could God permit Moses to make provision for divorce in the Old Testament (Deut 24:1-4)? And, if remarriage is never an option, how can those same verses in Deuteronomy speak of the divorced wife becoming "the wife of another man"? If A ("I hate divorce") means B ("No divorce can be permitted"), how could God, through Ezra, actually demand that members of the postexilic generation put away their foreign wives (Ezra 10:11)? (pp. 217-18)

Richards speaks as if God himself provided for both divorce and remarriage as indicated by Deuteronomy 24:1-3. He then reads the "permitted" in Jesus' statement that "Moses *permitted* you to divorce your wives because your hearts were hard" (Mt 19:8 NIV) as "provided for," and concludes that God "announced through Moses that marriages could be ended" (p. 223). My understanding of the Old

Testament teaching on divorce and the context of Matthew 19:8 persuades me to read the "permitted" as conceded or tolerated. Let me explain why.

Foundational to Richards's understanding of the biblical teaching on divorce and remarriage is the notion that the giving of the bill of divorce in Old Testament times was a practice instituted by God through Moses, his intermediary. But note that Deuteronomy 24:1-4 is laid out in the straightforward "*If . . . then . . .*" structure common to all of the case laws in the Mosaic writings. The "if" portion notes the relevant facts of the case that is being decided upon in the "then" portion. We read, for example, in Deuteronomy 24:7: "*If* a man is caught kidnapping any of his countrymen of the sons of Israel, and he deals with him violently, or sells him, *then* that thief shall die." No one would suggest from the "if" portion of this case that Moses is legislating the way in which a fellow Israelite should be kidnapped if a kidnapping takes place! Nor should one conclude from the "if" portion of Deuteronomy 24:1-4 (that is, vv. 1-3) that Moses is setting forth the proper procedure for divorce should a divorce take place. What makes Deuteronomy 24:1-4 less clear than the case ruled upon in verse 7 is that verses 1-3 record an already existing divorce procedure that Israel followed in accordance with the customs of the non-Israelite peoples. This is what Jesus says Moses "permitted": the continuance of the ancient Near Eastern "legal" practice of divorce and remarriage during the Mosaic period of concession and compromise.

If I were to adopt Larry's approach to this case law in Deuteronomy, then I could formulate an excellent argument for why polygamy should be sanctioned today. Divorce, like polygamy, was one of the marriage customs that Israel shared with her ancient Near Eastern neighbors. The Mosaic Law "permitted" polygamy in the same way it permitted the continuance of divorce. Though the creation ideal is clearly one woman for one man, we could, in Larry's understanding, argue for "God's willingness to deal graciously with humanity rather than hold lost people unconditionally responsible to live up to his ideal" and thereby permit polygamy.

As the outline of my chapter suggests, with the coming of Jesus the creation "ideal" is restored. Jesus adds to his statement that Moses did not "outlaw" but permitted divorce, "But it was not this way from the beginning." I believe that the grace of God and the gift of the Holy Spirit make indissoluble marriage a real possibility, a standard to be realized, not an impossible ideal. To speak of lifelong marriage as an "ideal" is to suggest that it can be ended when the going gets tough. I agree with Tony Lane, lecturer at London Bible College: "We need to differentiate between ideals and standards. The former are long-term goals; the latter one is expected to follow." He illustrates his point by saying that his college has a long-standing tradition that students do not beat up the faculty. This is a standard that every student must observe. But, says Lane, the moment people start talking about this standard as an ideal that is to be strived for and one day hopefully achieved, he is going to hire a bodyguard!

In the end I cannot agree with Richards when he says that his understanding of the biblical teaching on divorce and remarriage fit the three criteria of interpretation he mentions at the start of the chapter. Nevertheless, I find much in this chapter that I agree with. On one point in particular I am amazed at how clearly Richards, Laney and I agree. We each see in Hosea 1—3 an illustration of how to treat a wayward spouse. Richards says that "adultery may be grounds for forgiveness, but it is not grounds for divorce!" (p. 229). Here the three of us seem to stand in sharp contrast with what Edgar says about the sin of adultery:

> Although Jesus does not require divorce in such a case [adultery], he indicates that it is perfectly proper and without stigma on the part of the innocent party. . . . Unfaithfulness or adultery is regarded as such a serious sin that it alone is acceptable as grounds for a genuine severance of a marriage. . . . Adultery is . . . a heinous sin against the marriage relationship." (p. 166)

To conclude my response, I suppose that Richards would call my own views on this subject as a "retreat to legalism to deal with the heart-rendering issue of divorce and remarriage" (p. 228). Given my exegesis, however, I do not see how obedience to what I think is God's revealed will can be called legalism. I cannot bring myself to take the step to permit remarriage the way Richards does. To allow divorce in certain situations is one thing; but to permit remarriage is to sanction an attempt to break the union completely, to reverse what God has done, to put asunder the union that God himself established. Richards reads everything the Bible teaches about divorce and remarriage in the light of "Scripture's most basic context, that of the grace of God" (p. 219). My understanding of the grace of God simply does not permit me to do with the divorce texts what Richards's understanding allows him to do.

Note

[1]Moore, "The Prophet Malachi" in *Commentary on the Holy Scriptures: Minor Prophets,* ed. John Peter Lange, trans. and ed. Philip Schaff (Grand Rapids: Zondervan, n.d.), p. 18.

Response

Thomas R. Edgar

*I*n the nature of the case, due to the title of Richards's section, I would expect to have more areas of agreement with Richards, since he seems to allow some exceptions permitting divorce and remarriage, than with Laney or Heth. In the cases of Laney and Heth I disagree with their fundamental perspective that marriage is indissoluble. Since this doctrine exercises definitive control over their interpretation, I also disagreed with much of their discussion of the divorce passages. Since Richards's title seems to deny the indissolubility concept and, therefore, this should not dictate to his exegesis, I would not expect him to disallow the clear statements of Matthew 19:9 and the probable meaning of 1 Corinthians 7:15. However, as I will show, this expectation based on the title is not, in fact, realized.

I do agree with Richards that divorce is all too common, although

I doubt that it is as common in the Christian community as in the secular, as he seems to think (pp. 215-16). This is more so if we discount those divorces occurring before the persons were Christians. I also agree that we must not violate Scripture, nor merely develop a legalistic approach.

I also agree with Richards that Malachi 2:14 does not mean that God hates every divorce, but only those in the context. His statement that we must begin with the Word of God would, I assume, be agreeable to all the writers of this book. I concur with his levels of approach to Scripture, but would limit the third to grace as it is revealed and circumscribed in Scripture, not in terms of our views. I also commend Richards for his compassion on those who "hurt" in a divorce situation and for his desire to minister to them in their need. Having said all this, I must admit that the areas of disagreement were greater than I had anticipated.

I had hoped and expected a presentation of the view that, according to the Scripture, divorce and remarriage are acceptable in a more flexible view under a variety of circumstances. I believe that there are some passages which could be argued for such a perspective. However, it is clear that Richards is not presenting the view that divorce and remarriage are acceptable under a variety of circumstances if "acceptable" means they are not wrong. Richards states very clearly that he believes divorce is always sin and that remarriage is always adultery. If we look for any arguments that allow divorce and/or remarriage in any case, apart from sin, then we will be disappointed, since Richards does not support such a view. In this sense Richards does not support a fourth view, but promotes what amounts to a "no divorce, no remarriage" view of Scripture with a different application in real life. For this reason, I find that I frequently disagree with his section, particularly with regard to the exception passages. From some of his initial statements it seems reasonable to conclude that Richards also accepts the indissolubility of marriage concept. Rather than an equal number on both sides of this concept, I find that I am the only one who does not accept this dogma. The recognition that

Richards holds that divorce and remarriage are both always wrong will make it clear why I so frequently disagree with him. I further disagree with his application of what he thinks Scripture definitely teaches.

In his discussion of the context of Matthew 19:3–12 (p. 220), Richards argues that the overall context is one of loving relationship. He argues that the passage is to illustrate an improper route to spiritual greatness and that Jesus sketches these routes. From this he concludes that the real issue in Matthew 19:2–12 is not divorce and remarriage, but the Pharisees' legalism. From this, his ultimate conclusion in this section is that since some Pharisees sat on Jewish ecclesiastical courts, no ecclesiastical court can rule on such a personal matter. This leads to his deduction that the church and its leaders have no right to make any decisions regarding a divorce or remarriage, but this is solely up to the couple and the church must abide by their decision (p. 228). This is an entire edifice erected on sand.

Matthew 19:3–12 says nothing about ecclesiastical courts, nor is it correct to view this incident as a sketch of Jesus which is merely part of a literary section, in effect, something like a parable. Matthew 19:3–12 is an actual historical event which is different from those events surrounding it. There is no basis to assume it must agree with another event merely due to proximity in this historical account. The Pharisees were not helping Jesus create an illustration when they asked the question " 'Is it lawful for a man to divorce his wife for any and every reason?' " They were setting a trap for Jesus. When Jesus responds with an answer regarding marriage, followed by the Pharisees' objections based on a divorce passage (Deut 24:1–4), and this in turn is answered by Jesus with a discussion on divorce and remarriage, it is clearly contrary to the passage to imply that Jesus in the passage was not really concerned with divorce and remarriage and to bring in ecclesiastical courts and other non-apparent concepts. Yet this deduction regarding Jesus' "real" point and the reading in of "ecclesiastical courts" underlies much of Richards's following discussion and argument (p. 226). I would also disagree with his statement that the Pharisees asked the wrong question, that they should have asked, "How can a troubled marriage be saved?" This present book makes it clear that " 'Is it lawful to divorce?' " is a valid and crucial question. The first issue—before how to save the marriage—is "Does it need to be saved at all costs?"

Although I would agree with the idea that the Law is a lowered standard with regard to the ideal pre-Fall situation, I would disagree with the implication that in the post-Fall situation it is somehow "lower" to follow it (p. 223). And although I would agree that divorce and remarriage are primarily a personal matter, this is basically in the sense that the couple are accountable to God for their actions and cannot shift the ultimate responsibility to someone else.

I disagree with Richards's concept that the church has no right to render approval or disapproval regarding divorce or remarriage. The church must either approve or disapprove (implicitly or explicitly) all actions discussed in the Scripture. It seems too far from the tone of the Bible in general to describe the situation of divorce in Richards's words "God calls us to abandon our marriage," as if the initiative and responsibility were God's. To deny the exception in Matthew 19:9 must be done on the basis of syntax, not as Richards does on the supposition that Jesus is not really concerned with divorce but with legalism.

Richards's statements about the meaning of *porneia* (p. 230) are apparently not based on an indepth study of the words involved, but on a glance at a lexicon. It is simply inaccurate to say that *porneia* does not mean adultery. It is a common term for the woman (wife) involved in adultery, as well as for other illicit sex. The explicit word for adultery, *moicheia,* is not used as often to describe the woman's actions. It is surprising that Richards is so conformed to present secular thinking that he can argue that a clear and serious sin such as adultery is not grounds for divorce, yet allow divorce for reasons such as abuse, emotional disharmony, and so on (p. 229-30). Our "happiness" seems to be more significant than serious sin.

Richards quotes the *New International Dictionary of New Testament Theology,* apparently to show the possibility of meanings for *porneia* such as incestuous marriage (p. 230). However, there is not one biblical instance of *porneia* used for incestuous marriage, and despite Fitzmeyer's desperate attempt, no one has yet come up with one clear case where *z^enût (porneia)* refers to incestuous marriage. Richards's conclusion that we have no answer in Greek usage for the meaning of *porneia* is certainly wrong. In this passage it unquestionably has its normal literal meaning of "illicit sex." With regard to the various options he presents the first, "Does it refer to some previous sin that invalidates the marriage?" is hardly possible. If a marriage can be dissolved for sin before marriage, it certainly can be due to sin after marriage. Adultery is a more likely option. I have discussed this in my refutation of the "betrothal view." It does not even seem to be a reasonable possibility to agree with his second possibility, that in Matthew 19:9 *porneia* is an illustration of hardheartedness. With regard to Richards's last option, "Does it imply a special class of divorce and remarriage cases?" the answer is yes! The special cases are those divorced on the ground of illicit sex—the exception.

His handling of Matthew 5:32 is inconsistent (p. 232). He argues that the first part of the antithesis "you have heard" does not express God's highest standard regarding marriage. Therefore, divorce is still sin. However, this is one of six similar antitheses, all on a similar format. The first half of the antitheses does not imply that it is sinful to do what is described by "you have heard," as Richards implies. This would then require that to observe the commandments against murder, adultery, oaths, retribution and one's enemies is also sinful since each is contrasted with God's "ideal." Richards's concept that the passage teaches that observance of the Law (Deut 24:1-4) is sinful, is not in Matthew 5:31-32. Therefore, he has no support for his concept that biblically permissible divorce is still sinful. He also ignores the specifically stated exception in Matthew 5:32, as if it were not there. The second half of each antithesis "but I say unto you" expresses God's ideal. In this passage (Mt 5:31-32) the exception, *porneia*, is included in the "ideal," and divorce for *porneia* and subsequent remarriage are, in this ideal, explicitly excluded from being "adultery." Both of Richards's "deductions" from Matthew 5:31-32 are not only lacking in the passage, but are contrary to the passage.

In his discussion of Matthew 19:3-12 Richards stresses Jesus' comments regarding Deuteronomy 24:1-4, but gives little mention of Jesus' own view expressed in verse 9. He tends to ignore the exception in order to conclude that all divorce and remarriage are sin. Then he closes with the astounding observation that *porneia* is a valid exception, but that since we do not know what it means, in effect, we can forget it.

Richards lists five situations where his principles clearly apply in allowing divorce. The first three depend on *porneia* as an exception and the fourth depends on desertion. These have biblical support. His last is completely without explicit biblical support and seems to arise from a cultural perspective. However, he seems to relegate all five to insignificance when he states that God sanctions remarriage regardless of the reason for divorce. His opening the options for divorce to mental abuse, emotional desertion and so on would really mean a divorce for almost any reason is acceptable.

It is true, as Richards states, that the statements in 1 Corinthians 7:10-11 cannot be considered as "exceptionless," particularly since Paul refers back to Jesus' statement in Matthew 19:3-12 (p. 241). However, the fact that they include as "understood" a specifically stated exception does not make them mere "guiding principles." Does the fact that an ambulance is an "understood" exception (although not stated) to a posted speed limit, turn the speed-limit sign into a mere guiding principle?

Richards claims that he originally held the no-divorce and no-remarriage view, but has changed due to a restudy of the passages. How can this be? It does not take a restudy of the passages to change from the view that the Bible teaches that divorce is always sin and remarriage is always adultery to his present view that the Bible teaches that divorce is always sin and remarriage is always adultery but go ahead since God will forgive it. Did he need to restudy the Bible to be aware that God is merciful and gracious and will forgive sin? This is the only real difference in his position. All of the writers in this book would agree that God will forgive the sin of improper divorce; we would not all agree that this makes it a valid option.

I must admit that I am disappointed that Richards does not really present a fourth view of what the Scripture teaches regarding divorce and remarriage. His approach is really a very prevalent one today; that is, that the Bible teaches that divorce is sin, but we must modify this to fit today's situation. In the overall analysis Richards, rather than arguing that the Bible allows more flexibility, argues that all divorce and remarriage are sin. However, he seems to feel that since we cannot be expected to live under great stress, we may divorce and remarry anyway and rely on God's grace to forgive our sin. The church has no right to an opinion regarding such actions (even though they are sin), since it is purely one's own personal business. This view can hardly be described as "biblical." It is merely a specific application of the concept, "Go ahead and sin; God will forgive you."

We all agree that God will forgive the believer's sin, but he will also forgive adultery, theft, and other sins. However, that does not make adultery or theft valid options for the believer. Neither does the fact that God will forgive improper divorce and remarriage make it a viable option for the believer. Only in the case of those exceptions which Scripture indicates are not sin, that is in the case of adultery or desertion, is divorce and remarriage a "biblical" option.

About the contributors

H. Wayne House, former assistant professor of systematic theology at Dallas Theological Seminary, is academic dean and professor of theology at Western Baptist College, Salem, Oregon. In addition to writing scholarly articles, he has coauthored *Dominion Theology: Blessing or Curse* and *The Christian Confronts His Culture* as well as serving as the editor of *Schooling Choices: An Examination of Public, Private, and Home Education.*

J. Carl Laney serves as professor of Biblical literature at Western Conservative Baptist Seminary. The author of many magazine and journal articles and a frequent contributor to *Bibliotheca Sacra,* he has written eight books, including *A Guide to Church Discipline* and *The Divorce Myth,* a biblical examination of divorce and remarriage.

William A. Heth is assistant professor of New Testament and Greek at Taylor University, Upland, Indiana. With Gordon J. Wenham he is the coauthor of *Jesus & Divorce: The Problem with the Evangelical Consensus.*

Thomas R. Edgar is professor of New Testament at Capital Bible Seminary in Lanham, Maryland. He is also the author of the book *Miraculous Gifts: Are They for Today?*

Lawrence O. (Larry) Richards taught at Wheaton College, Wheaton, Illinois, for several years and authored textbooks in Christian education that are widely used. Now a full-time writer, he has written over one hundred books, including *Expository Dictionary of Bible Words, The Teacher's Commentary* and the *Revell Essential Bible Dictionary.* Richards has also written many devotional books for young people and adults, and authored the notes for the bestselling *Adventure Bible.*